LOG HORIZON
THE WEST WIND BRIGADE

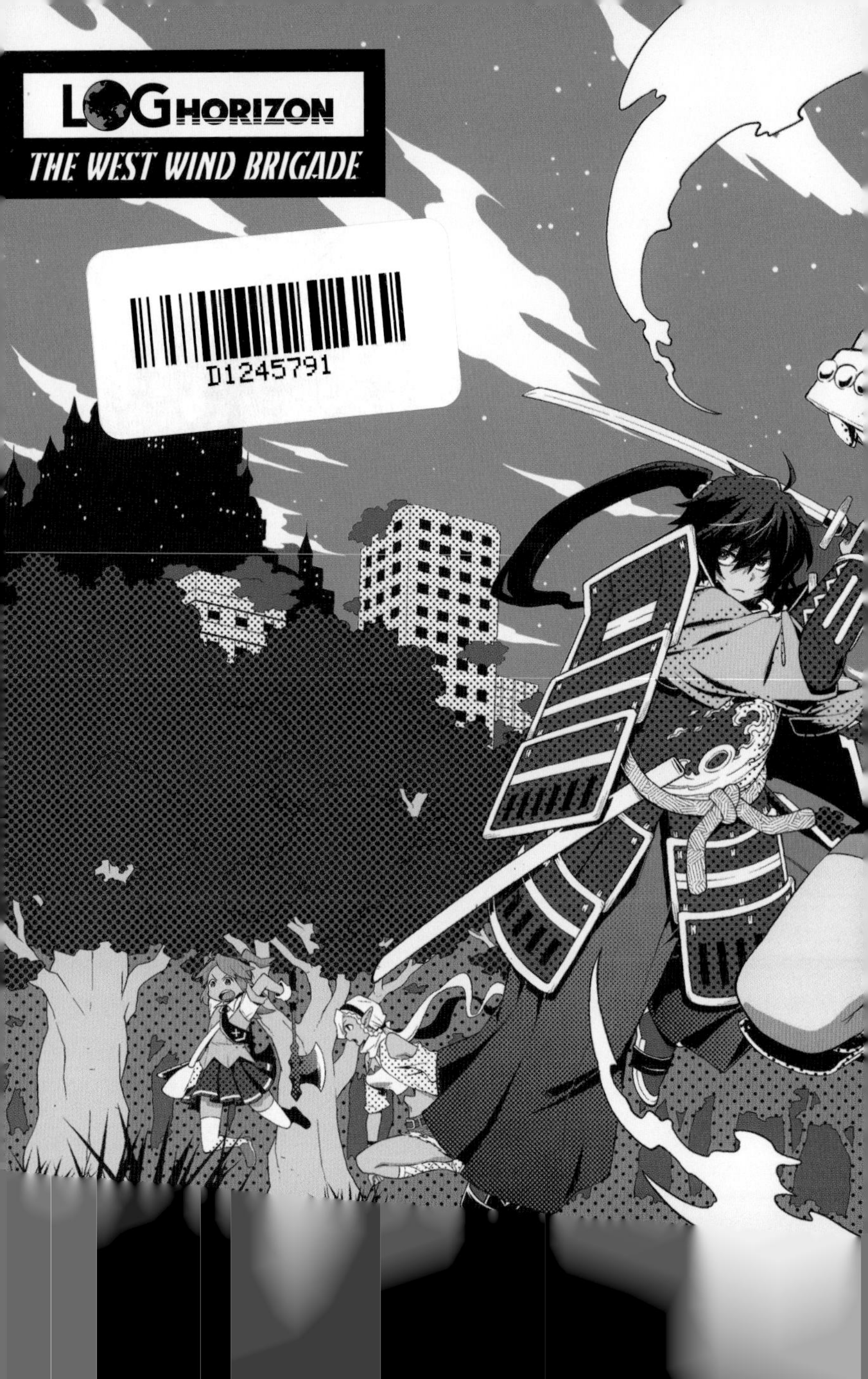

[CONTENTS]

LOG HORIZON **THE WEST WIND BRIGADE** 7

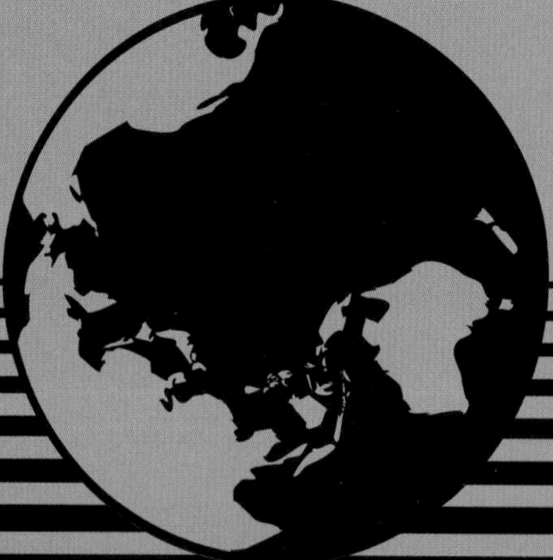

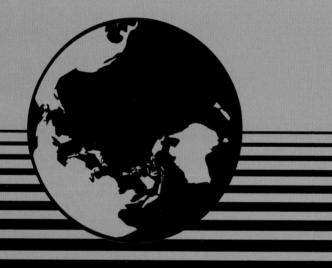

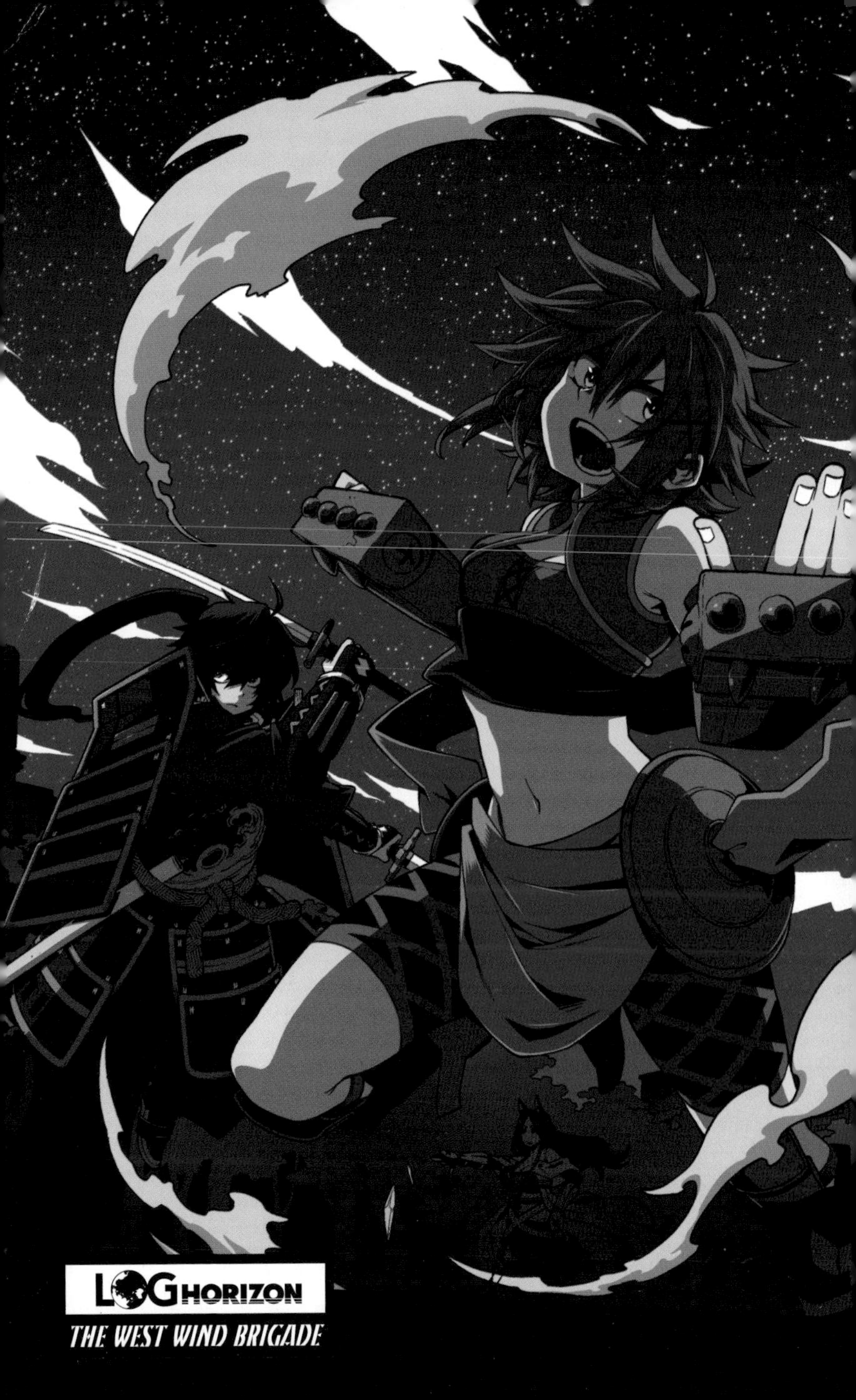
LOG HORIZON
THE WEST WIND BRIGADE

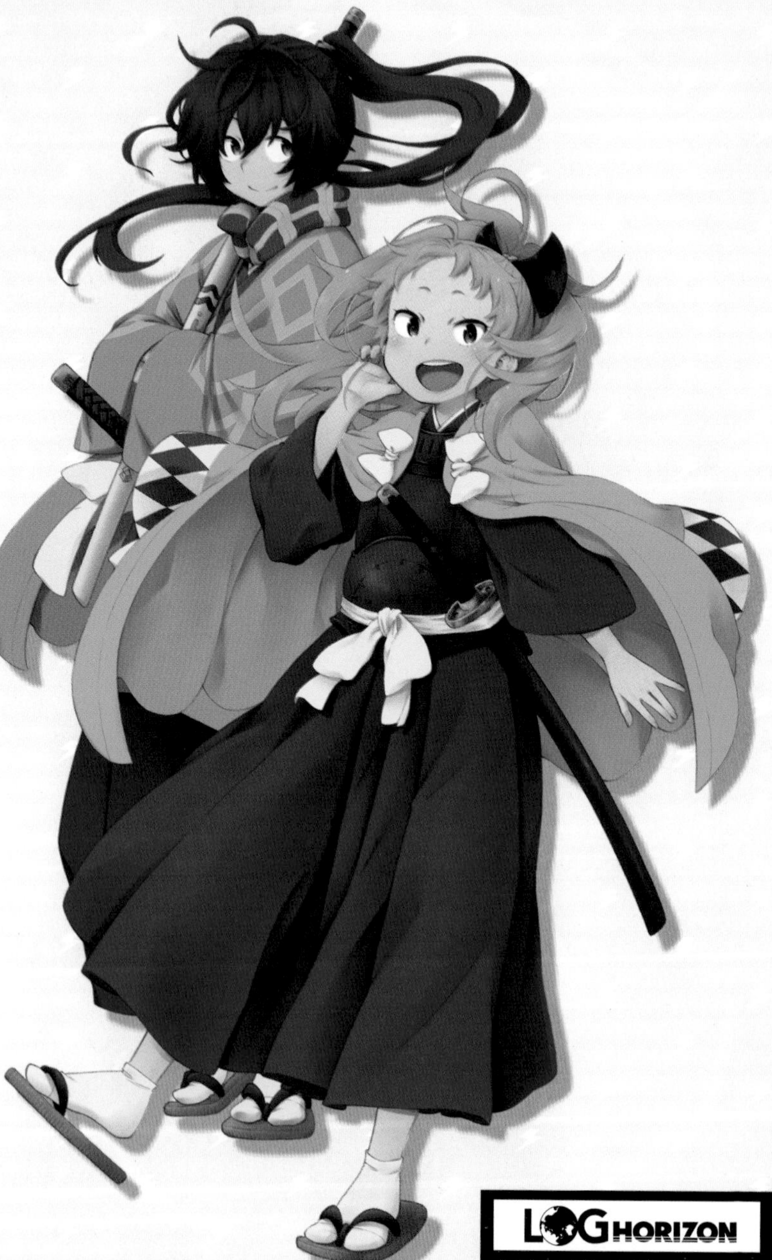

LOG HORIZON
THE WEST WIND BRIGADE

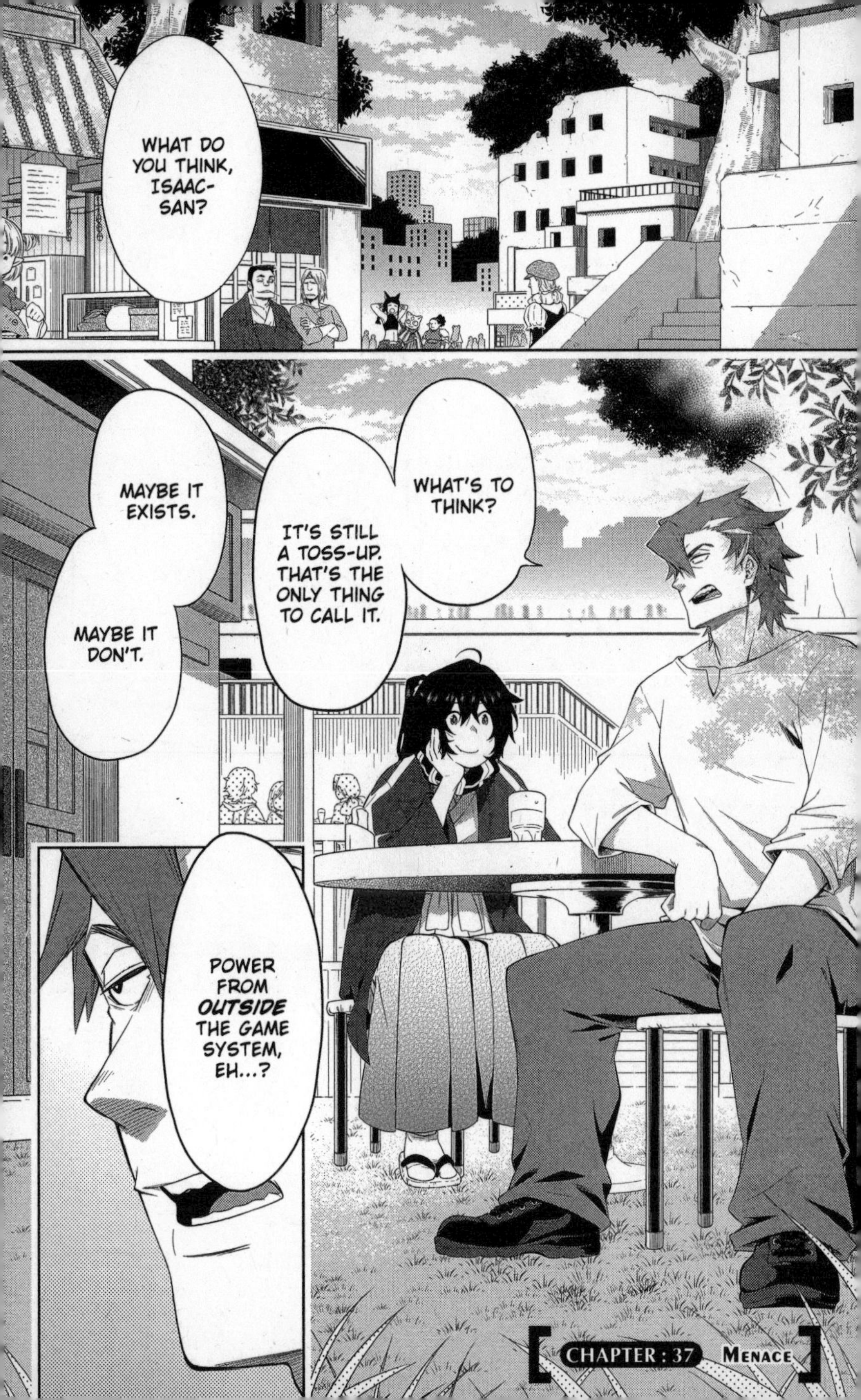
WHAT DO YOU THINK, ISAAC-SAN?
WHAT'S TO THINK?
IT'S STILL A TOSS-UP. THAT'S THE ONLY THING TO CALL IT.
MAYBE IT EXISTS.
MAYBE IT DON'T.
POWER FROM *OUTSIDE* THE GAME SYSTEM, EH...?
CHAPTER : 37 MENACE

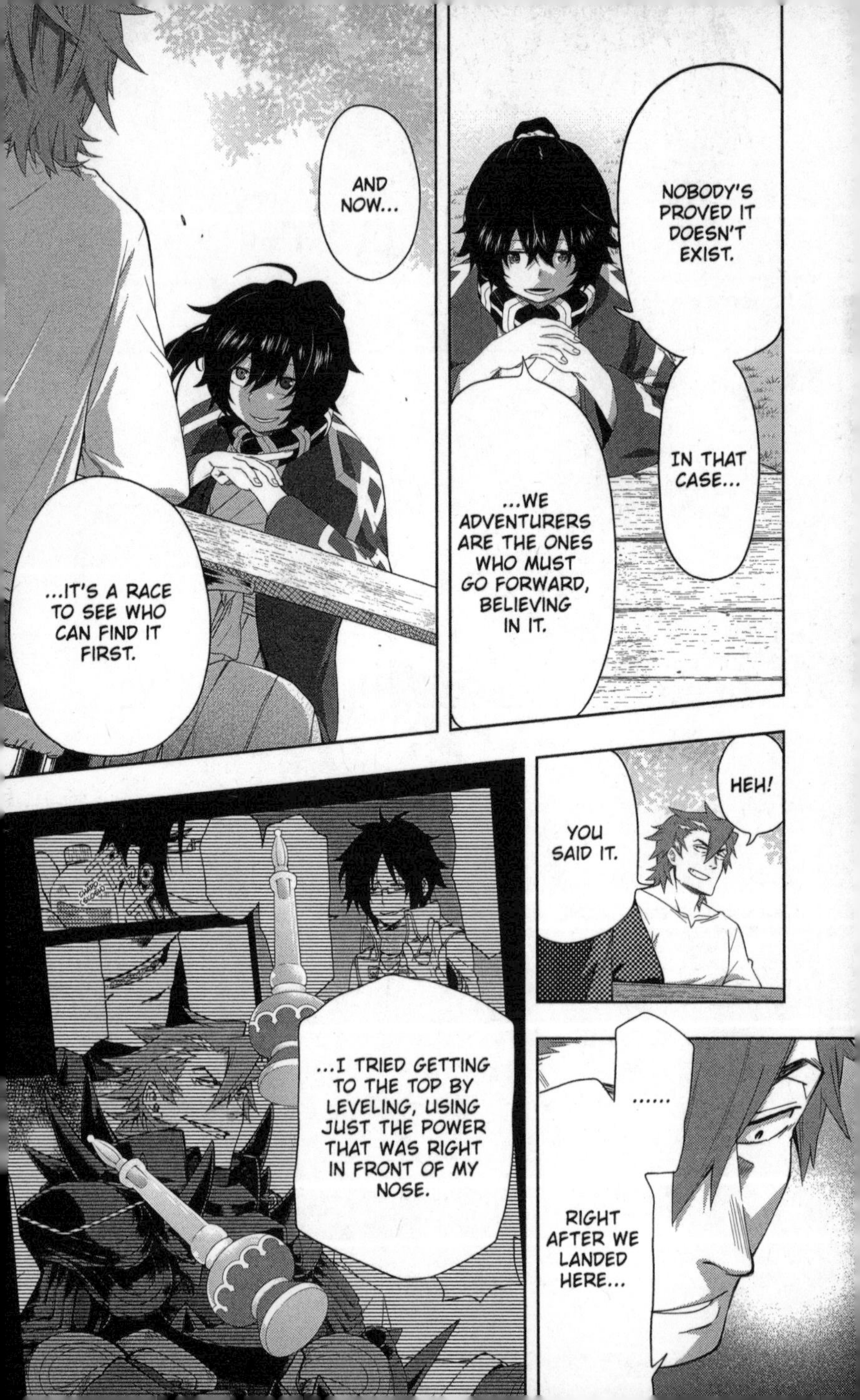
NOBODY'S PROVED IT DOESN'T EXIST.
IN THAT CASE...
...WE ADVENTURERS ARE THE ONES WHO MUST GO FORWARD, BELIEVING IN IT.
AND NOW...
...IT'S A RACE TO SEE WHO CAN FIND IT FIRST.
HEH!
YOU SAID IT.
......
RIGHT AFTER WE LANDED HERE...
...I TRIED GETTING TO THE TOP BY LEVELING, USING JUST THE POWER THAT WAS RIGHT IN FRONT OF MY NOSE.

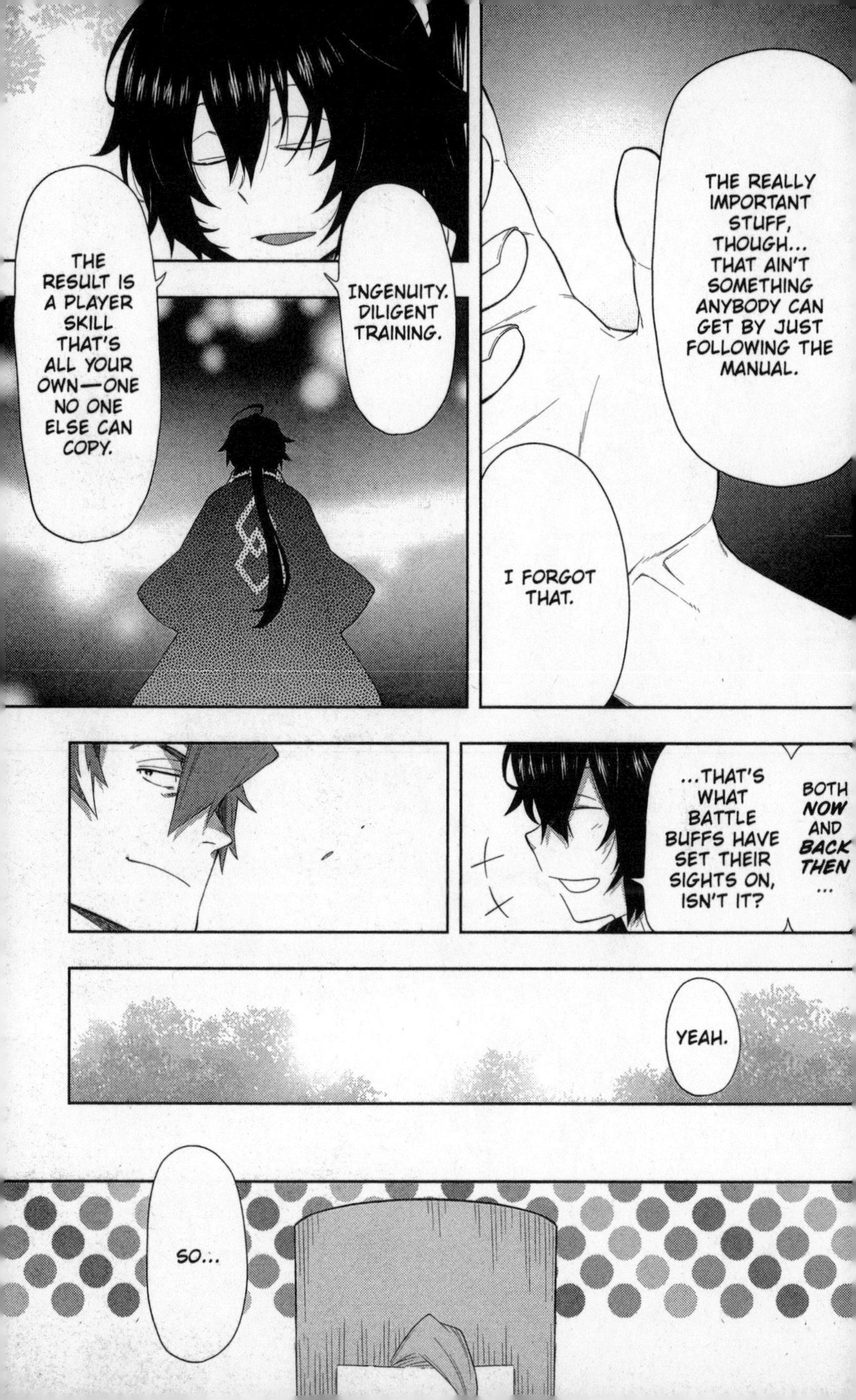
THE REALLY IMPORTANT STUFF, THOUGH... THAT AIN'T SOMETHING ANYBODY CAN GET BY JUST FOLLOWING THE MANUAL.
I FORGOT THAT.
INGENUITY. DILIGENT TRAINING.
THE RESULT IS A PLAYER SKILL THAT'S ALL YOUR OWN—ONE NO ONE ELSE CAN COPY.
BOTH *NOW* AND *BACK THEN*...
...THAT'S WHAT BATTLE BUFFS HAVE SET THEIR SIGHTS ON, ISN'T IT?
YEAH.
SO...

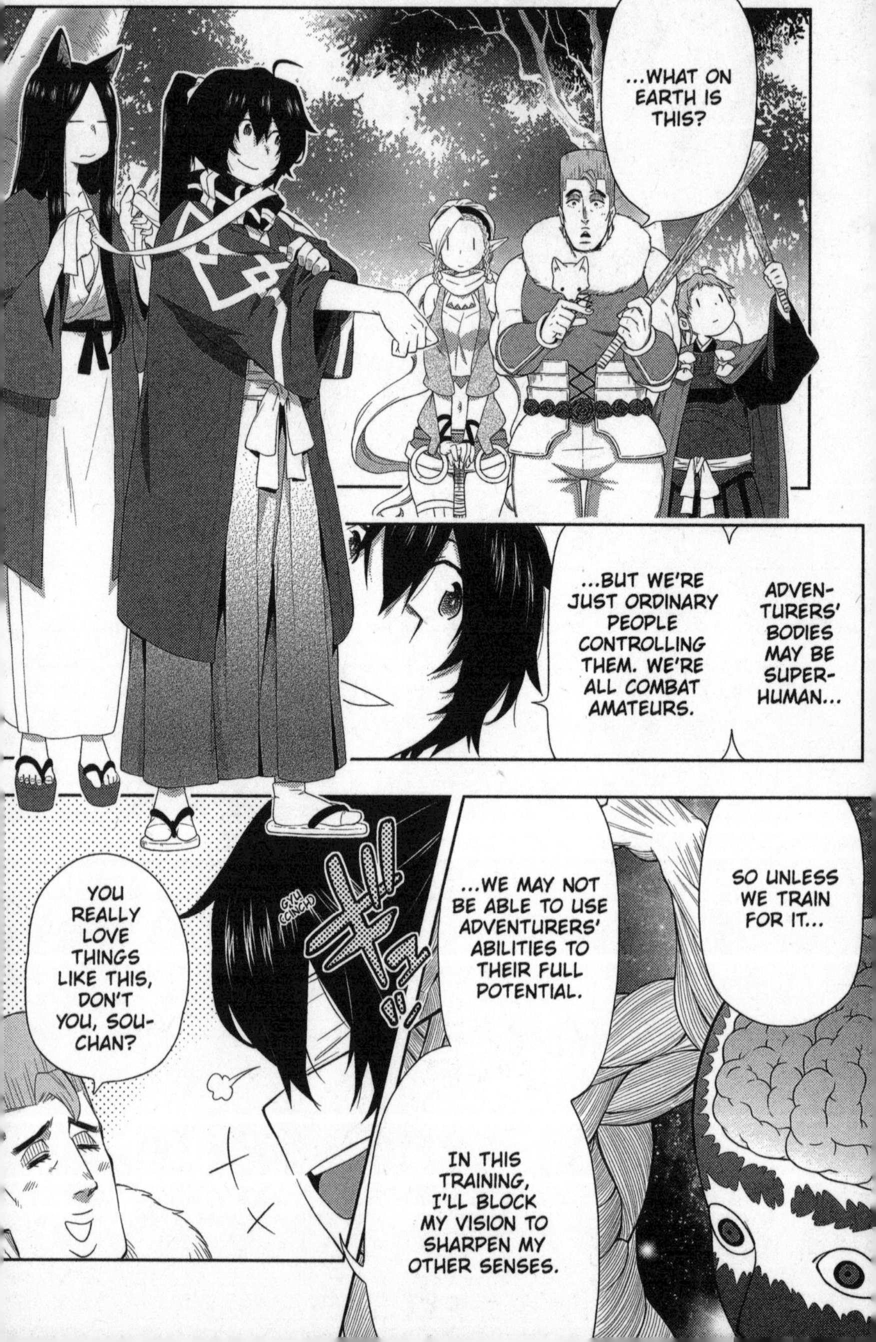
...WHAT ON EARTH IS THIS?
ADVENTURERS' BODIES MAY BE SUPERHUMAN...
...BUT WE'RE JUST ORDINARY PEOPLE CONTROLLING THEM. WE'RE ALL COMBAT AMATEURS.
SO UNLESS WE TRAIN FOR IT...
...WE MAY NOT BE ABLE TO USE ADVENTURERS' ABILITIES TO THEIR FULL POTENTIAL.
IN THIS TRAINING, I'LL BLOCK MY VISION TO SHARPEN MY OTHER SENSES.
GYU (CINCH)
YOU REALLY LOVE THINGS LIKE THIS, DON'T YOU, SOU-CHAN?

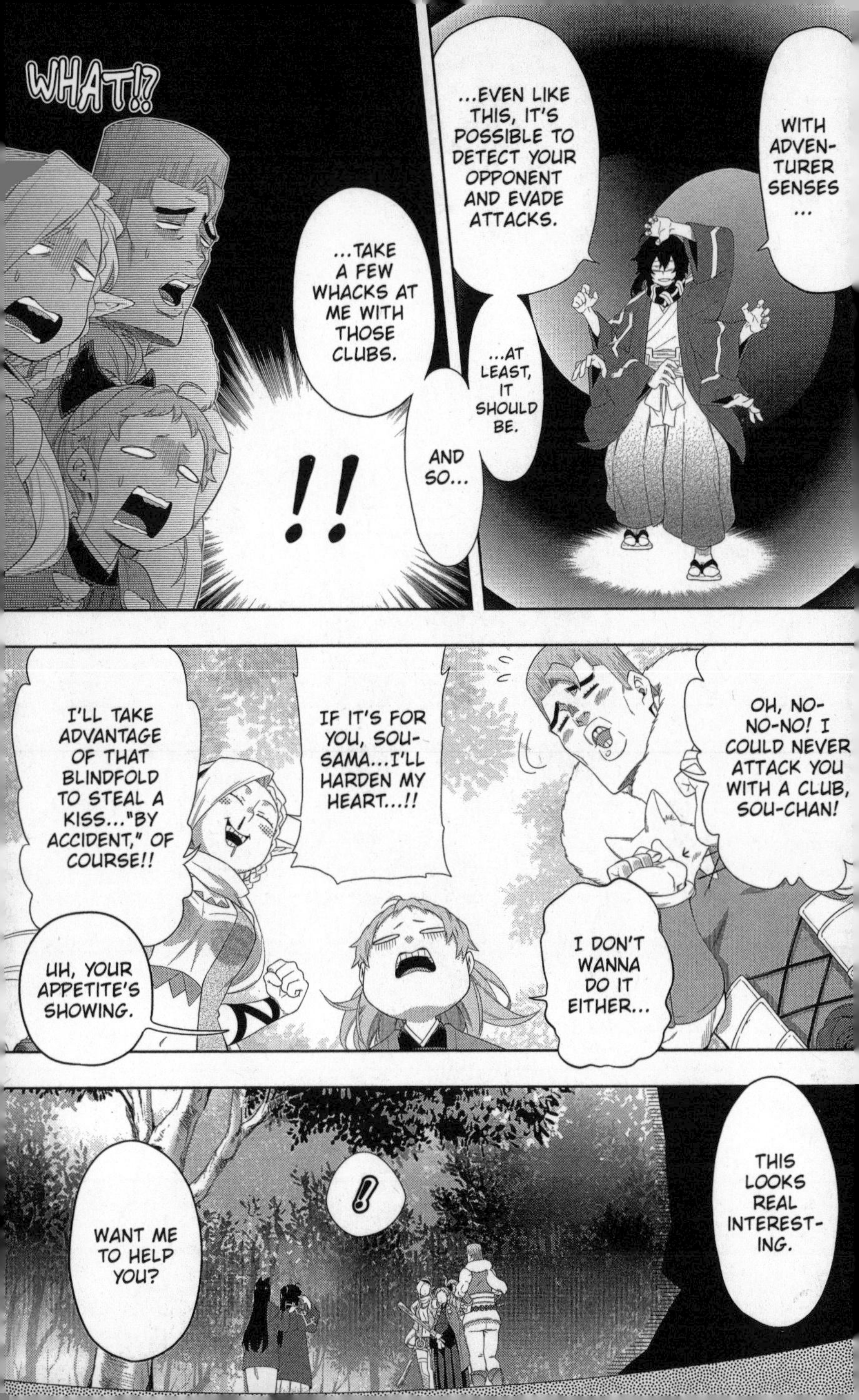
WITH ADVENTURER SENSES...
...EVEN LIKE THIS, IT'S POSSIBLE TO DETECT YOUR OPPONENT AND EVADE ATTACKS.
...AT LEAST, IT SHOULD BE.
AND SO...
...TAKE A FEW WHACKS AT ME WITH THOSE CLUBS.
!!
WHAT!?
OH, NO-NO-NO! I COULD NEVER ATTACK YOU WITH A CLUB, SOU-CHAN!
IF IT'S FOR YOU, SOU-SAMA...I'LL HARDEN MY HEART...!!
I'LL TAKE ADVANTAGE OF THAT BLINDFOLD TO STEAL A KISS..."BY ACCIDENT," OF COURSE!!
I DON'T WANNA DO IT EITHER...
UH, YOUR APPETITE'S SHOWING.
THIS LOOKS REAL INTERESTING.
!
WANT ME TO HELP YOU?

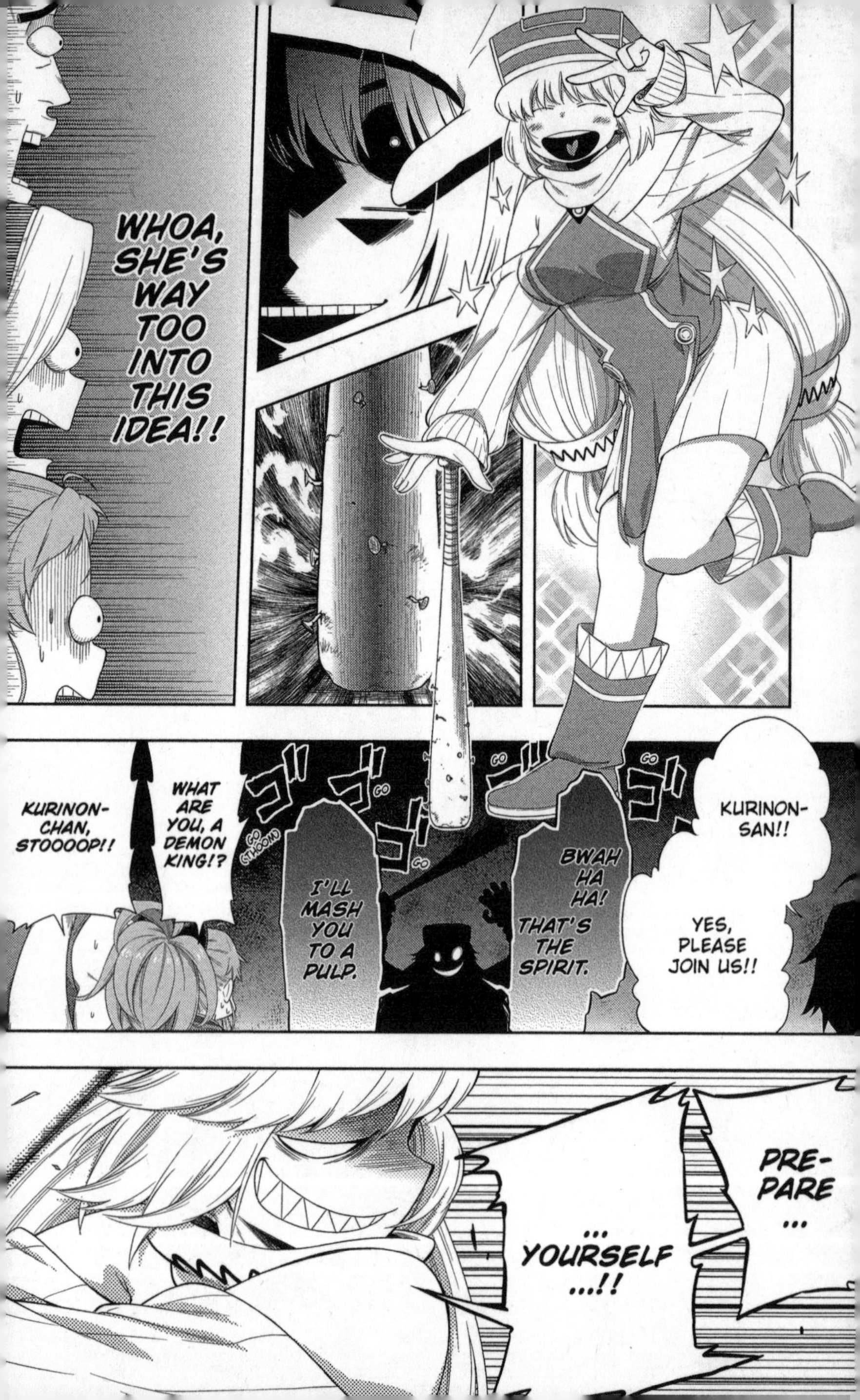
WHOA, SHE'S WAY TOO INTO THIS IDEA!!
KURINON-SAN!!
YES, PLEASE JOIN US!!
GO
GO
BWAH HA HA! THAT'S THE SPIRIT.
I'LL MASH YOU TO A PULP.
GO
GO (THOOM)
WHAT ARE YOU, A DEMON KING!?
KURINON-CHAN, STOOOOP!!
PRE-PARE...
...YOURSELF...!!

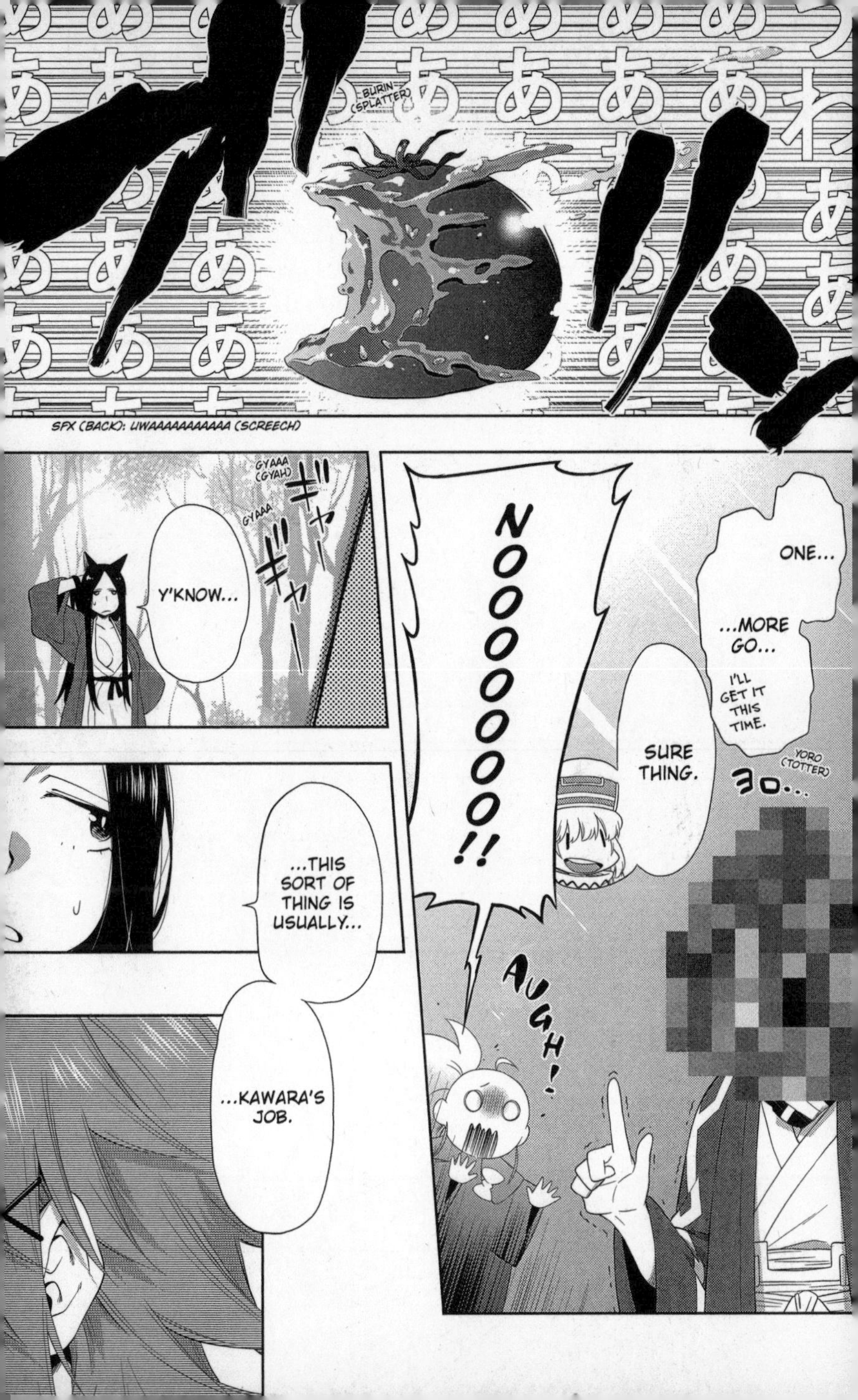
BURIN (SPLATTER)
SFX (BACK): UWAAAAAAAAAAAA (SCREECH)
ONE...
...MORE GO...
I'LL GET IT THIS TIME.
YORO (TOTTER)
SURE THING.
NOOOOOOOOOO!!
AUGH!
GYAAA (GYAH)
GYAAA
Y'KNOW...
...THIS SORT OF THING IS USUALLY...
...KAWARA'S JOB.

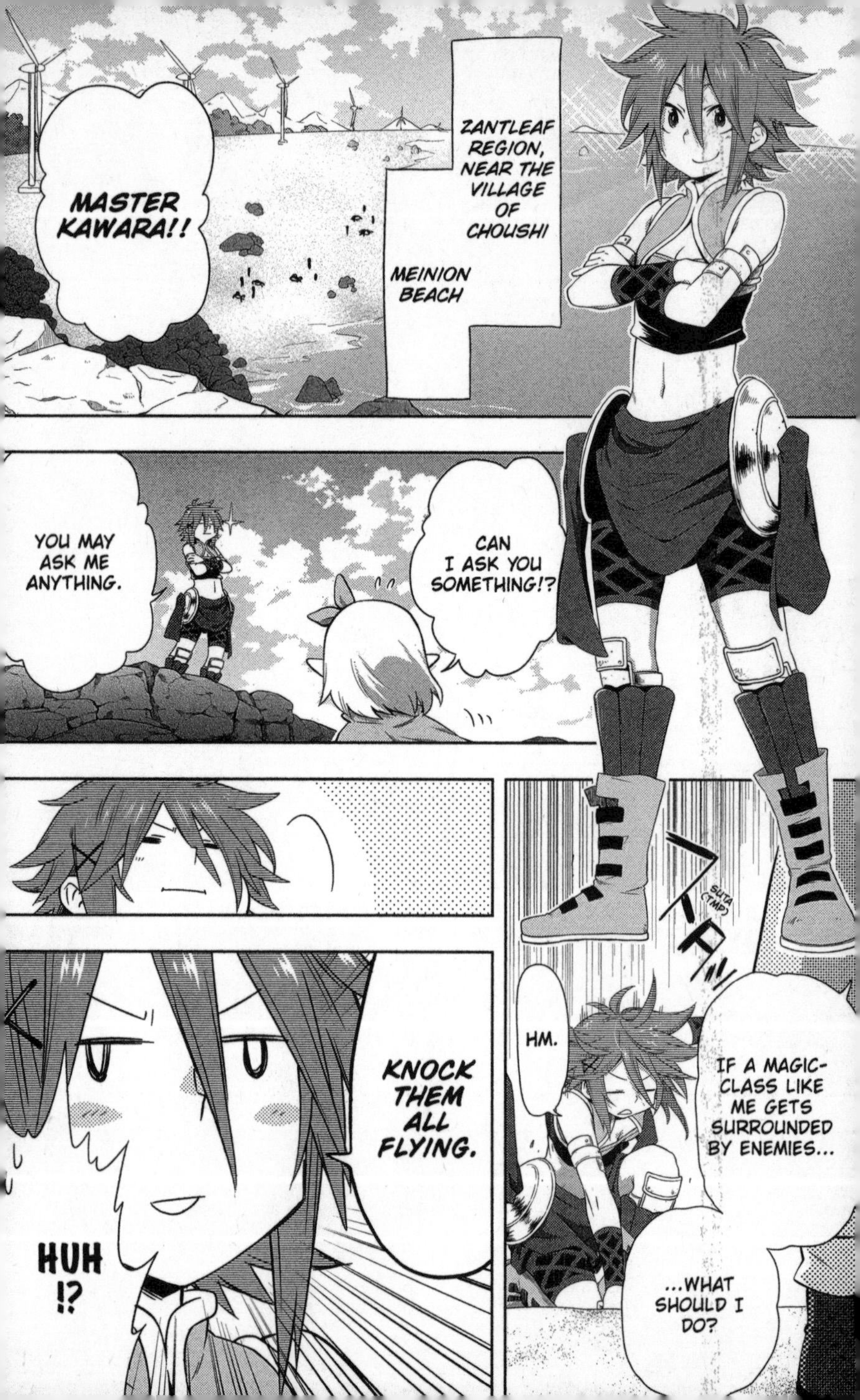
ZANTLEAF REGION, NEAR THE VILLAGE OF CHOUSHI
MEINION BEACH
MASTER KAWARA!!
CAN I ASK YOU SOMETHING!?
YOU MAY ASK ME ANYTHING.
SUTA (TMP)
IF A MAGIC-CLASS LIKE ME GETS SURROUNDED BY ENEMIES...
...WHAT SHOULD I DO?
HM.
KNOCK THEM ALL FLYING.
HUH!?

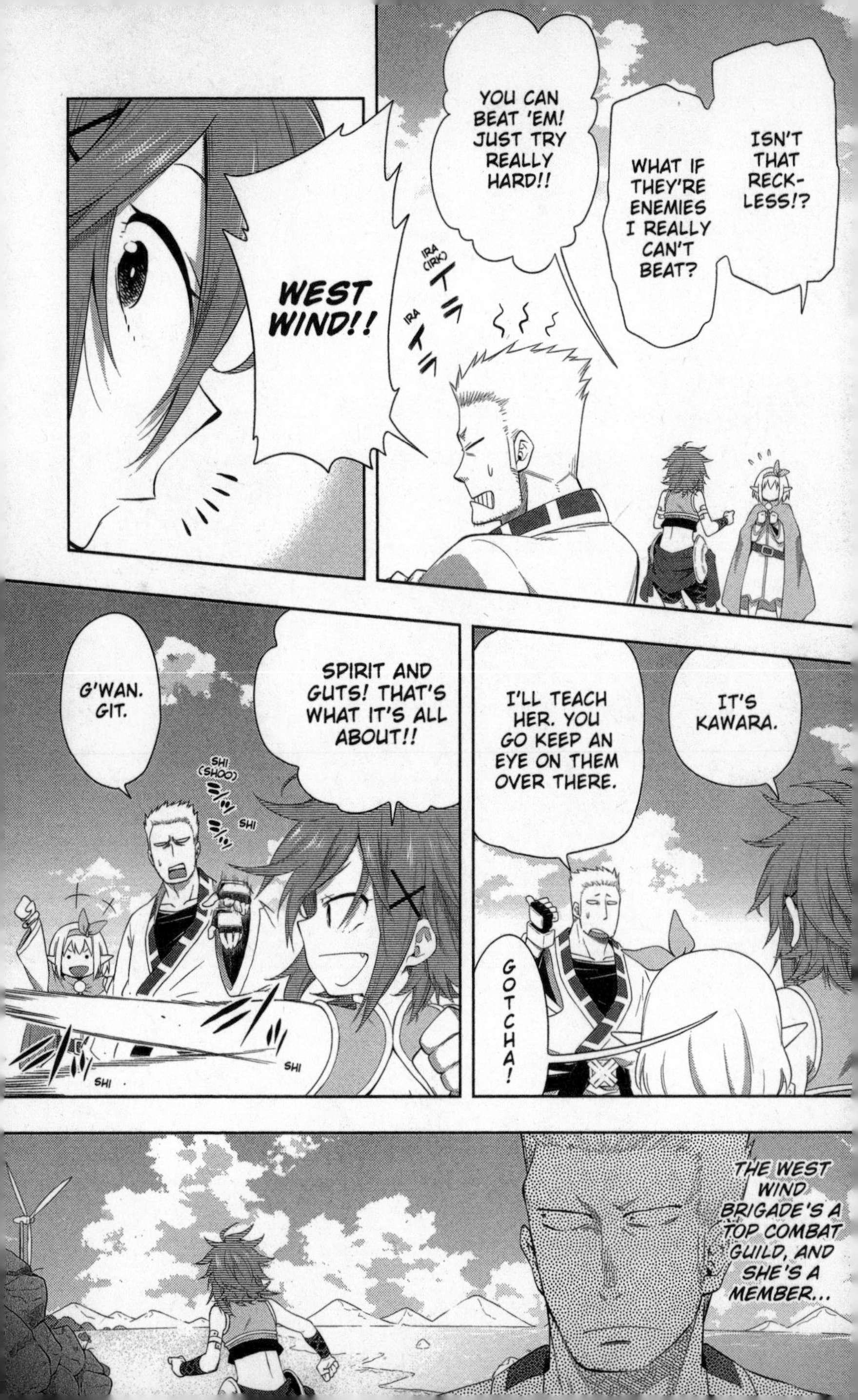
ISN'T THAT RECK-LESS!?
WHAT IF THEY'RE ENEMIES I REALLY CAN'T BEAT?
YOU CAN BEAT 'EM! JUST TRY REALLY HARD!!
IRA (IRK)
IRA
WEST WIND!!
IT'S KAWARA.
I'LL TEACH HER. YOU GO KEEP AN EYE ON THEM OVER THERE.
GOTCHA!
SPIRIT AND GUTS! THAT'S WHAT IT'S ALL ABOUT!!
G'WAN. GIT.
SHI (SHOO)
SHI
SHI
SHI
THE WEST WIND BRIGADE'S A TOP COMBAT GUILD, AND SHE'S A MEMBER...

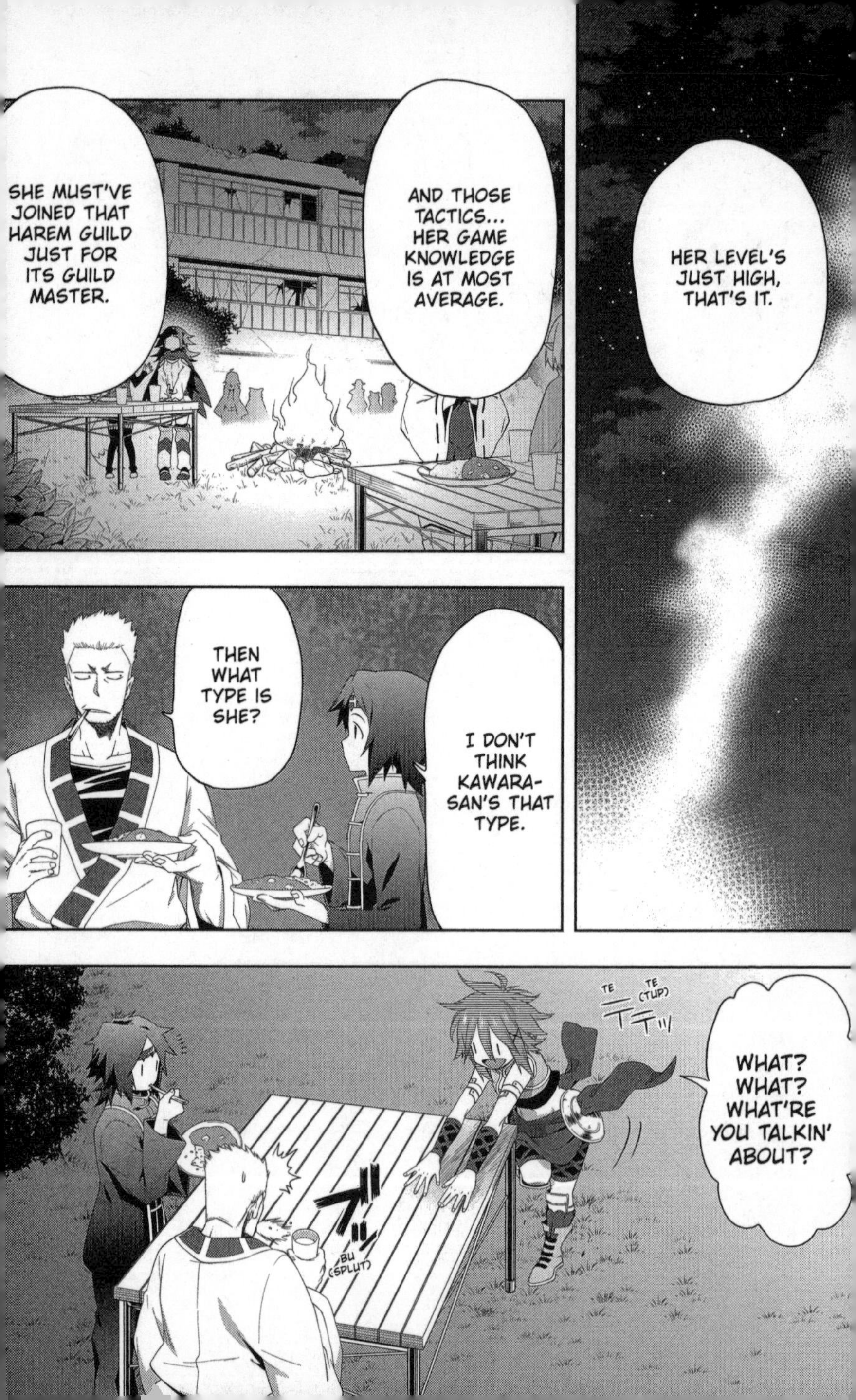
HER LEVEL'S JUST HIGH, THAT'S IT.
AND THOSE TACTICS... HER GAME KNOWLEDGE IS AT MOST AVERAGE.
SHE MUST'VE JOINED THAT HAREM GUILD JUST FOR ITS GUILD MASTER.
I DON'T THINK KAWARA-SAN'S THAT TYPE.
THEN WHAT TYPE IS SHE?
TE TE (TUP)
WHAT? WHAT? WHAT'RE YOU TALKIN' ABOUT?
BU (SPLUT)

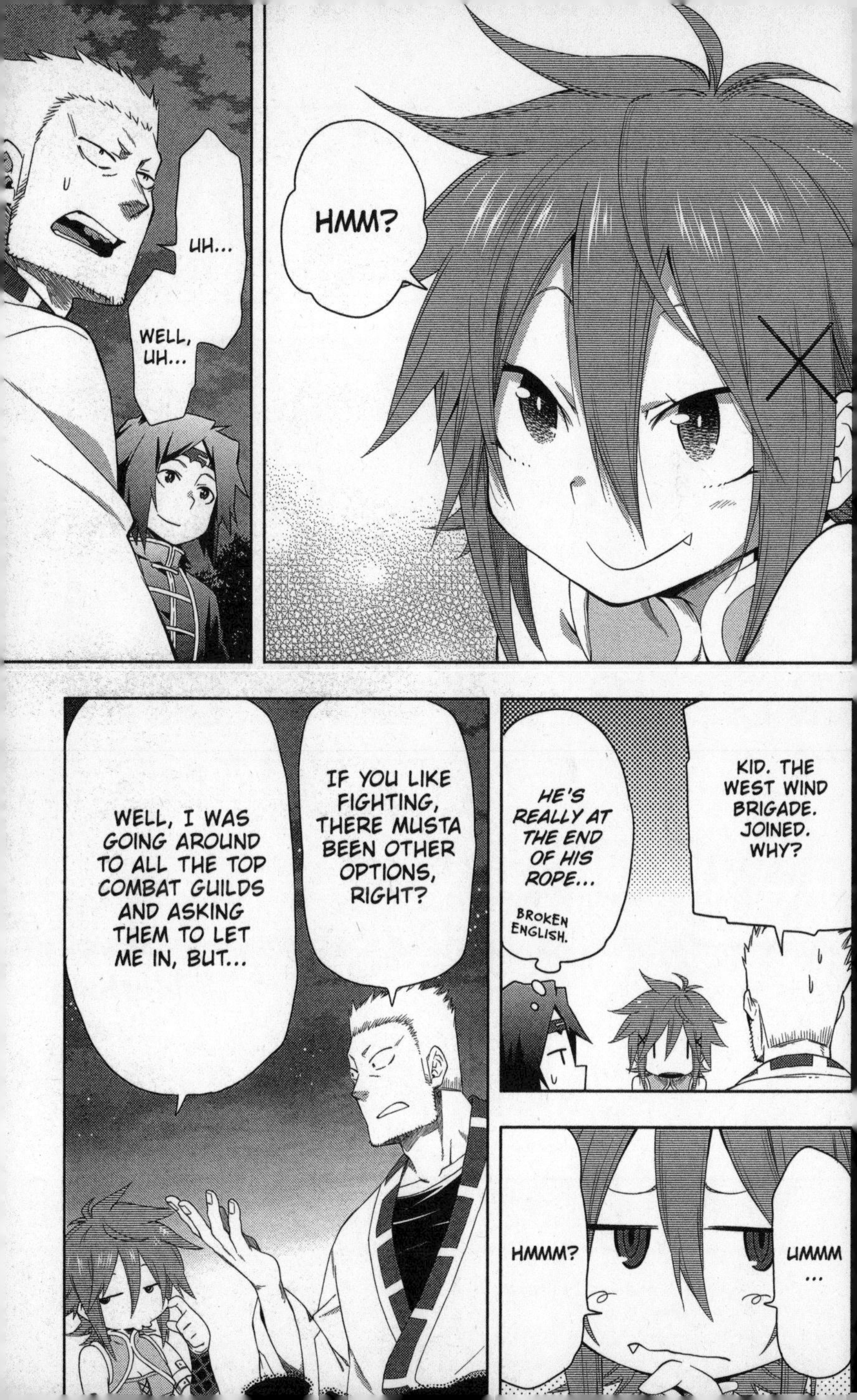
HMM?
UH...
WELL, UH...
KID. THE WEST WIND BRIGADE. JOINED. WHY?
HE'S REALLY AT THE END OF HIS ROPE...
BROKEN ENGLISH.
UMMM ...
HMMM?
IF YOU LIKE FIGHTING, THERE MUSTA BEEN OTHER OPTIONS, RIGHT?
WELL, I WAS GOING AROUND TO ALL THE TOP COMBAT GUILDS AND ASKING THEM TO LET ME IN, BUT...

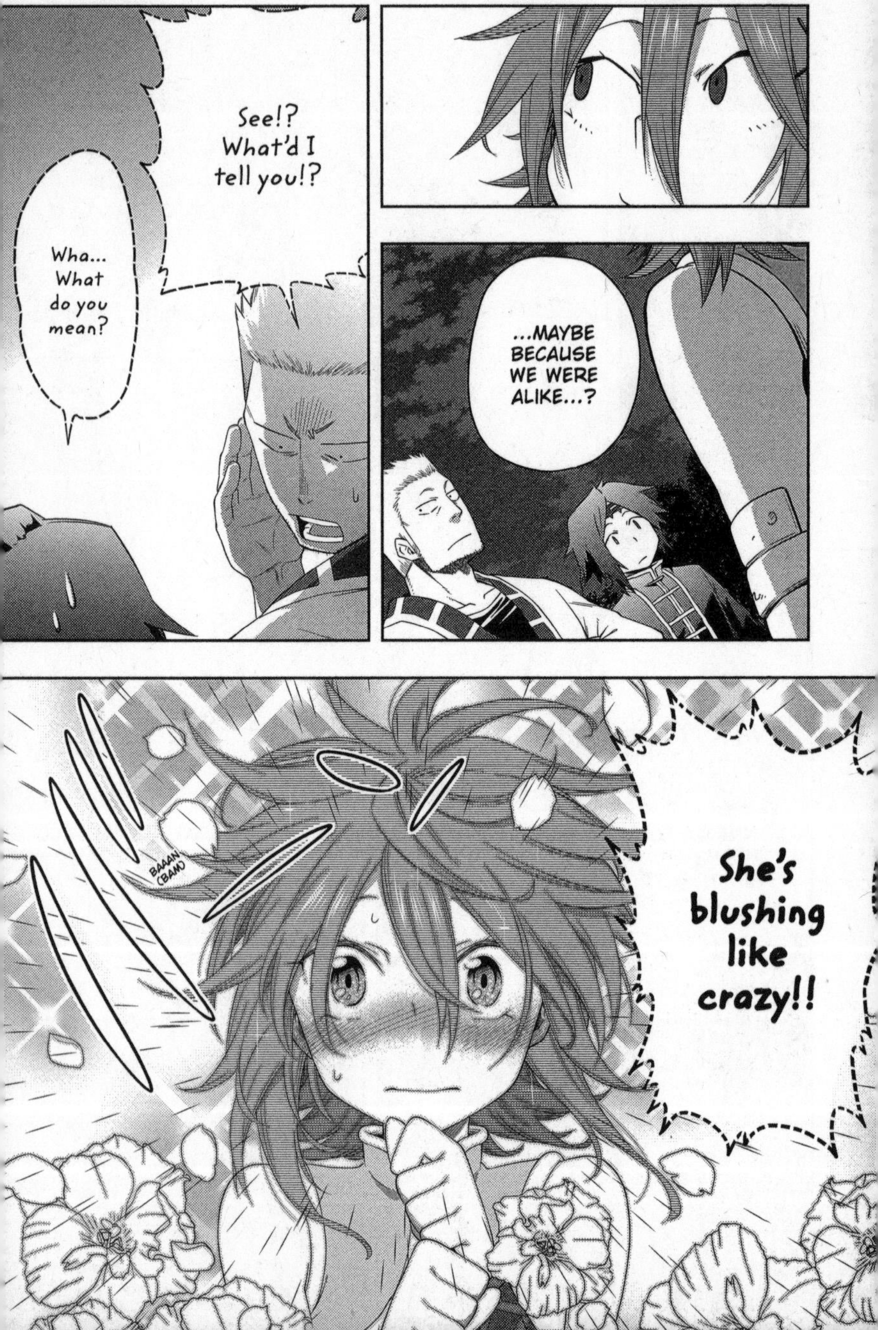
...MAYBE BECAUSE WE WERE ALIKE...?
See!? What'd I tell you!?
Wha... What do you mean?
She's blushing like crazy!!
BAAAN (BAM)

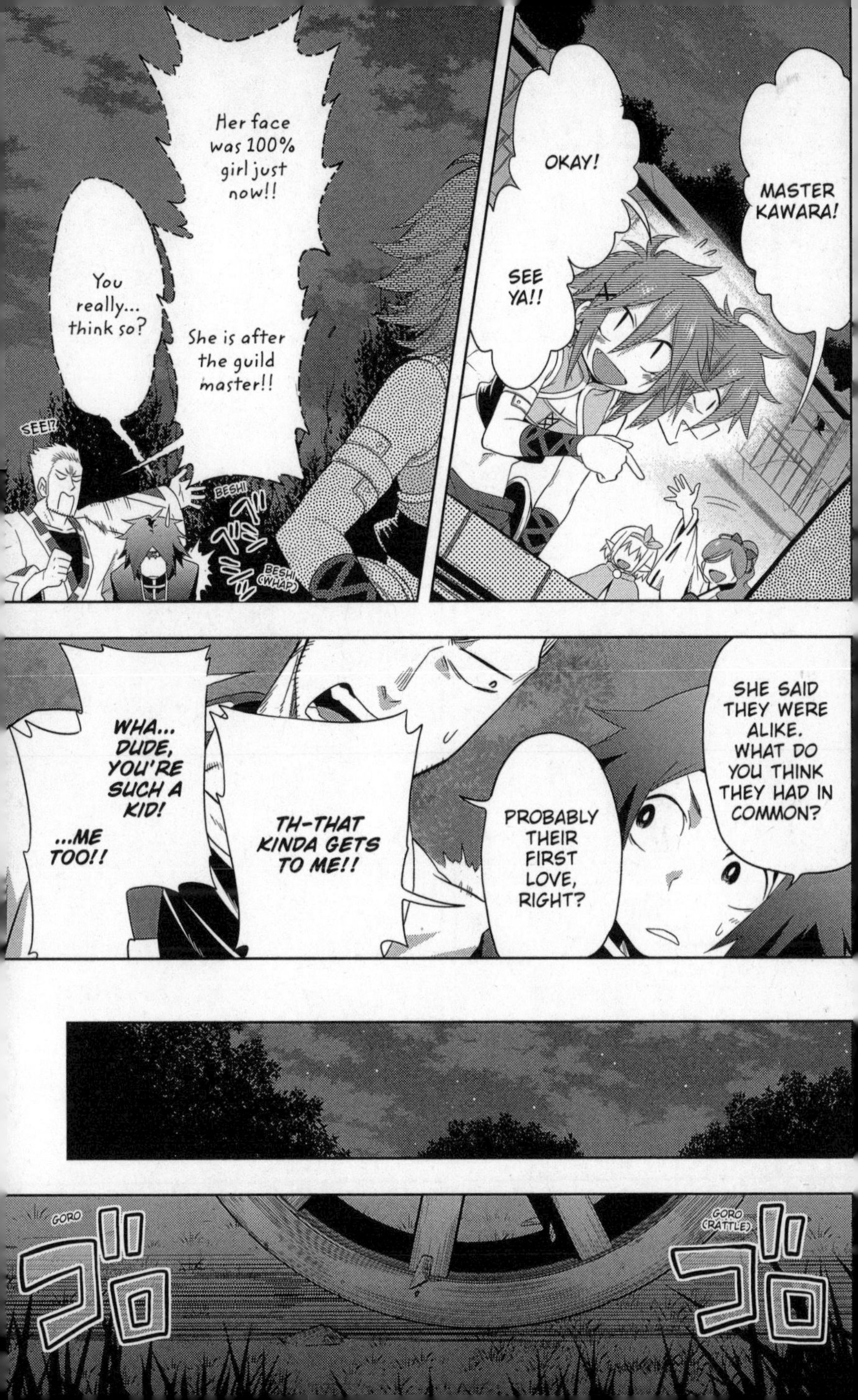
MASTER KAWARA!
OKAY!
SEE YA!!
Her face was 100% girl just now!!
She is after the guild master!!
You really... think so?
SEE!?
BESHI
BESHI (WHAP)
SHE SAID THEY WERE ALIKE. WHAT DO YOU THINK THEY HAD IN COMMON?
PROBABLY THEIR FIRST LOVE, RIGHT?
TH-THAT KINDA GETS TO ME!!
WHA... DUDE, YOU'RE SUCH A KID!
...ME TOO!!
GORO (RATTLE)
ゴロ
GORO
ゴロ

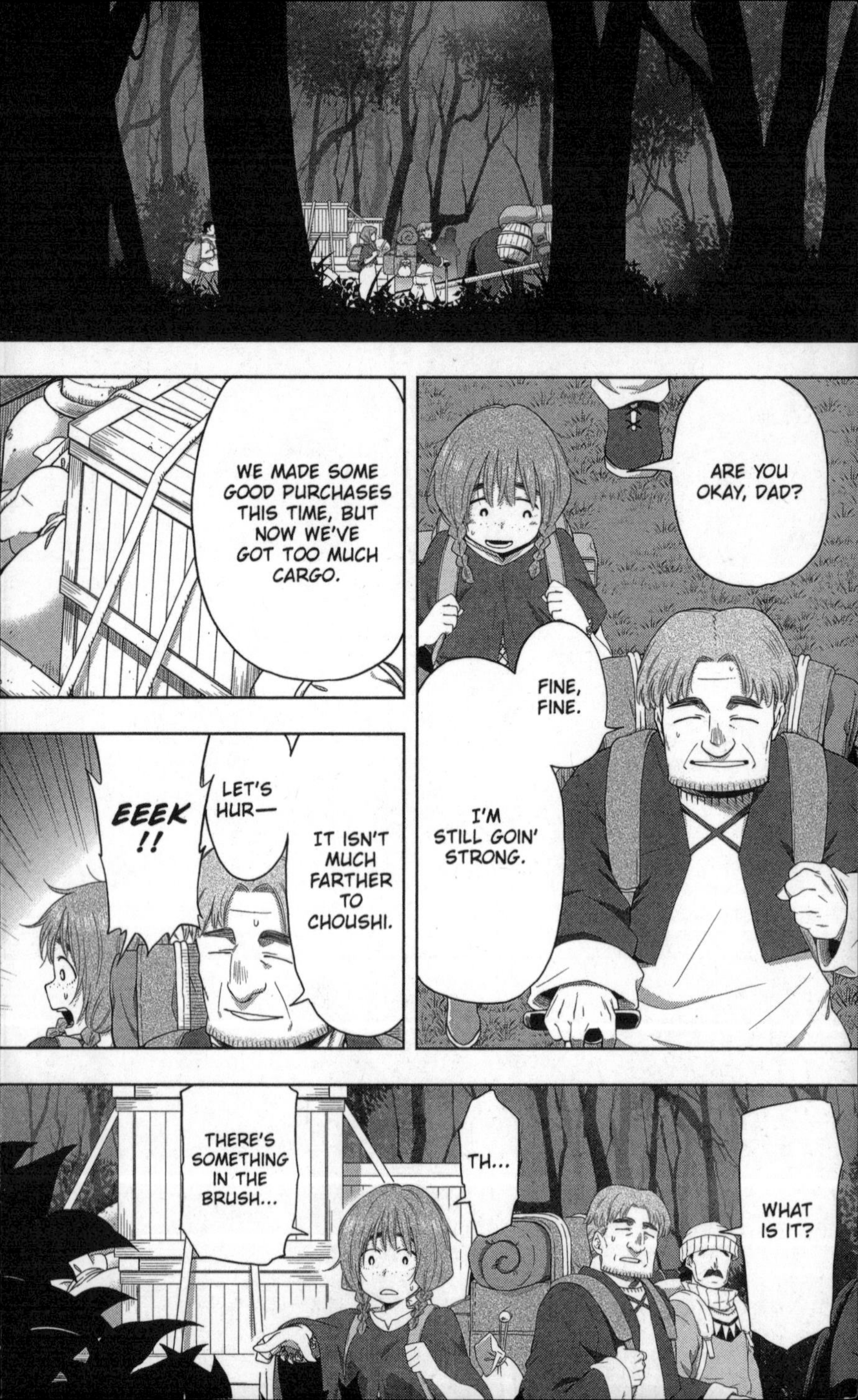
ARE YOU OKAY, DAD?
FINE, FINE.
I'M STILL GOIN' STRONG.
WE MADE SOME GOOD PURCHASES THIS TIME, BUT NOW WE'VE GOT TOO MUCH CARGO.
IT ISN'T MUCH FARTHER TO CHOUSHI.
LET'S HUR—
EEEK!!
WHAT IS IT?
TH...
THERE'S SOMETHING IN THE BRUSH...

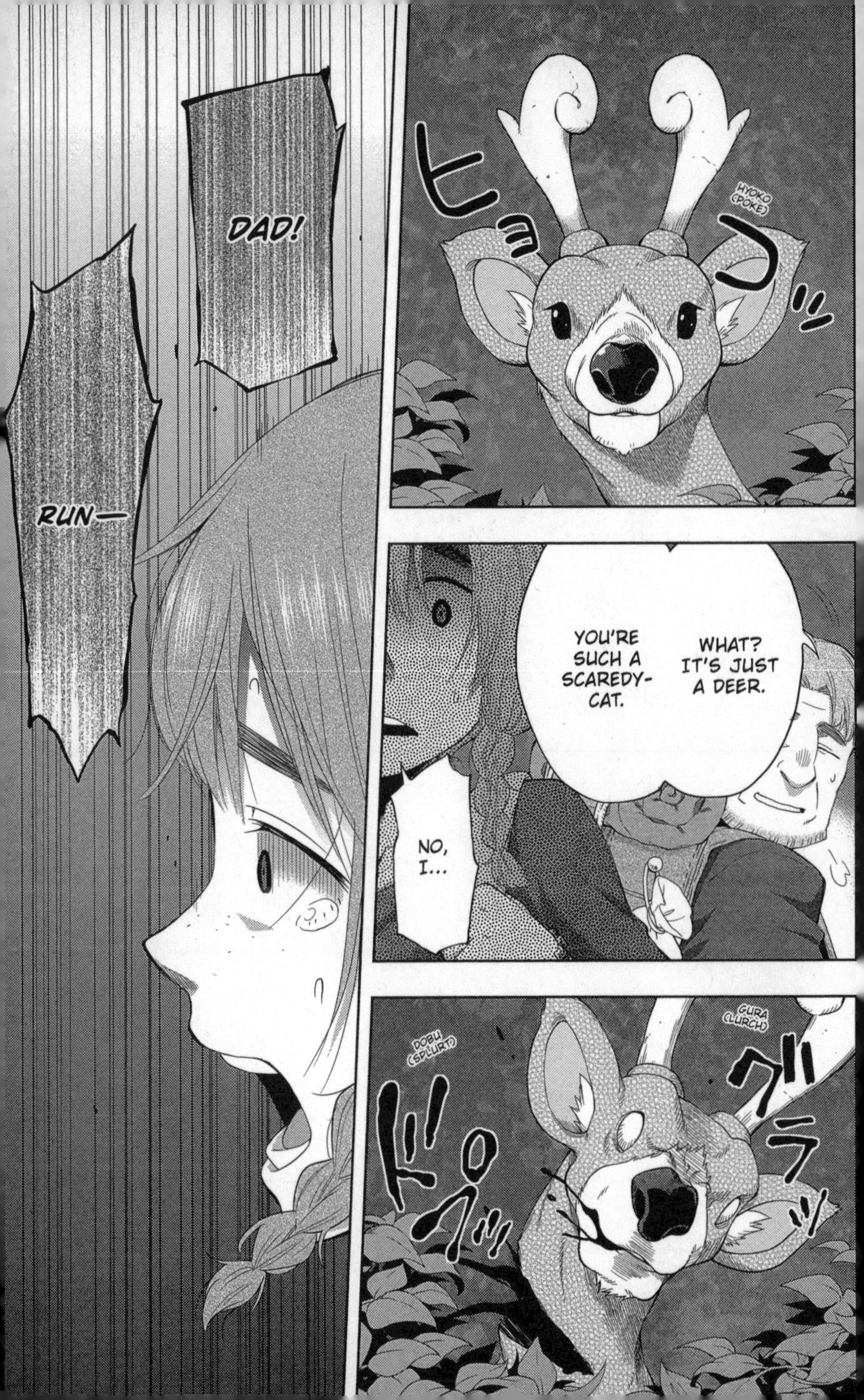

ヒョコッ
HYOKO (POKE)
WHAT? IT'S JUST A DEER.
YOU'RE SUCH A SCAREDY-CAT.
NO, I...
グラッ
GURA (LURCH)
ドプッ
DOBU (SPLURT)
DAD!
RUN—

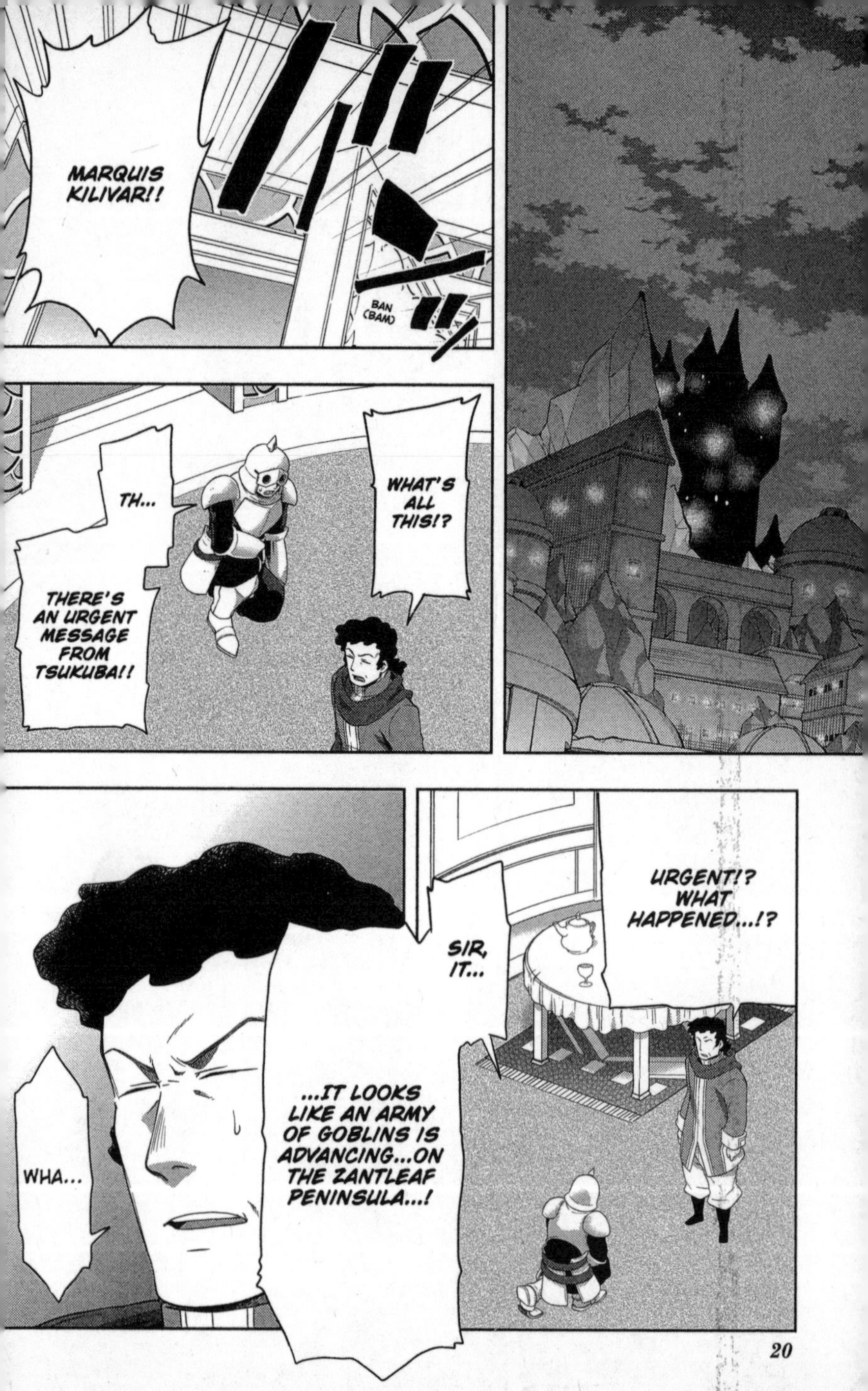
MARQUIS KILIVAR!!
BAN (BAM)
WHAT'S ALL THIS!?
TH...
THERE'S AN URGENT MESSAGE FROM TSUKUBA!!
URGENT!? WHAT HAPPENED...!?
SIR, IT...
...IT LOOKS LIKE AN ARMY OF GOBLINS IS ADVANCING...ON THE ZANTLEAF PENINSULA...!
WHA...

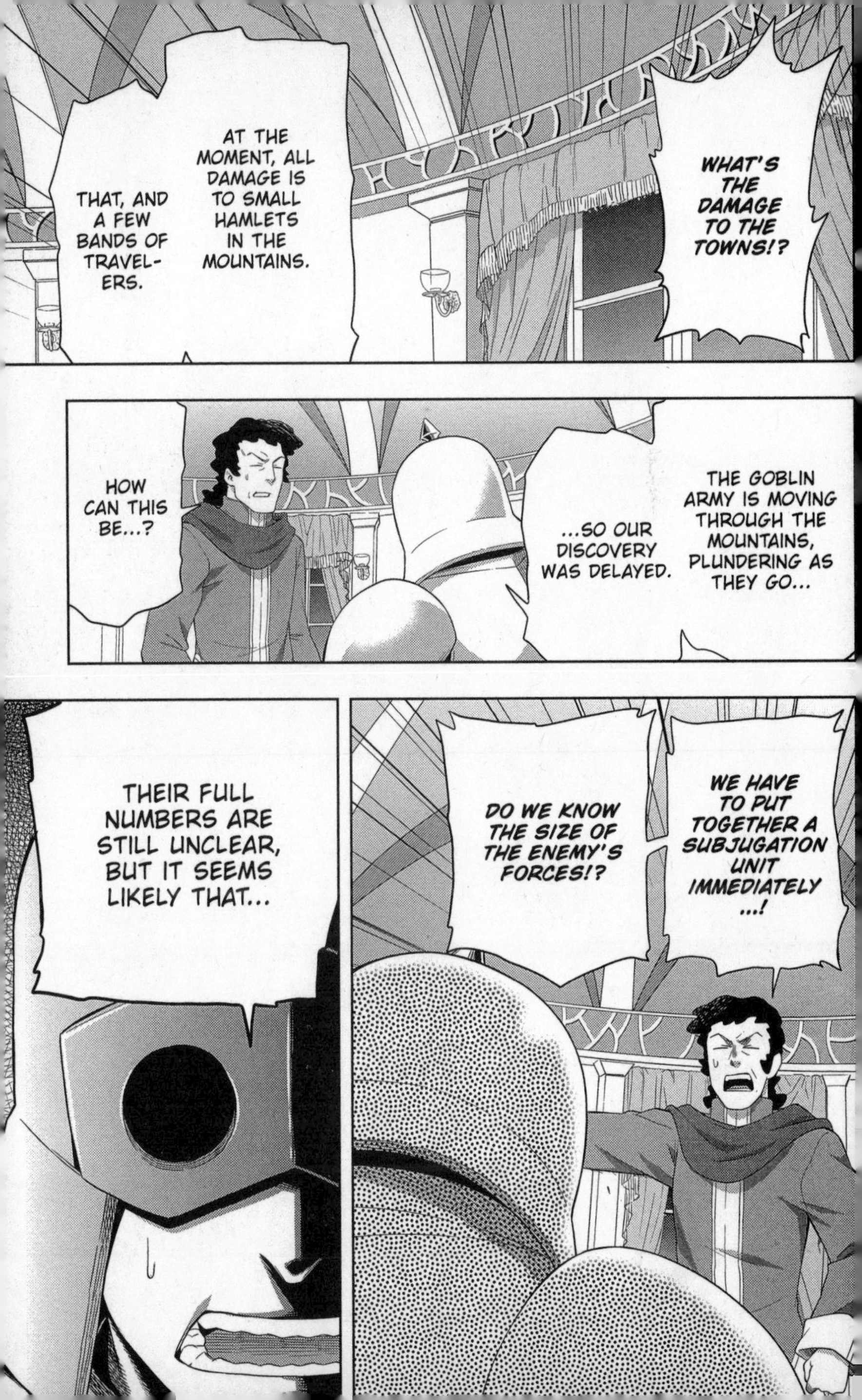
WHAT'S THE DAMAGE TO THE TOWNS!?
AT THE MOMENT, ALL DAMAGE IS TO SMALL HAMLETS IN THE MOUNTAINS.
THAT, AND A FEW BANDS OF TRAVEL-ERS.
THE GOBLIN ARMY IS MOVING THROUGH THE MOUNTAINS, PLUNDERING AS THEY GO...
...SO OUR DISCOVERY WAS DELAYED.
HOW CAN THIS BE...?
WE HAVE TO PUT TOGETHER A SUBJUGATION UNIT IMMEDIATELY ...!
DO WE KNOW THE SIZE OF THE ENEMY'S FORCES!?
THEIR FULL NUMBERS ARE STILL UNCLEAR, BUT IT SEEMS LIKELY THAT...

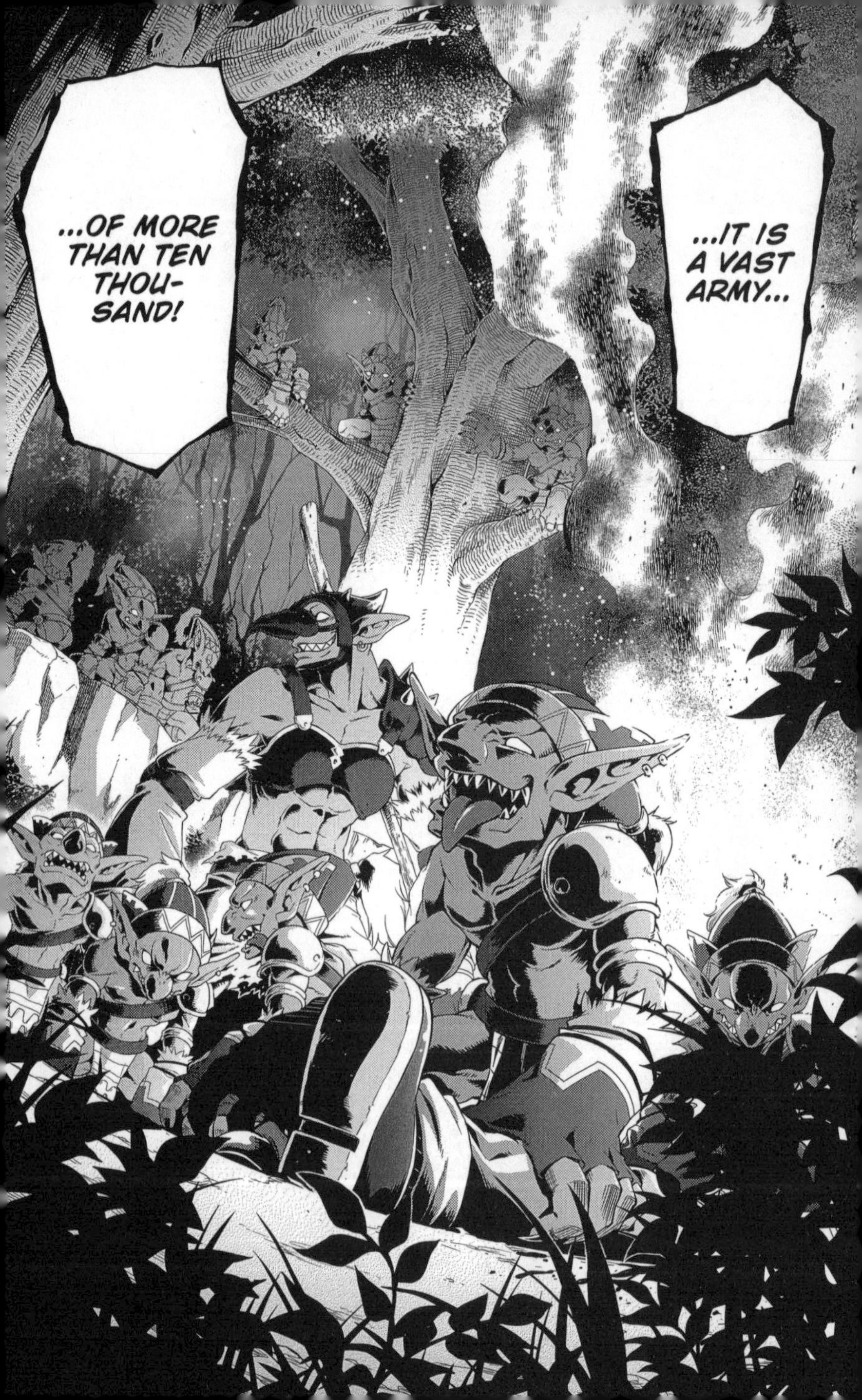
...IT IS A VAST ARMY...
...OF MORE THAN TEN THOU-SAND!

LOG HORIZON
THE WEST WIND BRIGADE

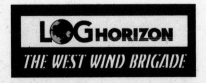

LOG HORIZON

THE WEST WIND BRIGADE

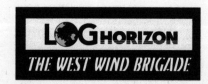

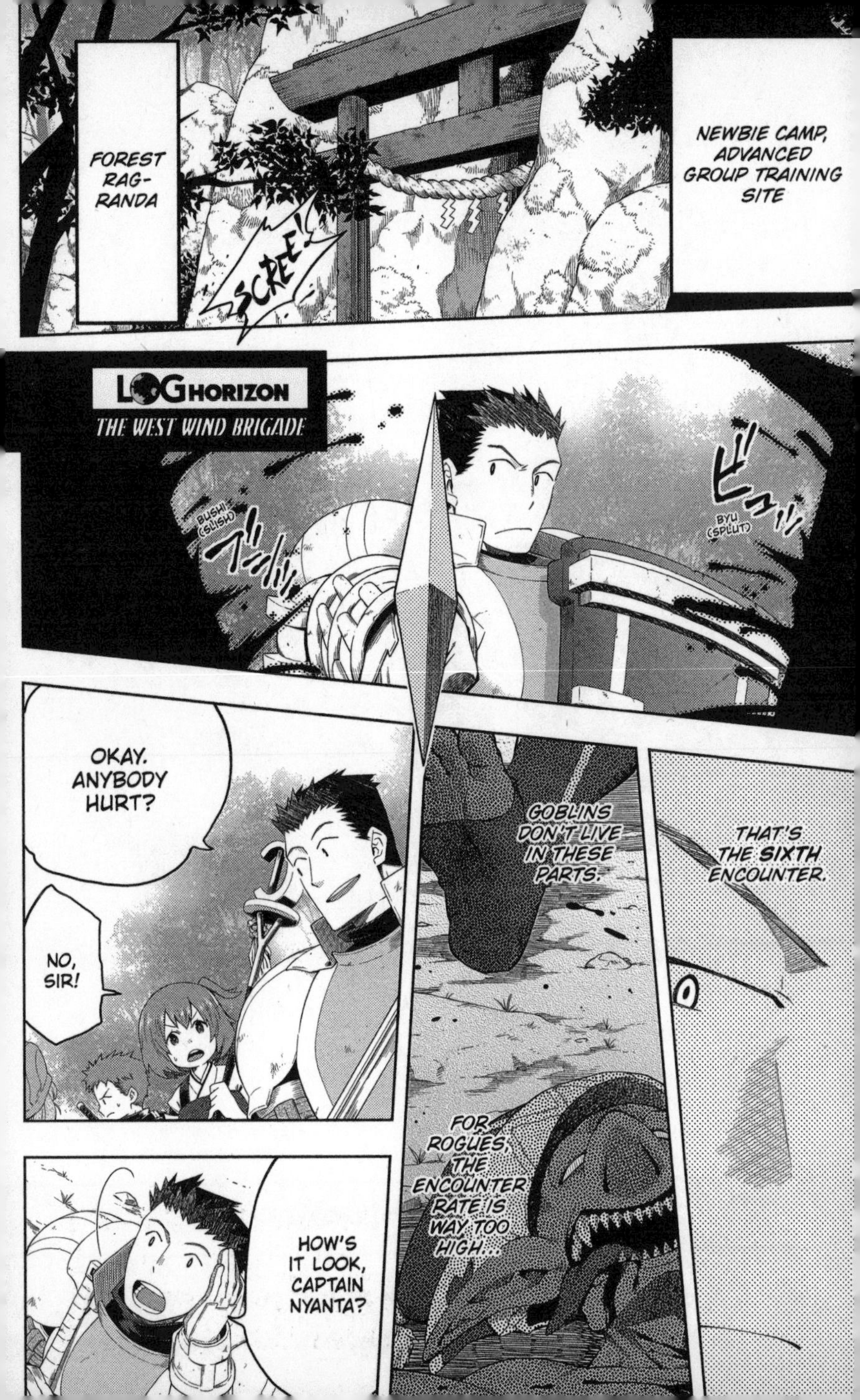
NEWBIE CAMP, ADVANCED GROUP TRAINING SITE
FOREST RAG-RANDA
SCREE!
LOG HORIZON
THE WEST WIND BRIGADE
ビュッ
BYU (SPLUT)
ブシュッ
BUSHI (SLISH)
THAT'S THE SIXTH ENCOUNTER.
GOBLINS DON'T LIVE IN THESE PARTS.
FOR ROGUES, THE ENCOUNTER RATE IS WAY TOO HIGH...
OKAY. ANYBODY HURT?
NO, SIR!
HOW'S IT LOOK, CAPTAIN NYANTA?

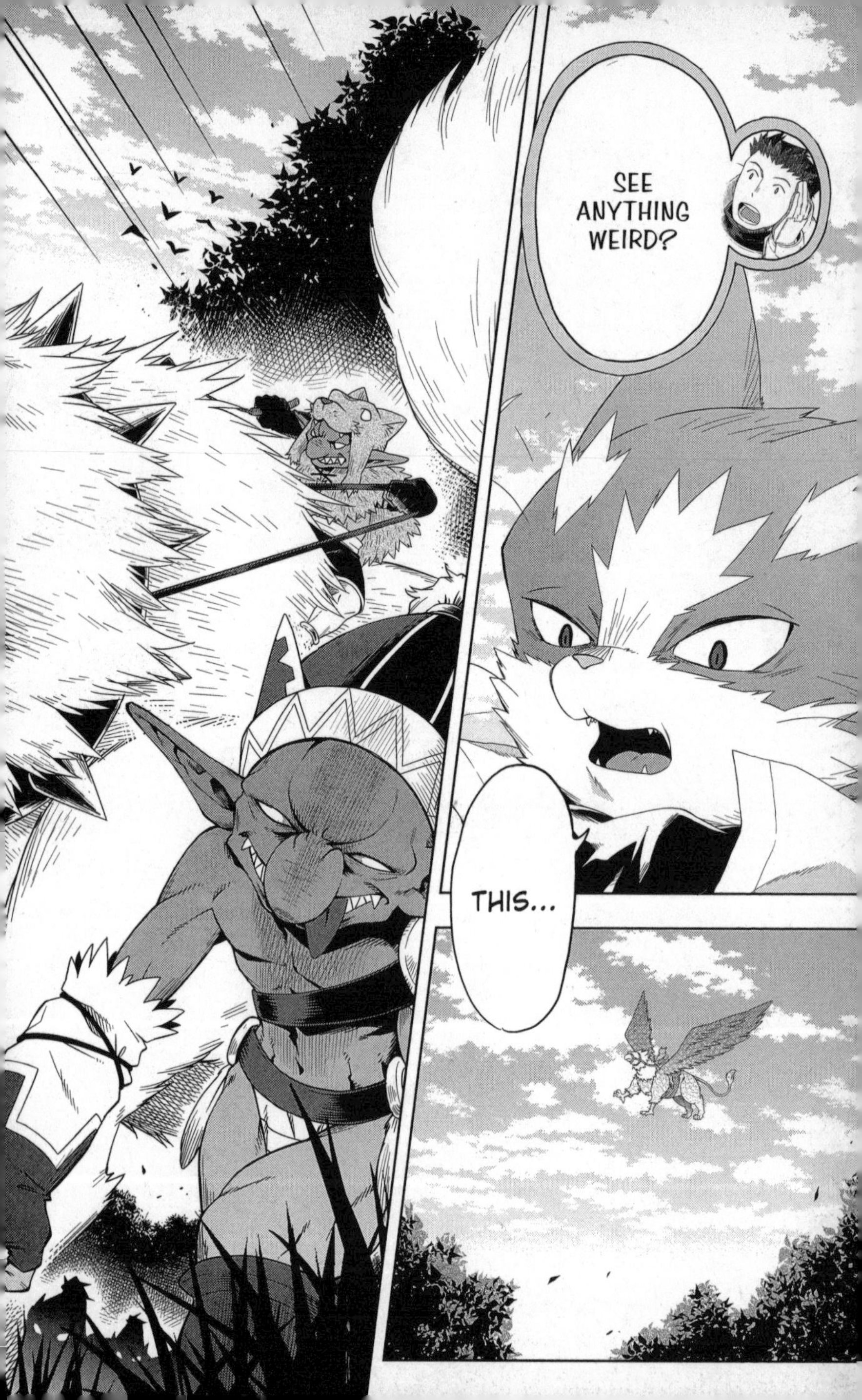
SEE ANYTHING WEIRD?
THIS...

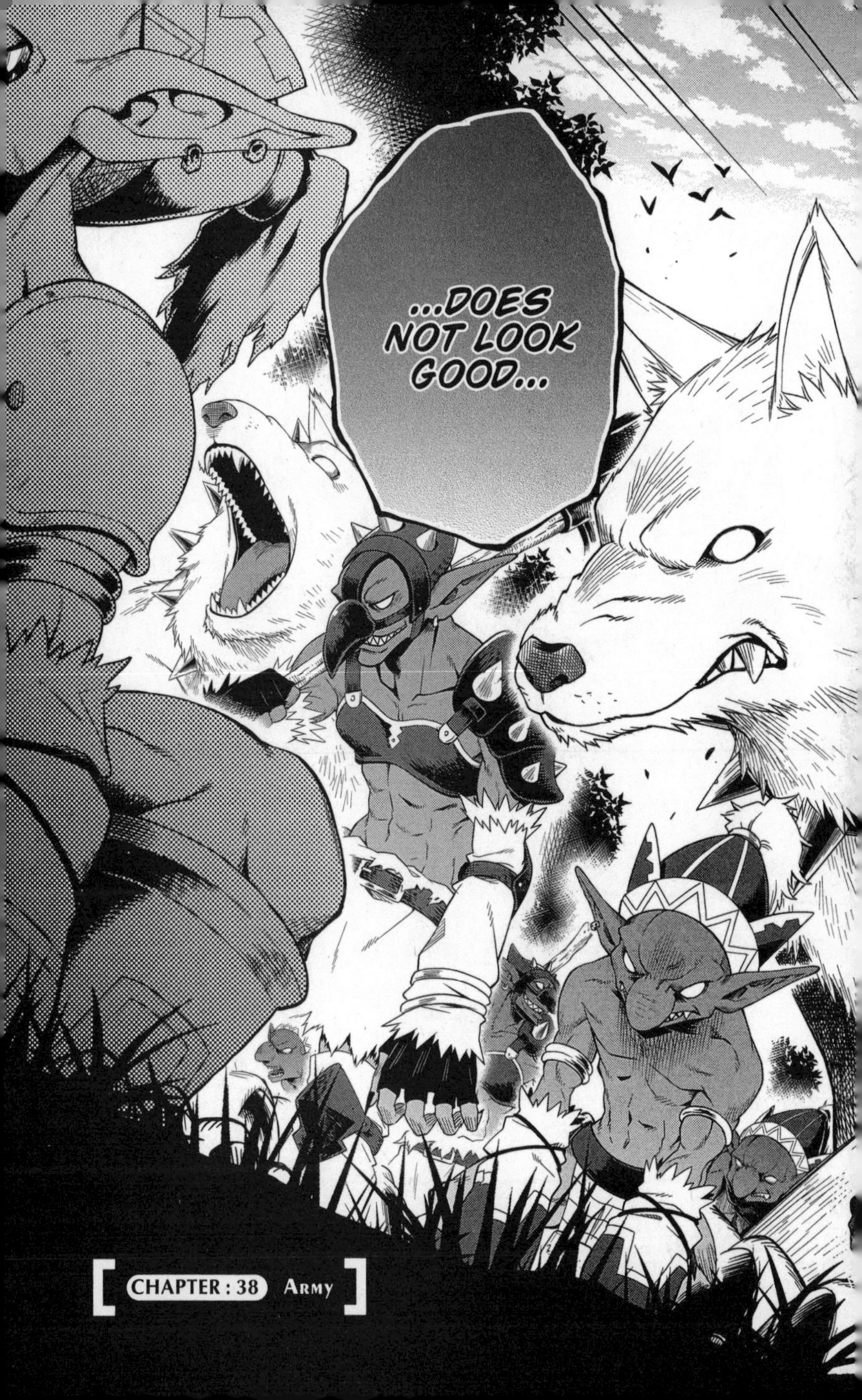
...DOES NOT LOOK GOOD...
CHAPTER : 38 Army

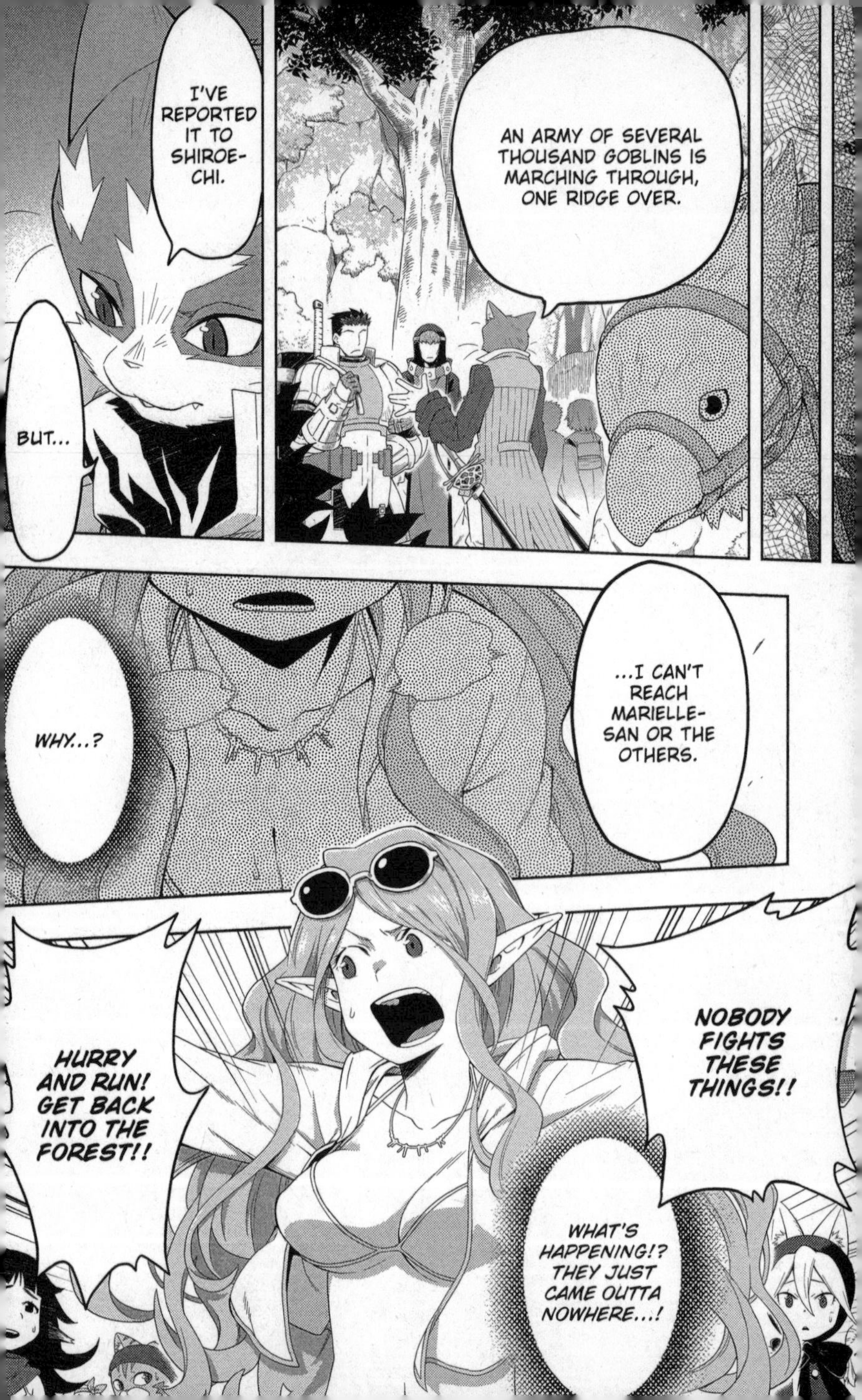
AN ARMY OF SEVERAL THOUSAND GOBLINS IS MARCHING THROUGH, ONE RIDGE OVER.
I'VE REPORTED IT TO SHIROE-CHI.
BUT...
...I CAN'T REACH MARIELLE-SAN OR THE OTHERS.
WHY...?
NOBODY FIGHTS THESE THINGS!!
HURRY AND RUN! GET BACK INTO THE FOREST!!
WHAT'S HAPPENING!? THEY JUST CAME OUTTA NOWHERE...!

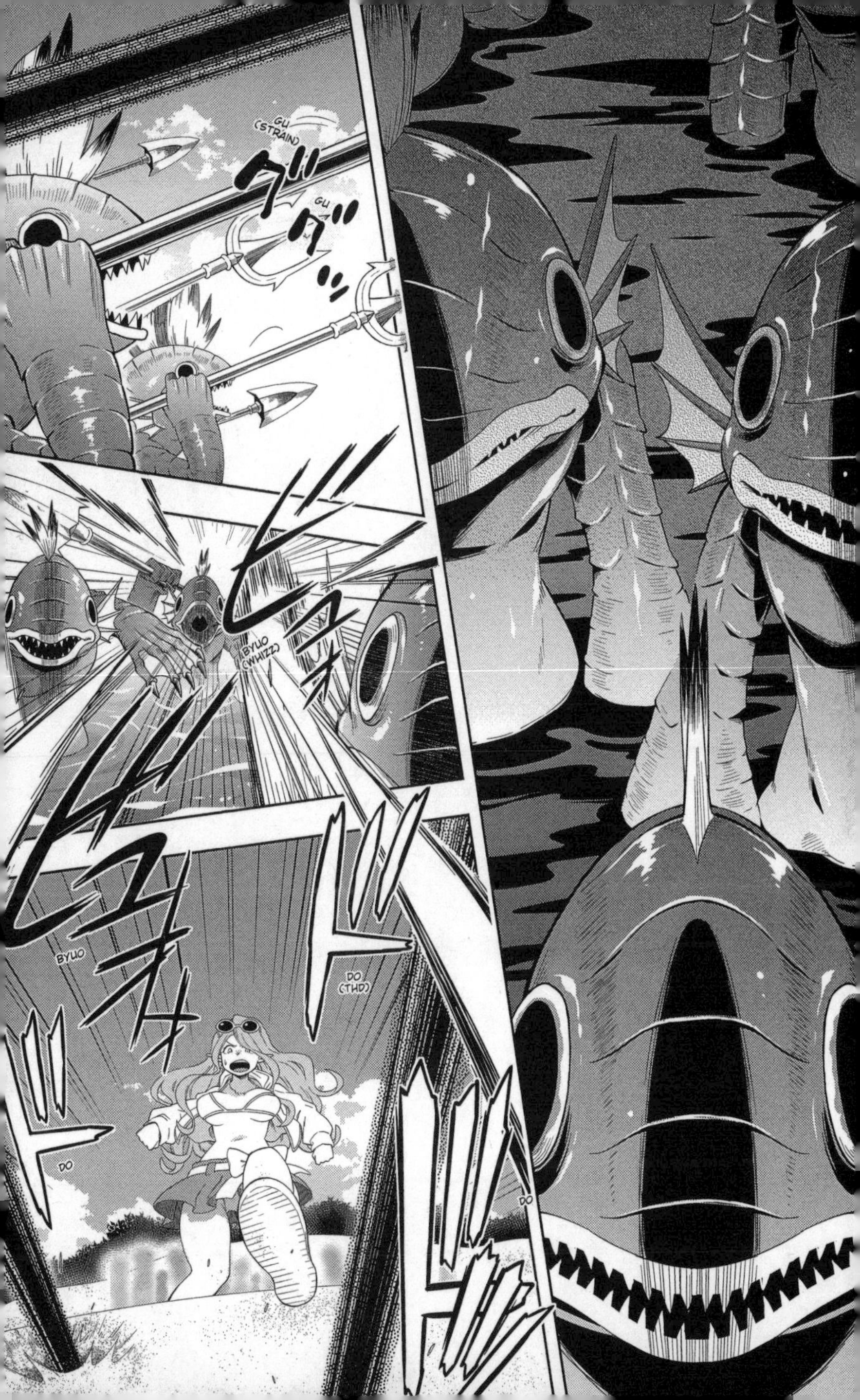
DO
GU (STRAIN)
GU
BYUO (WHIZZ)
DO (THD)
BYUO
DO

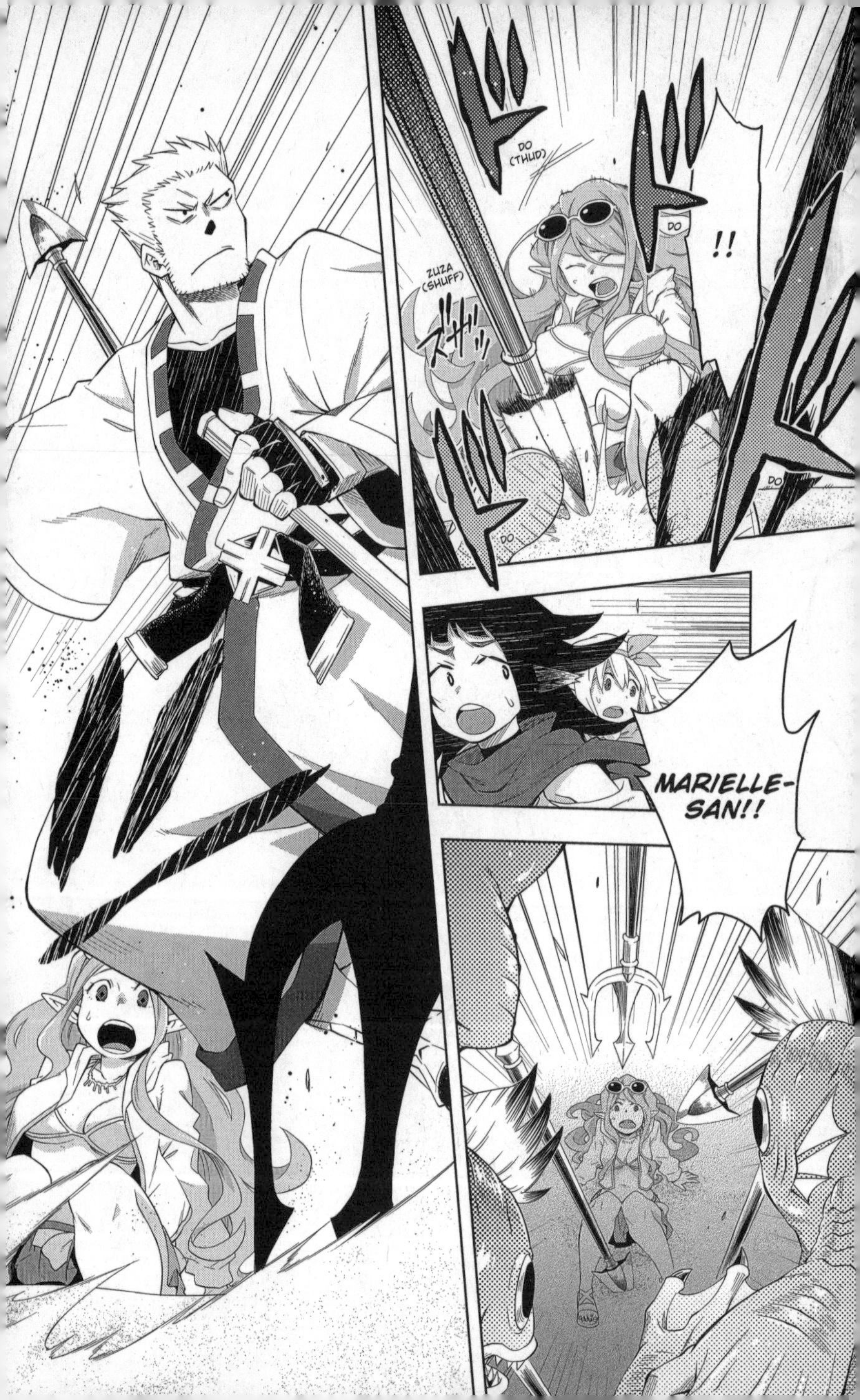

!!
DO
DO (THUD)
ZUZA (SHUFF)
ズザッ
DO
DO
MARIELLE-SAN!!

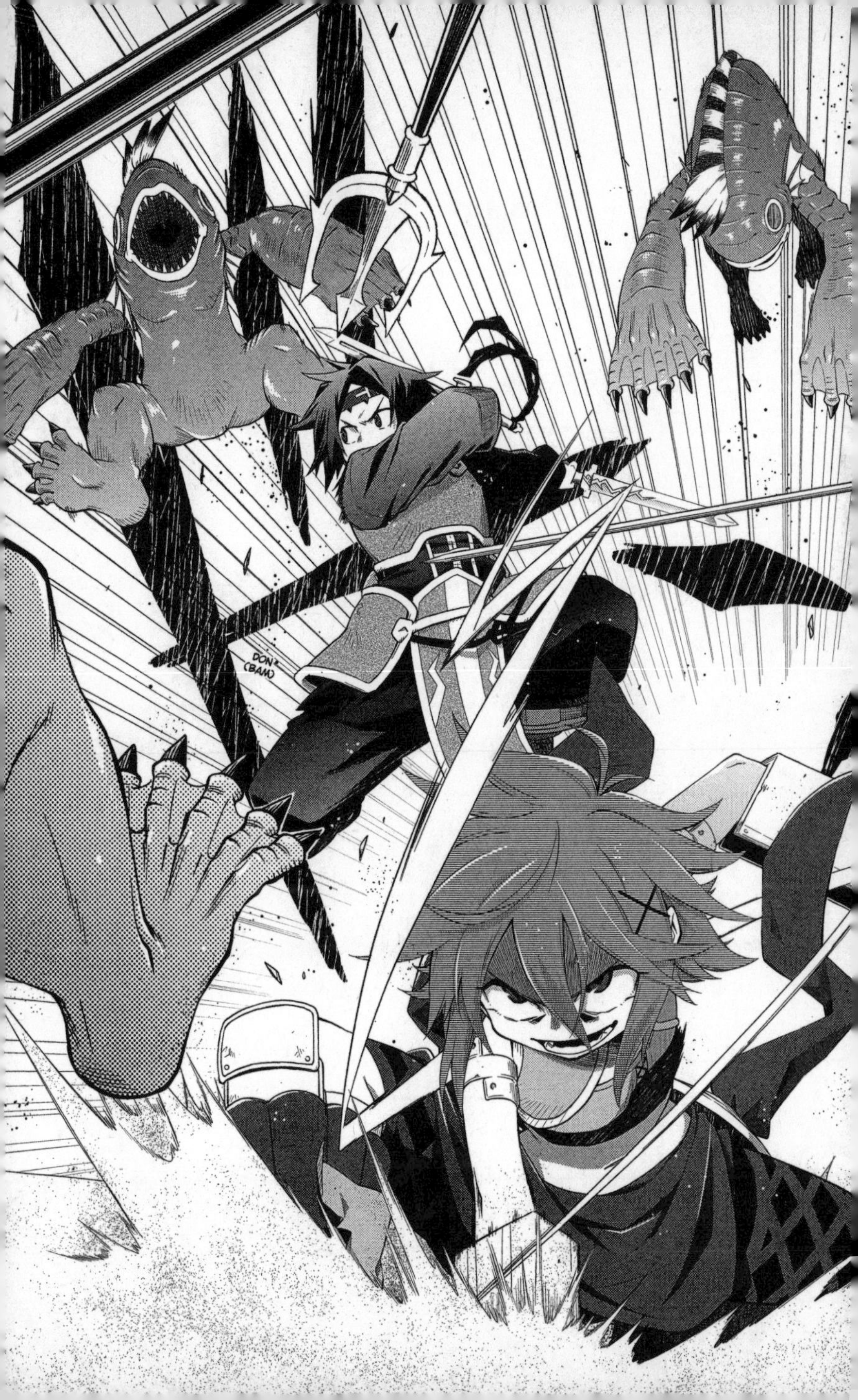
DON (BAM)

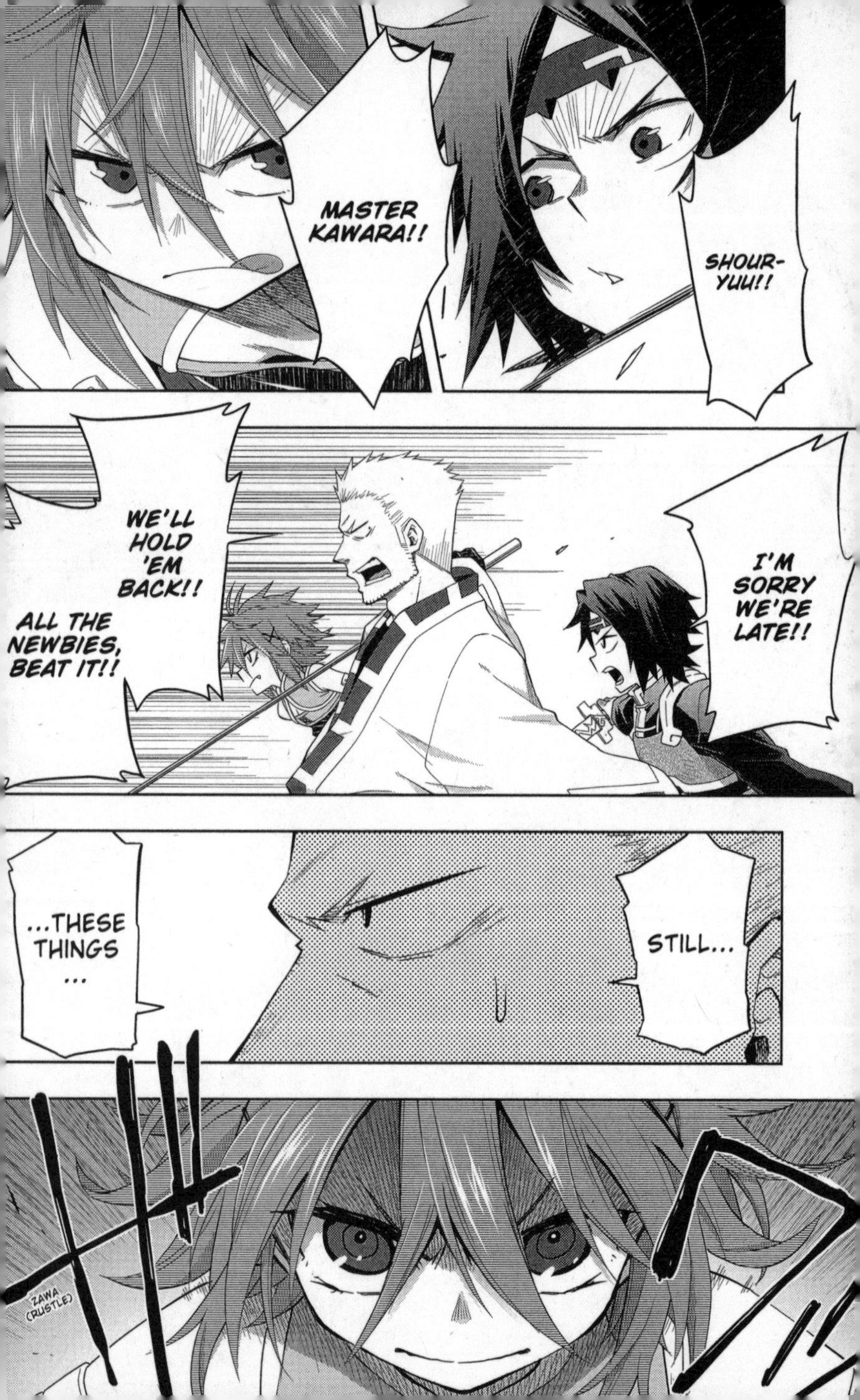
SHOUR-YUU!!
MASTER KAWARA!!
I'M SORRY WE'RE LATE!!
WE'LL HOLD 'EM BACK!!
ALL THE NEWBIES, BEAT IT!!
STILL...
...THESE THINGS ...
ZAWA (RUSTLE)

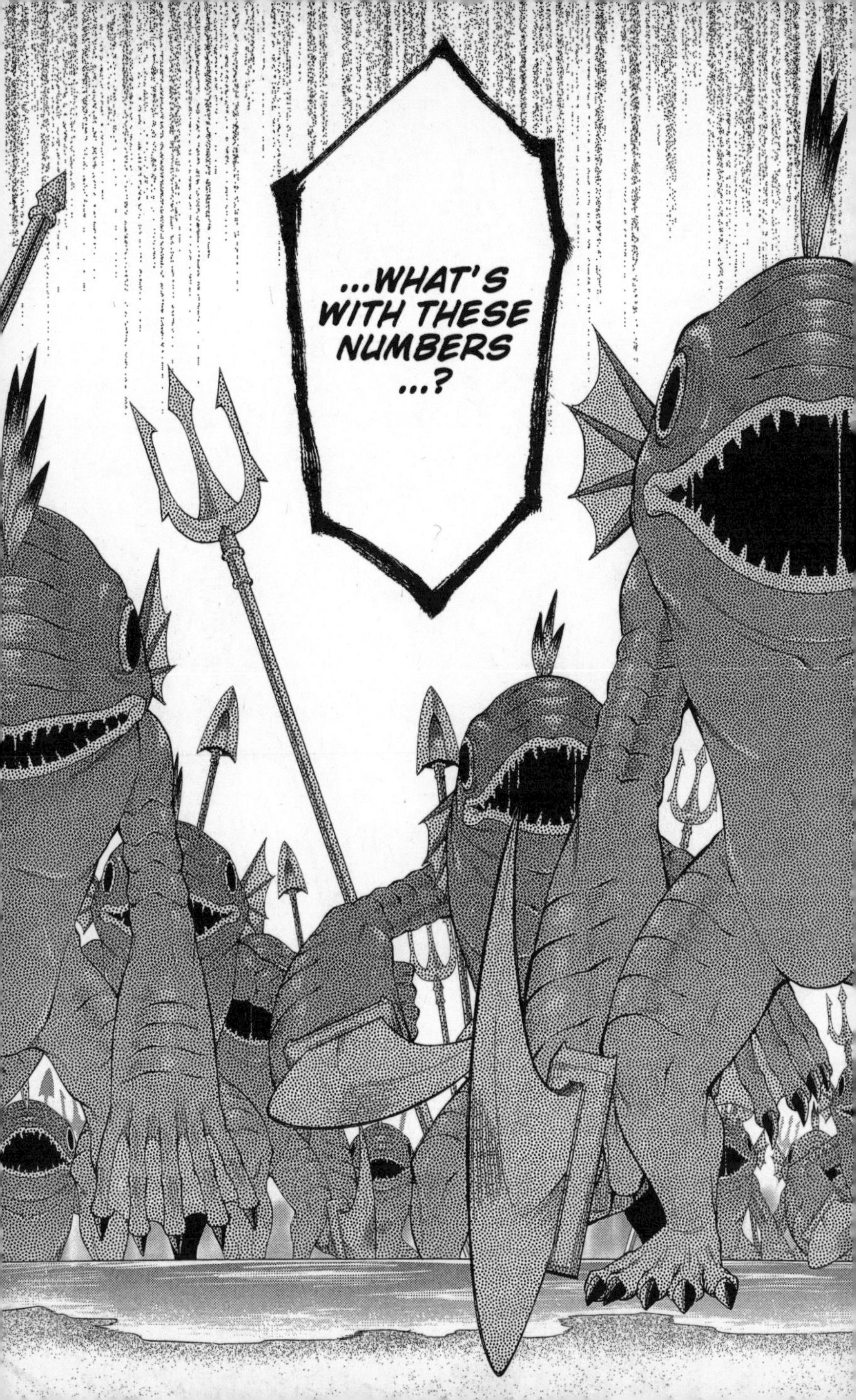
...WHAT'S WITH THESE NUMBERS ...?

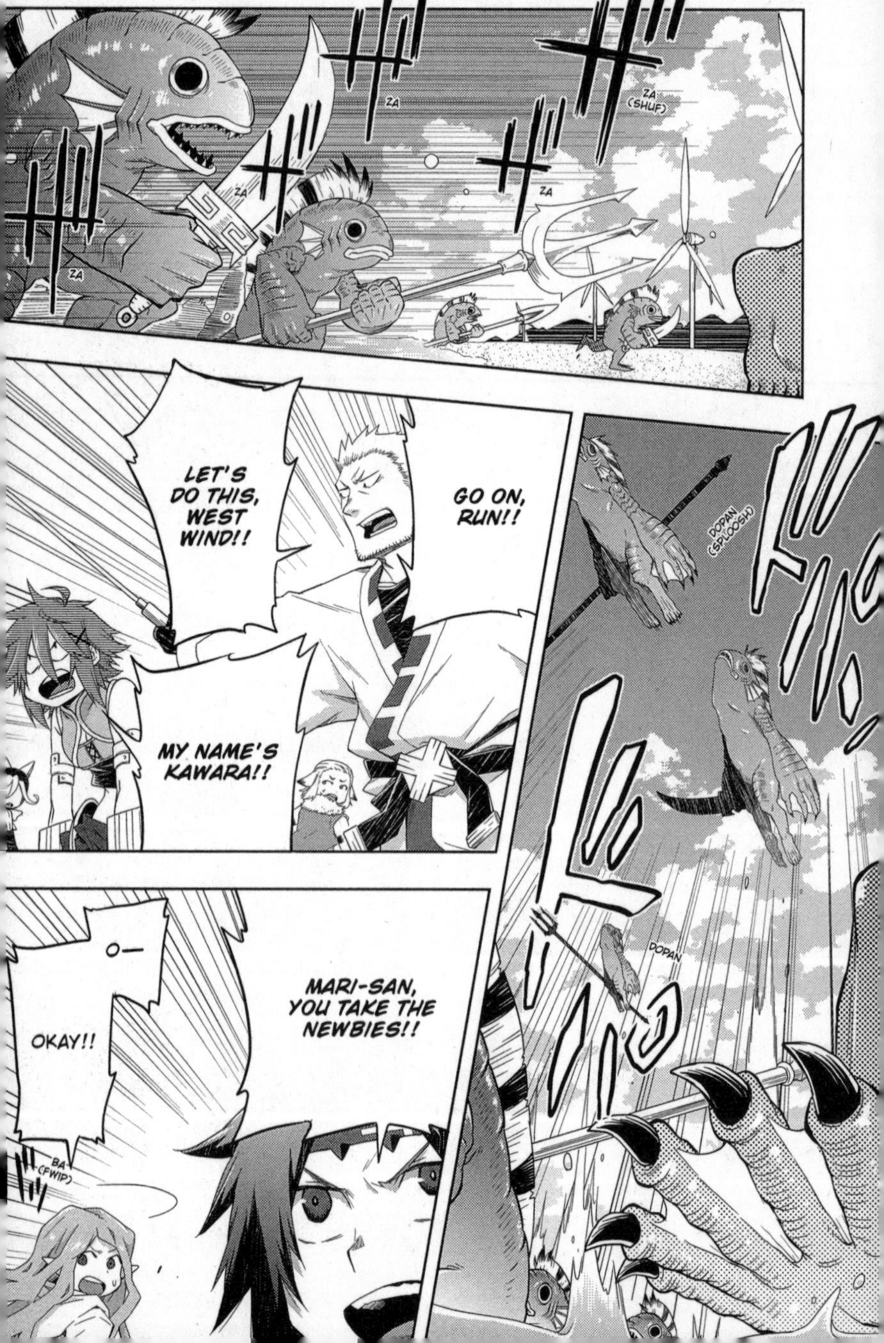
ZA (SHUF)
ZA
ZA
ZA
ZA
DOPAN (SPLOOSH)
DOPAN
GO ON, RUN!!
LET'S DO THIS, WEST WIND!!
MY NAME'S KAWARA!!
MARI-SAN, YOU TAKE THE NEWBIES!!
O—
OKAY!!
BA (FWIP)

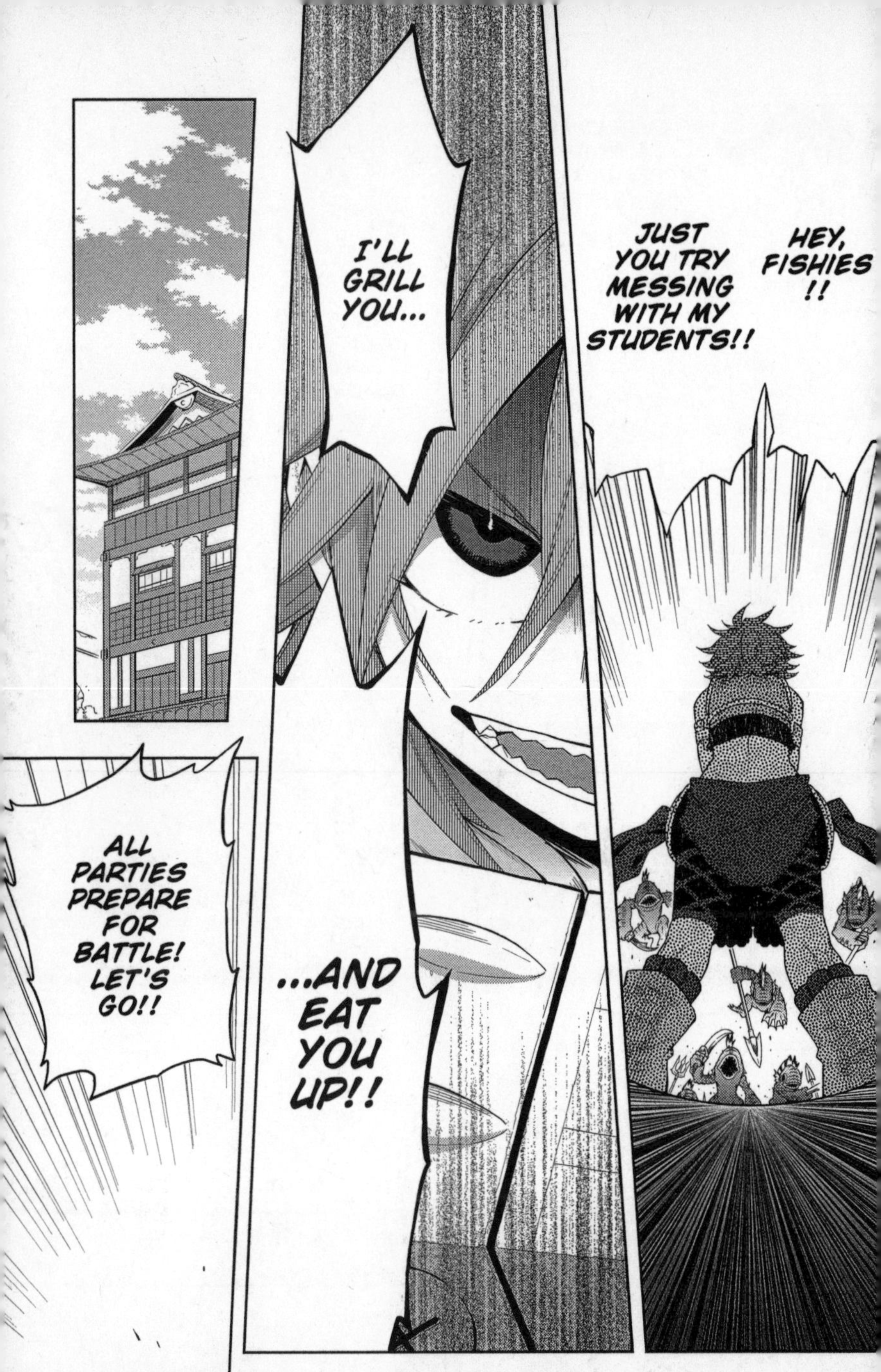
HEY, FISHIES!!
JUST YOU TRY MESSING WITH MY STUDENTS!!
I'LL GRILL YOU...
...AND EAT YOU UP!!
ALL PARTIES PREPARE FOR BATTLE! LET'S GO!!

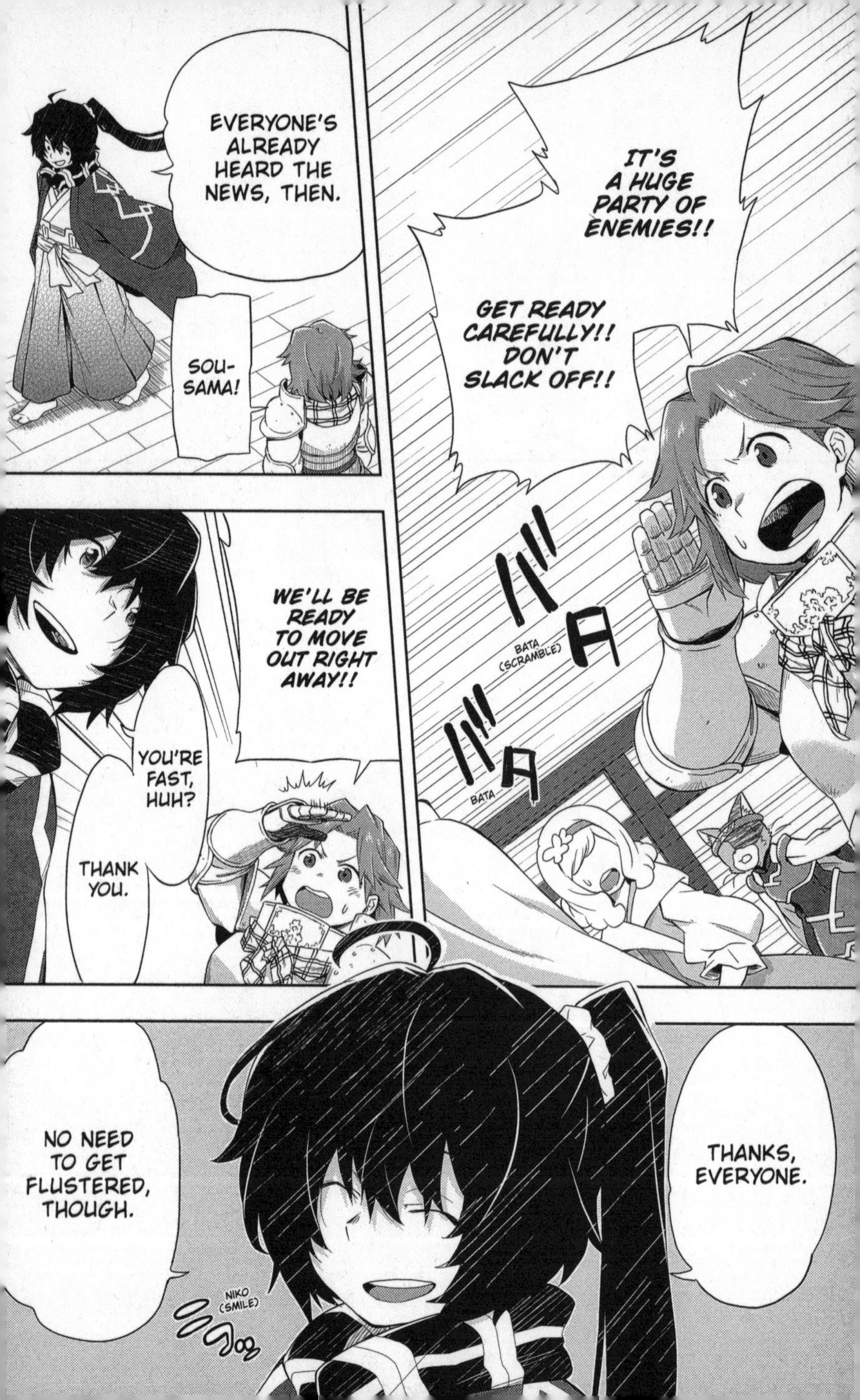
IT'S A HUGE PARTY OF ENEMIES!!
GET READY CAREFULLY!! DON'T SLACK OFF!!
BATA (SCRAMBLE)
BATA
EVERYONE'S ALREADY HEARD THE NEWS, THEN.
SOU-SAMA!
WE'LL BE READY TO MOVE OUT RIGHT AWAY!!
YOU'RE FAST, HUH?
THANK YOU.
THANKS, EVERYONE.
NO NEED TO GET FLUSTERED, THOUGH.
NIKO (SMILE)

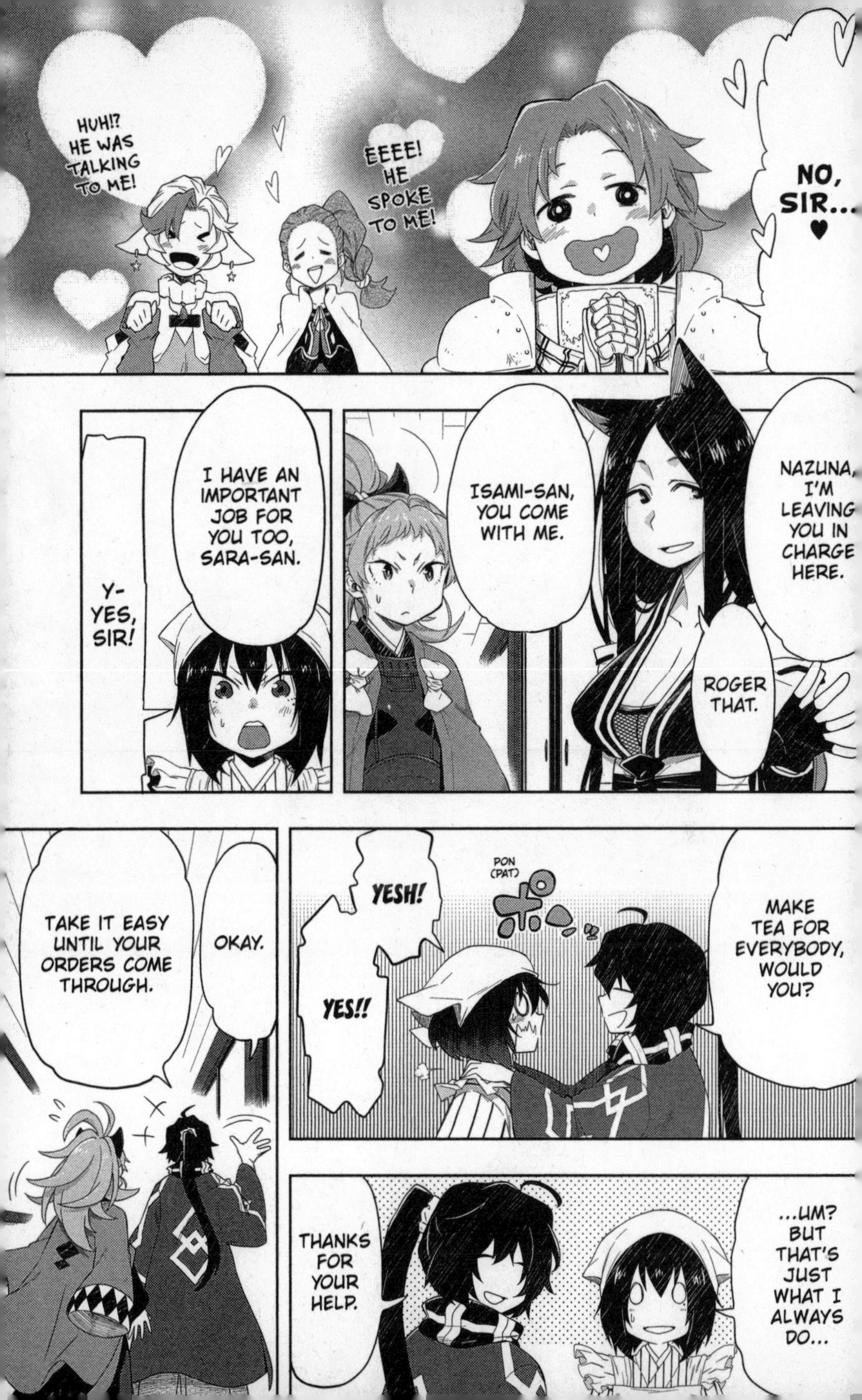
NO, SIR... ♥
EEEE! HE SPOKE TO ME!
HUH!? HE WAS TALKING TO ME!
NAZUNA, I'M LEAVING YOU IN CHARGE HERE.
ROGER THAT.
ISAMI-SAN, YOU COME WITH ME.
I HAVE AN IMPORTANT JOB FOR YOU TOO, SARA-SAN.
Y-YES, SIR!
MAKE TEA FOR EVERYBODY, WOULD YOU?
PON (PAT)
YESH!
YES!!
...UM? BUT THAT'S JUST WHAT I ALWAYS DO...
THANKS FOR YOUR HELP.
OKAY.
TAKE IT EASY UNTIL YOUR ORDERS COME THROUGH.

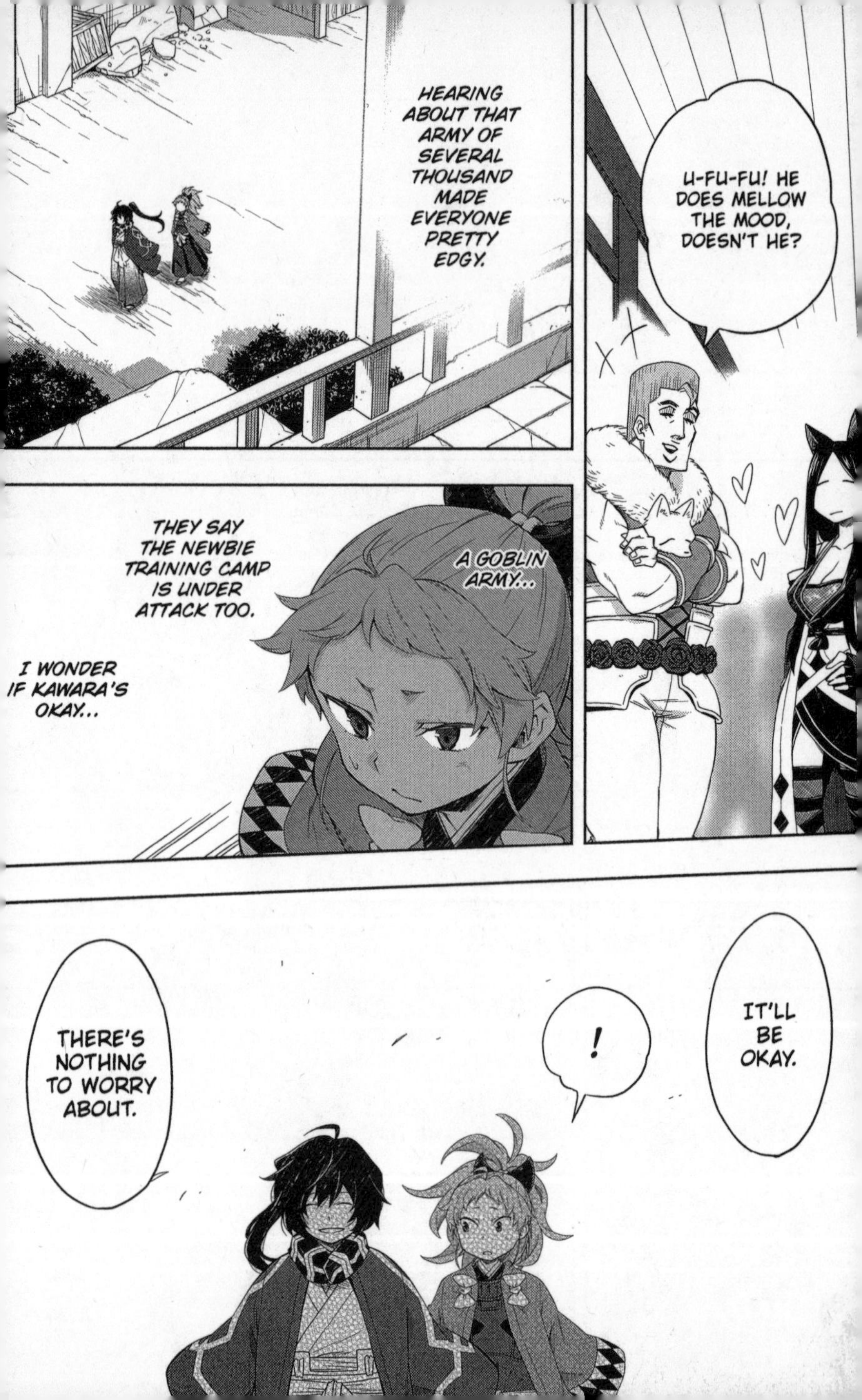
U-FU-FU! HE DOES MELLOW THE MOOD, DOESN'T HE?
HEARING ABOUT THAT ARMY OF SEVERAL THOUSAND MADE EVERYONE PRETTY EDGY.
A GOBLIN ARMY...
THEY SAY THE NEWBIE TRAINING CAMP IS UNDER ATTACK TOO.
I WONDER IF KAWARA'S OKAY...
IT'LL BE OKAY.
!
THERE'S NOTHING TO WORRY ABOUT.

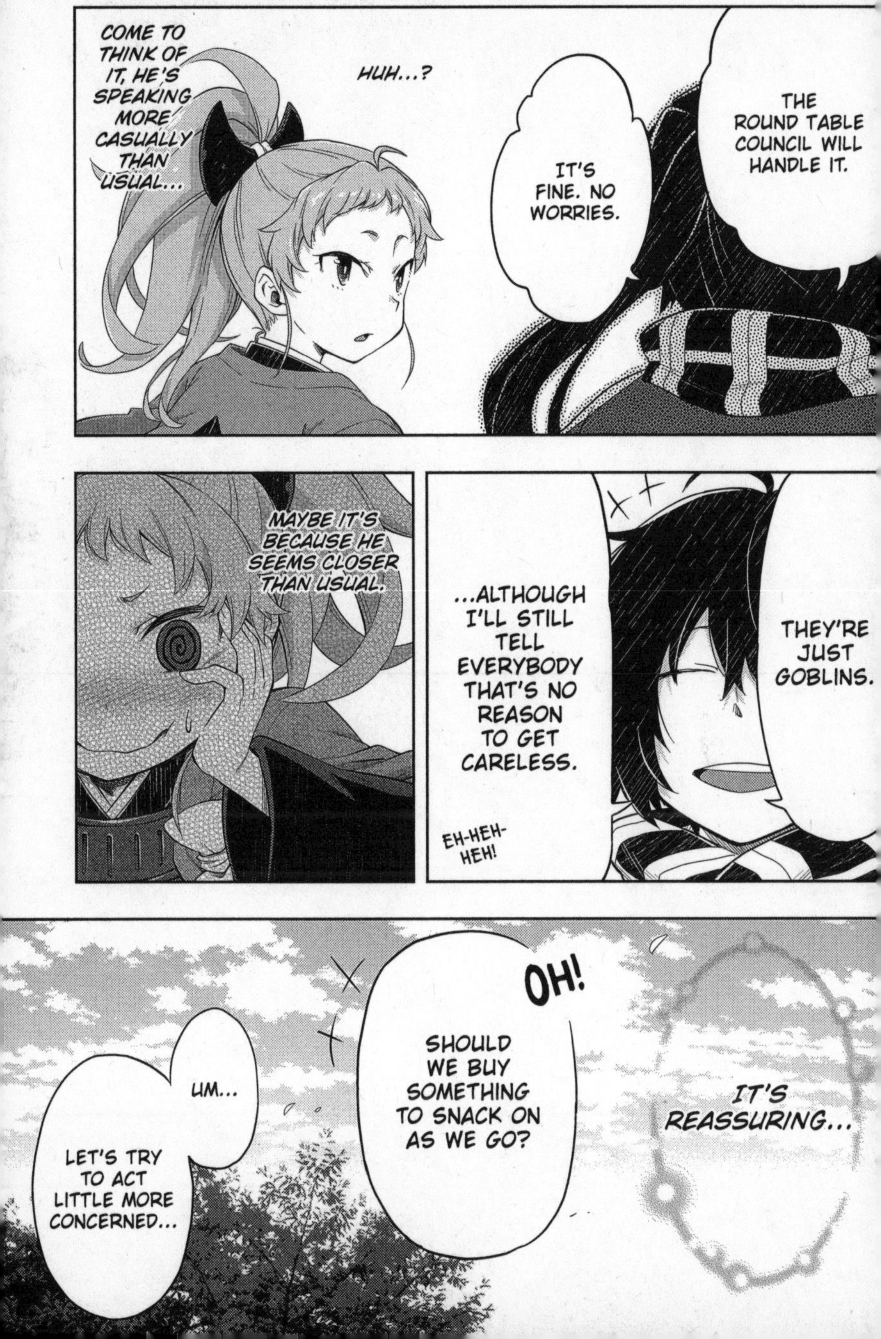
THE ROUND TABLE COUNCIL WILL HANDLE IT.
IT'S FINE. NO WORRIES.
HUH...?
COME TO THINK OF IT, HE'S SPEAKING MORE CASUALLY THAN USUAL...
THEY'RE JUST GOBLINS.
...ALTHOUGH I'LL STILL TELL EVERYBODY THAT'S NO REASON TO GET CARELESS.
EH-HEH-HEH!
MAYBE IT'S BECAUSE HE SEEMS CLOSER THAN USUAL.
IT'S REASSURING...
OH!
SHOULD WE BUY SOMETHING TO SNACK ON AS WE GO?
UM...
LET'S TRY TO ACT LITTLE MORE CONCERNED...

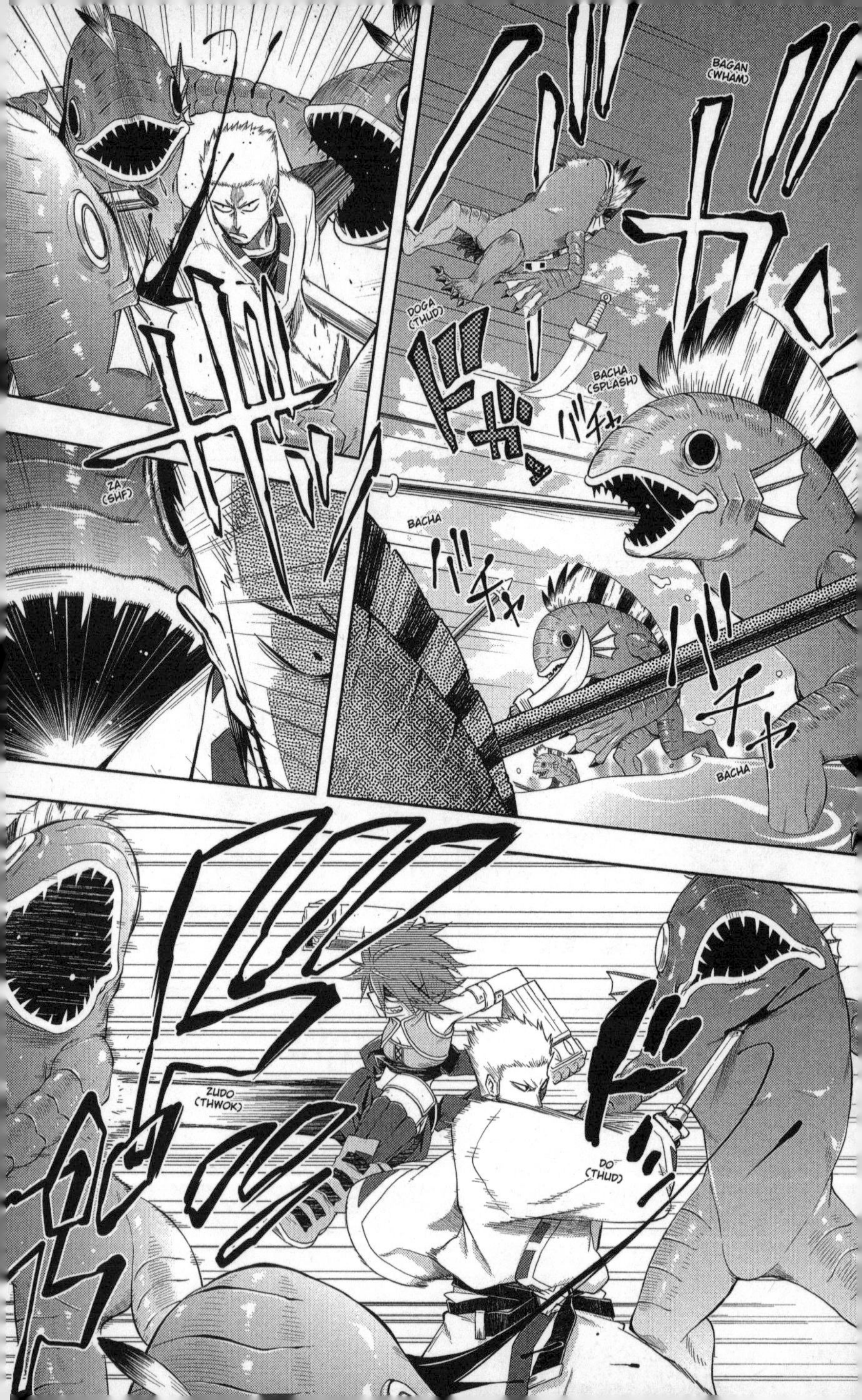
BAGAN (WHAM)
BACHA (SPLASH)
DOGA (THUD)
BACHA
BACHA
ZA (SHF)
DO (THUD)
ZUDO (THWOK)

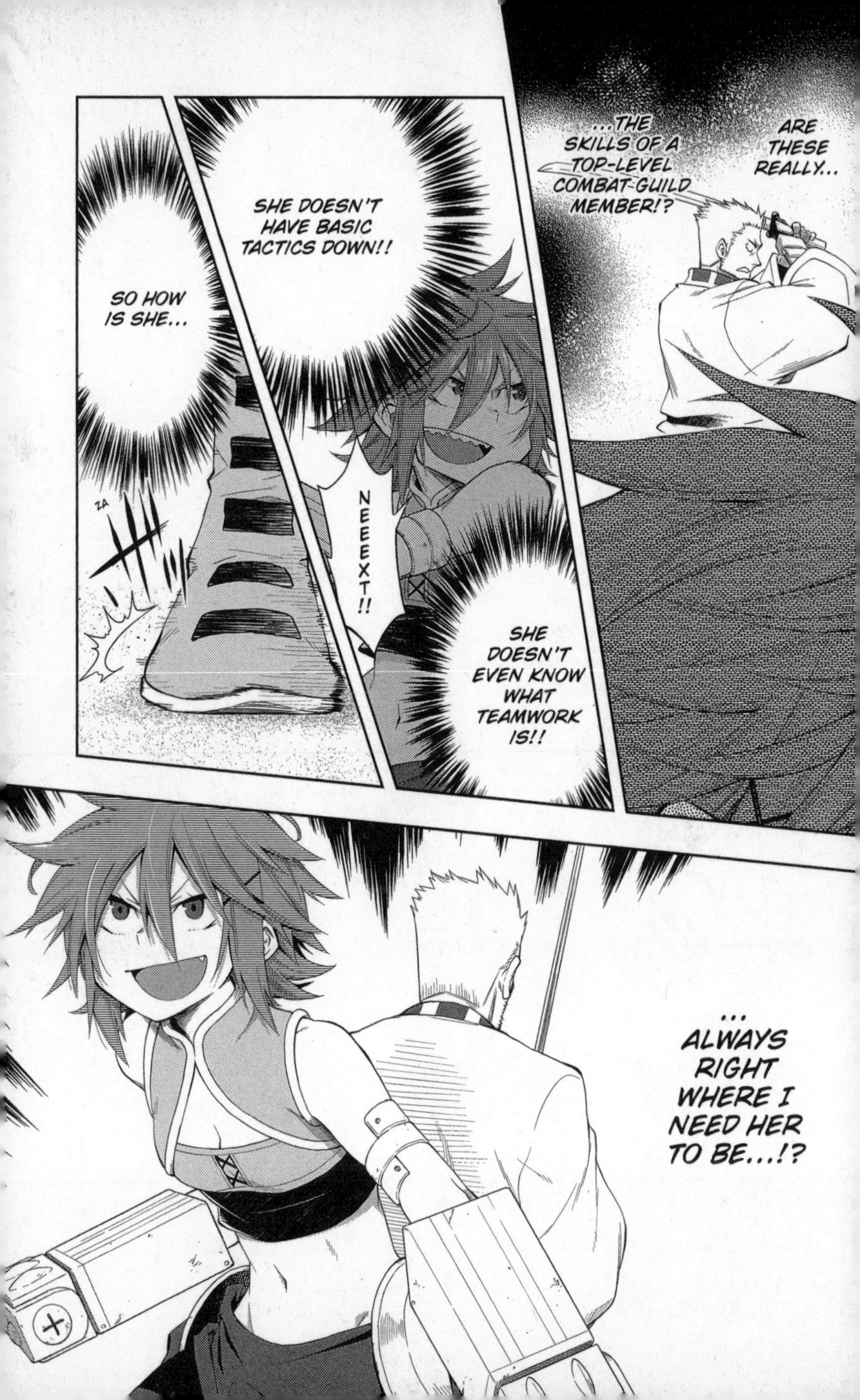
ARE THESE REALLY...
...THE SKILLS OF A TOP-LEVEL COMBAT-GUILD MEMBER!?
SHE DOESN'T HAVE BASIC TACTICS DOWN!!
NEEEEXT!!
SHE DOESN'T EVEN KNOW WHAT TEAMWORK IS!!
SO HOW IS SHE...
ZA
...ALWAYS RIGHT WHERE I NEED HER TO BE...!?

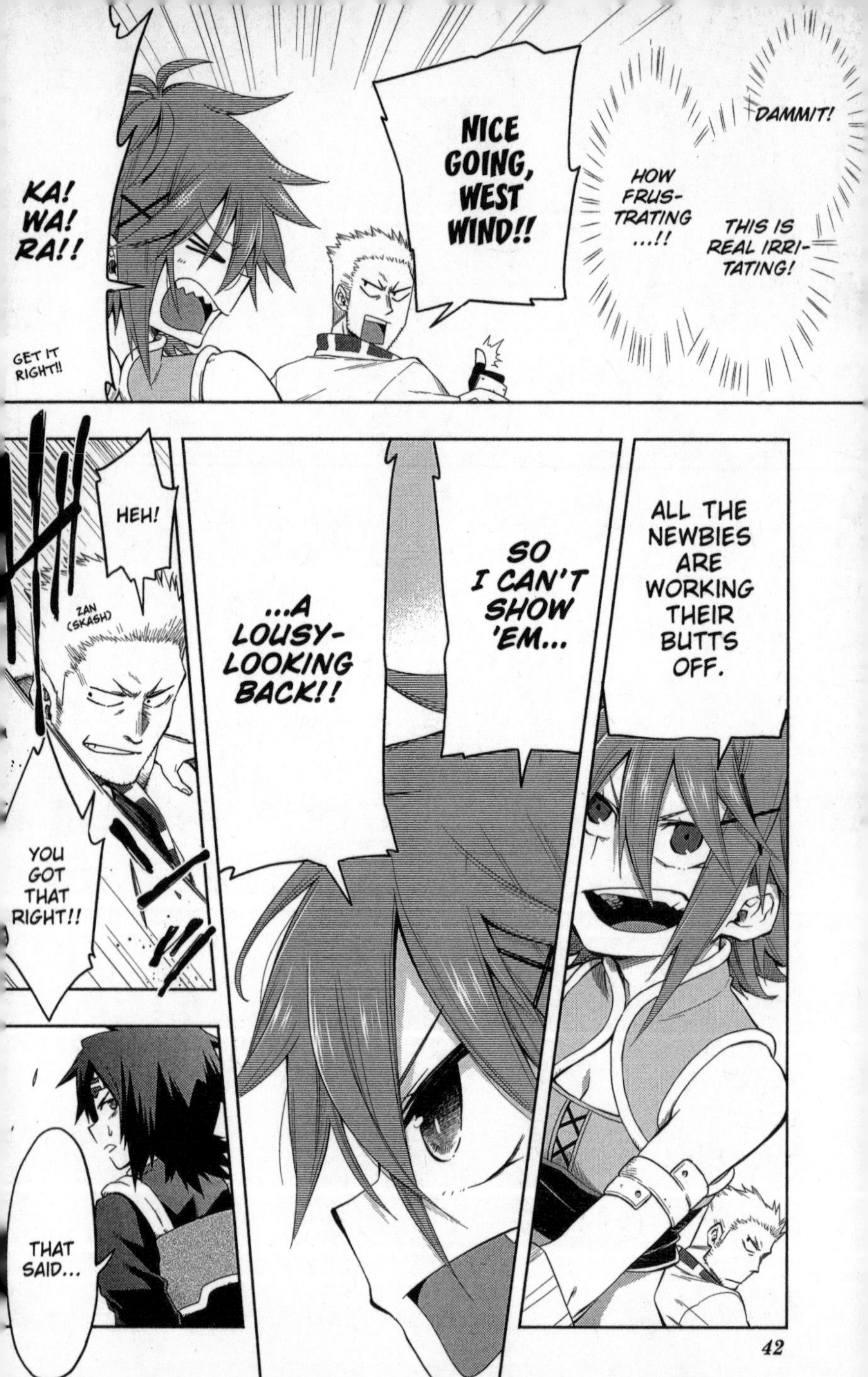
DAMMIT!
THIS IS REAL IRRITATING!
HOW FRUS-TRATING ...!!
NICE GOING, WEST WIND!!
KA! WA! RA!!
GET IT RIGHT!!
ALL THE NEWBIES ARE WORKING THEIR BUTTS OFF.
SO I CAN'T SHOW 'EM...
...A LOUSY-LOOKING BACK!!
HEH!
ZAN (SKASH)
YOU GOT THAT RIGHT!!
THAT SAID...

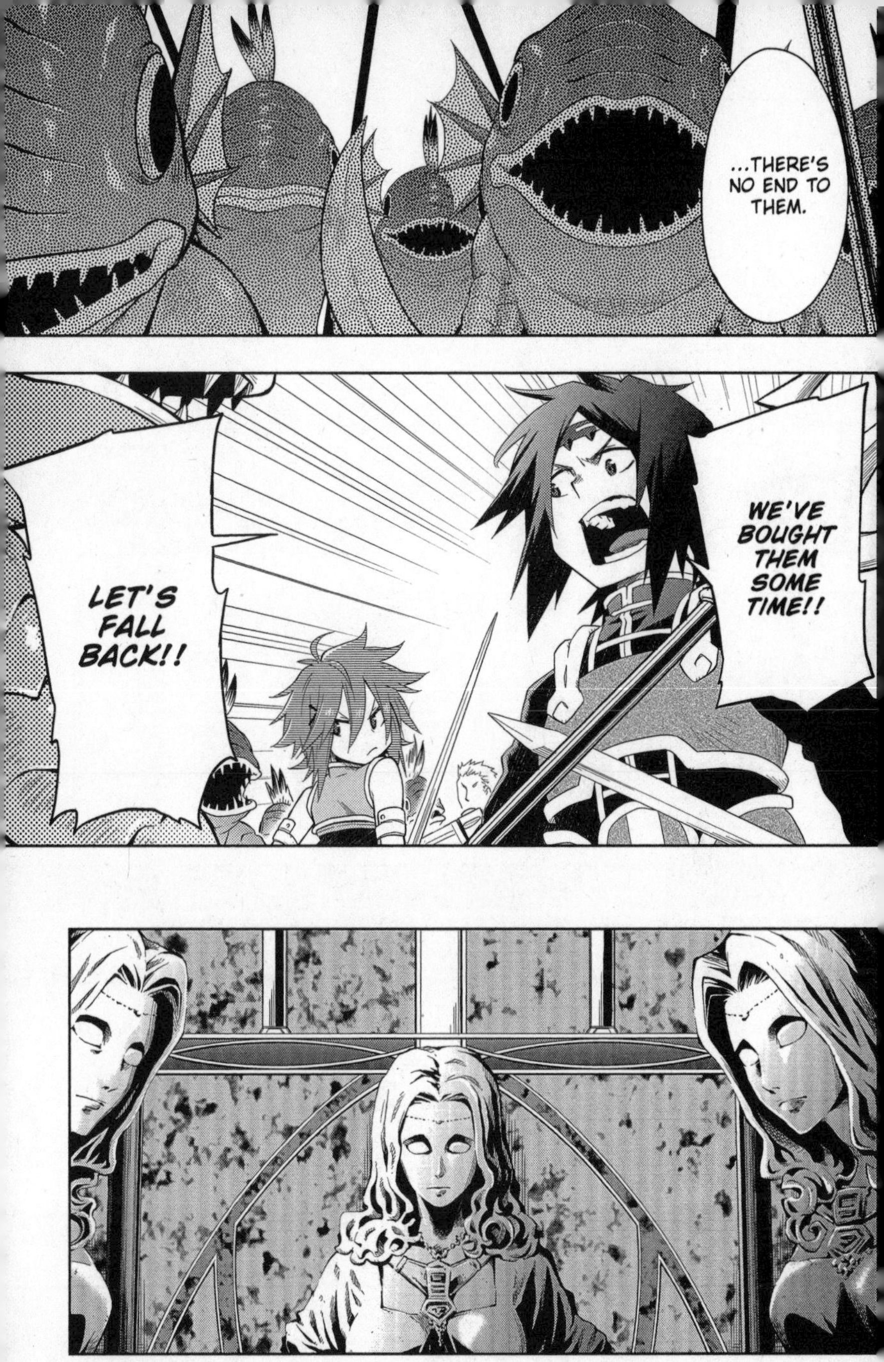
...THERE'S NO END TO THEM.
WE'VE BOUGHT THEM SOME TIME!!
LET'S FALL BACK!!

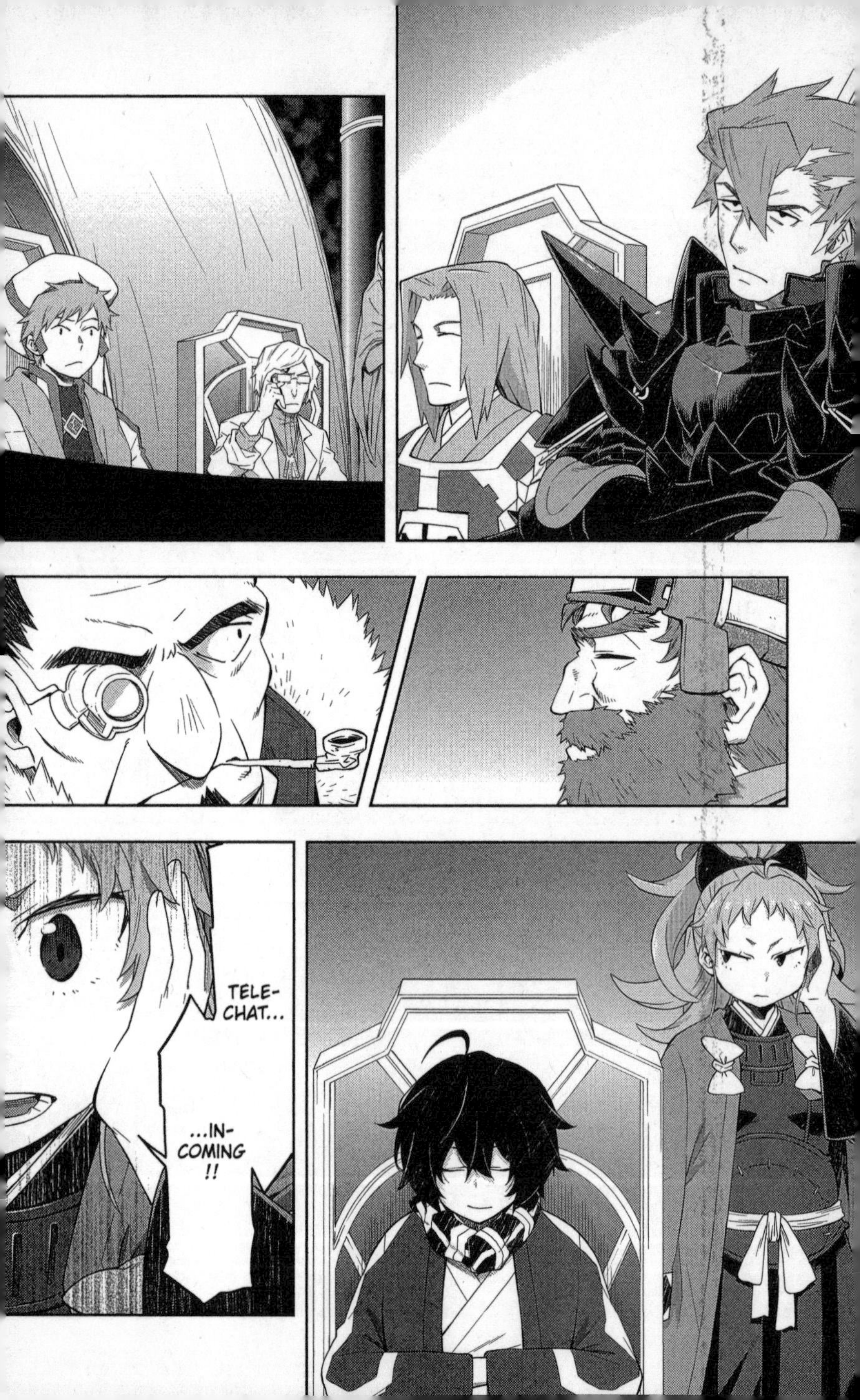
TELE-
CHAT...
...IN-
COMING
!!

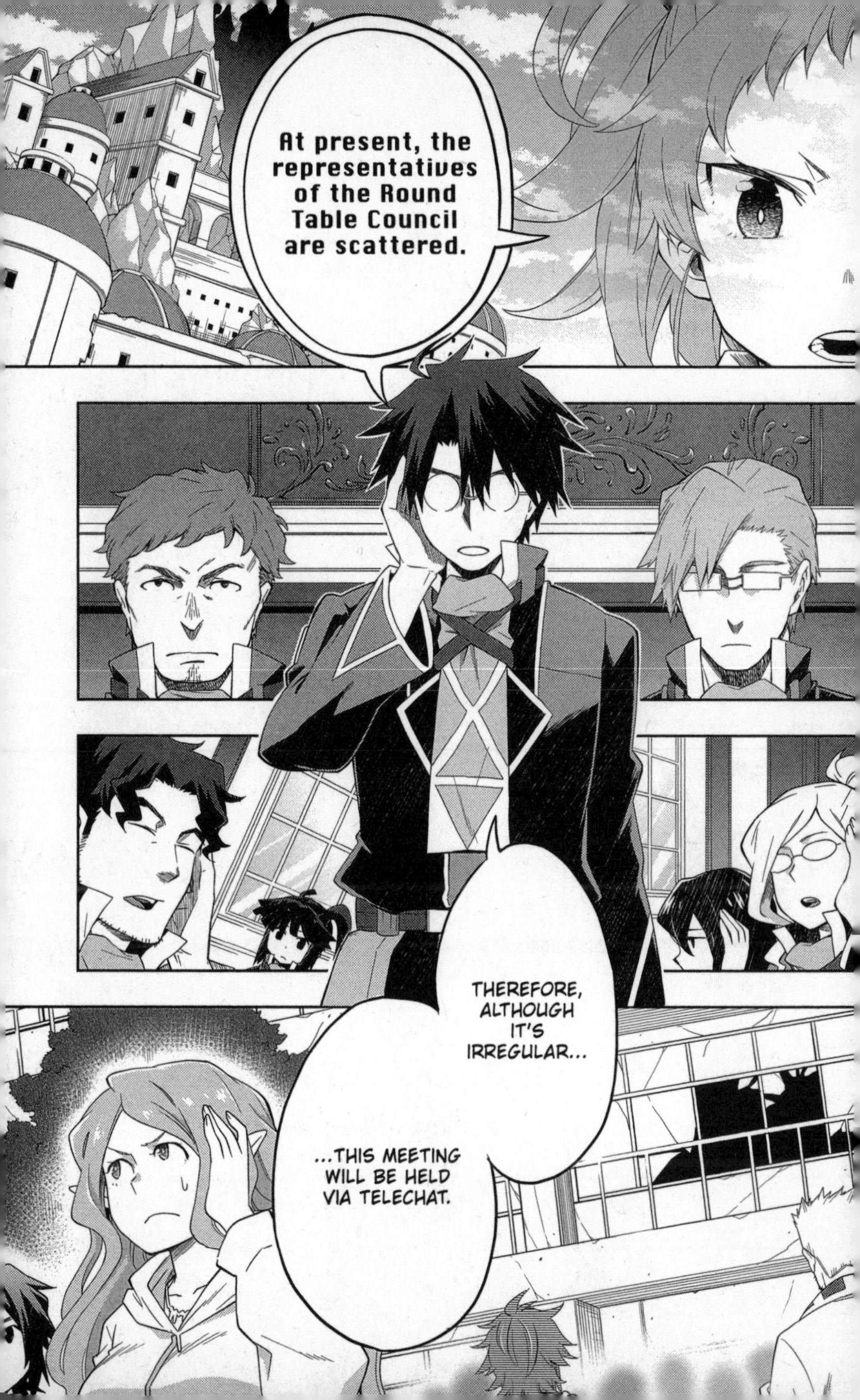
At present, the representatives of the Round Table Council are scattered.
THEREFORE, ALTHOUGH IT'S IRREGULAR...
...THIS MEETING WILL BE HELD VIA TELECHAT.

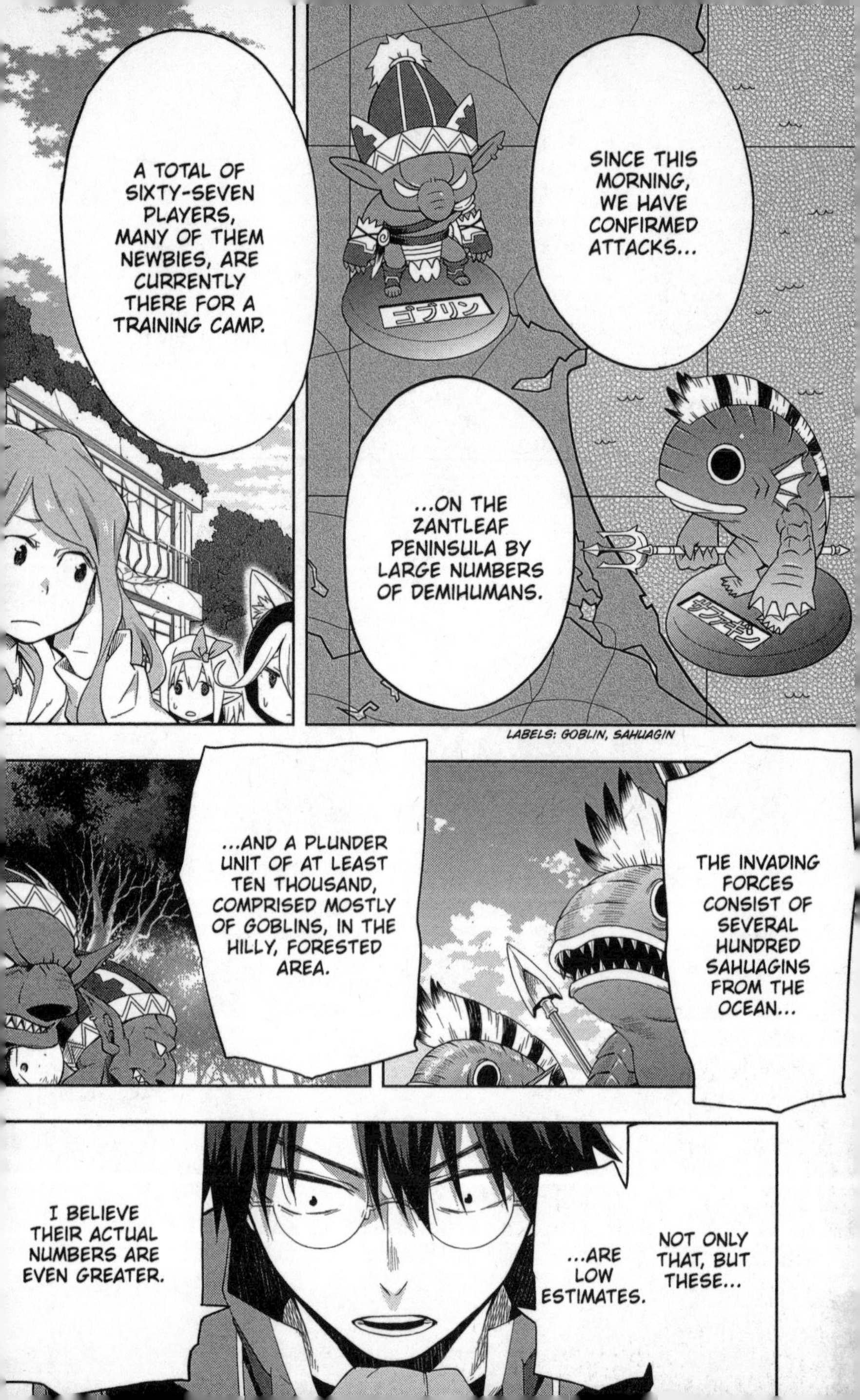
SINCE THIS MORNING, WE HAVE CONFIRMED ATTACKS...
...ON THE ZANTLEAF PENINSULA BY LARGE NUMBERS OF DEMIHUMANS.
ゴブリン
A TOTAL OF SIXTY-SEVEN PLAYERS, MANY OF THEM NEWBIES, ARE CURRENTLY THERE FOR A TRAINING CAMP.
LABELS: GOBLIN, SAHUAGIN
THE INVADING FORCES CONSIST OF SEVERAL HUNDRED SAHUAGINS FROM THE OCEAN...
...AND A PLUNDER UNIT OF AT LEAST TEN THOUSAND, COMPRISED MOSTLY OF GOBLINS, IN THE HILLY, FORESTED AREA.
NOT ONLY THAT, BUT THESE...
...ARE LOW ESTIMATES.
I BELIEVE THEIR ACTUAL NUMBERS ARE EVEN GREATER.

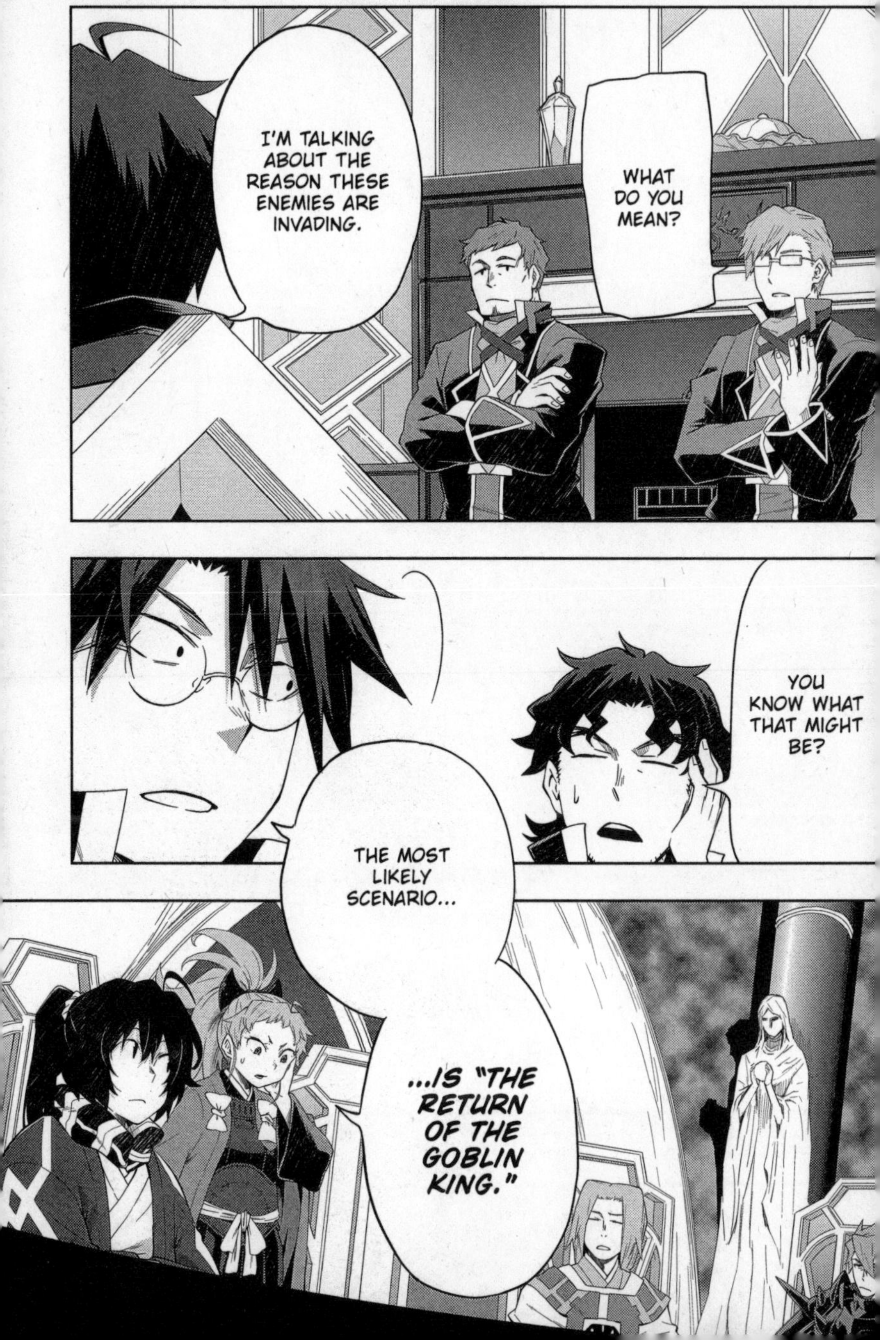
WHAT DO YOU MEAN?
I'M TALKING ABOUT THE REASON THESE ENEMIES ARE INVADING.
YOU KNOW WHAT THAT MIGHT BE?
THE MOST LIKELY SCENARIO...
...IS "THE RETURN OF THE GOBLIN KING."

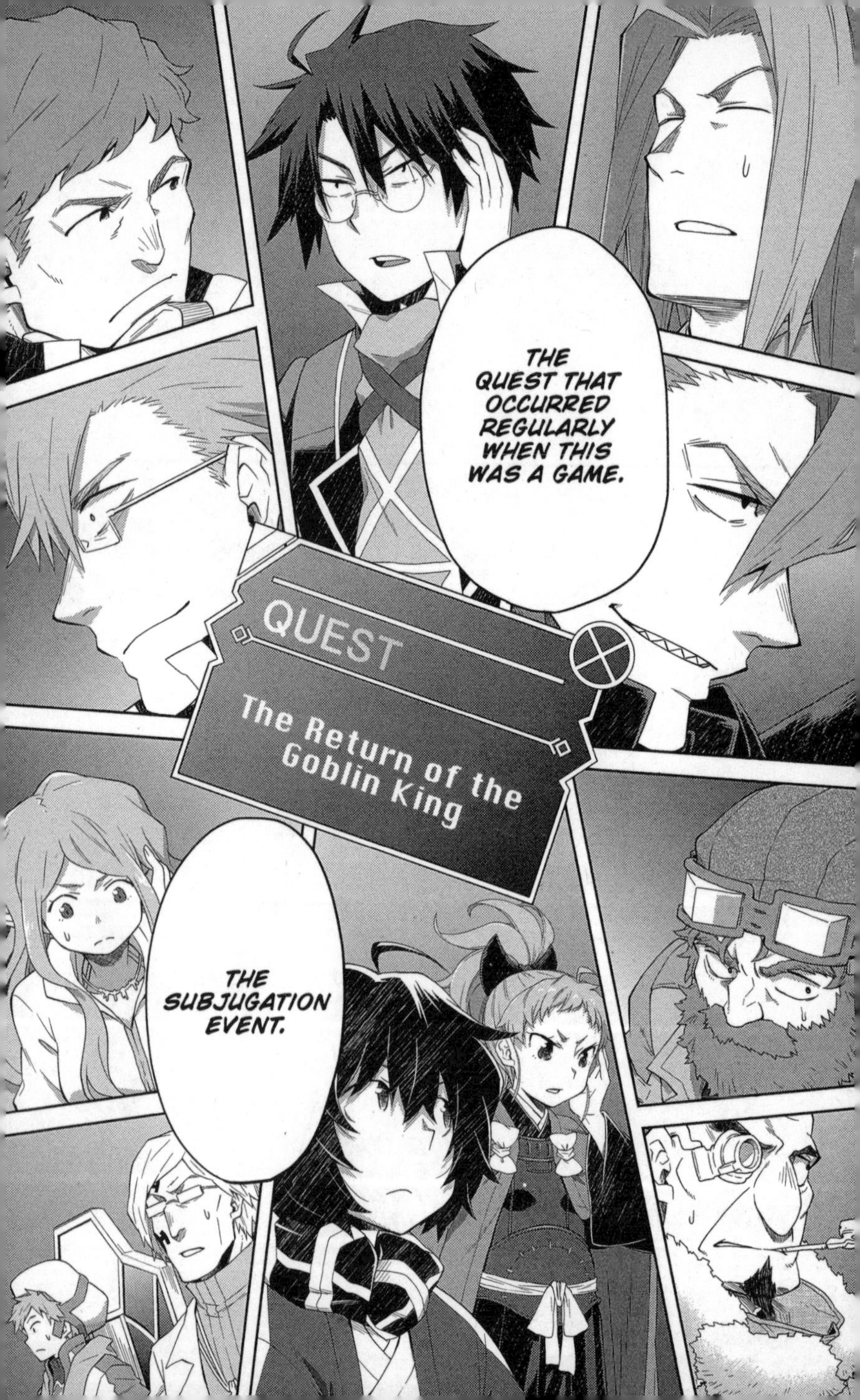
THE QUEST THAT OCCURRED REGULARLY WHEN THIS WAS A GAME.
QUEST
The Return of the Goblin King
THE SUBJUGATION EVENT.

LOG HORIZON

THE WEST WIND BRIGADE

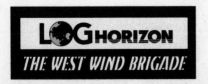

LOG HORIZON

THE WEST WIND BRIGADE

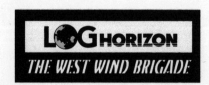

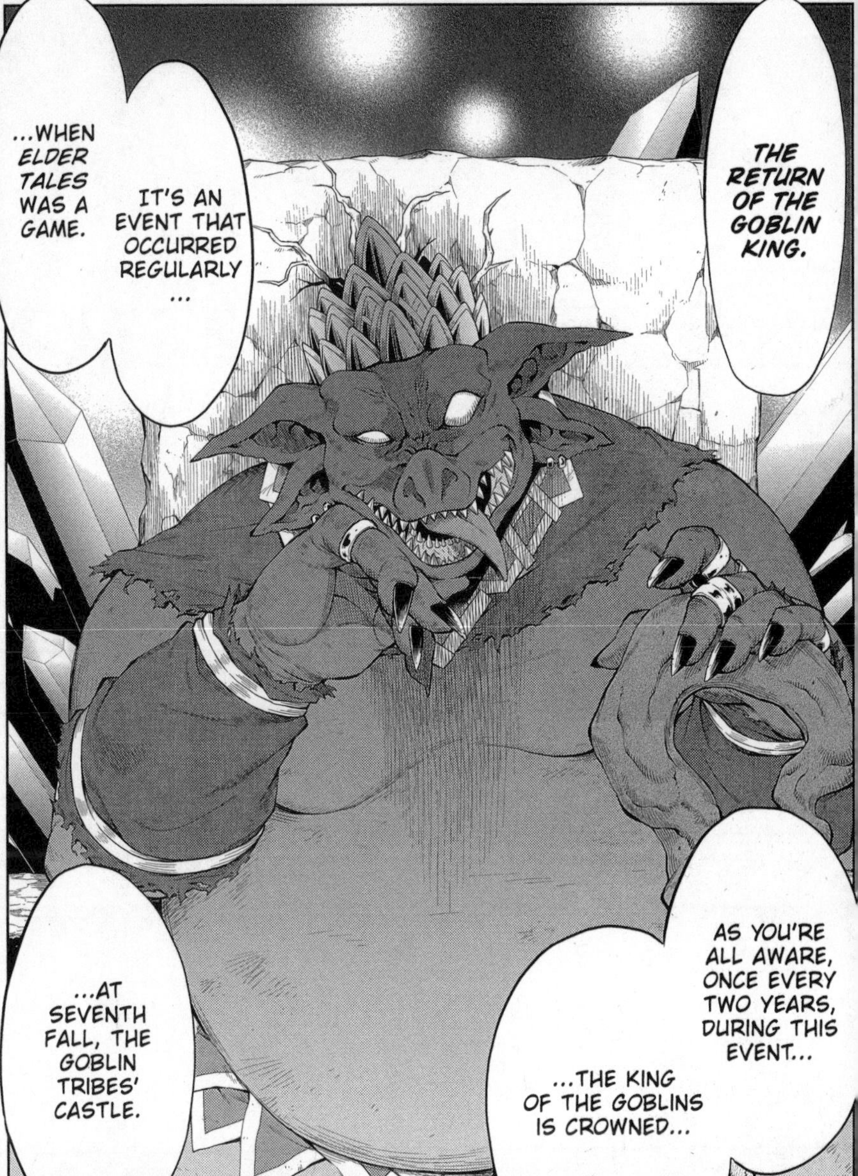
THE RETURN OF THE GOBLIN KING.
IT'S AN EVENT THAT OCCURRED REGULARLY...
...WHEN ELDER TALES WAS A GAME.
AS YOU'RE ALL AWARE, ONCE EVERY TWO YEARS, DURING THIS EVENT...
...THE KING OF THE GOBLINS IS CROWNED...
...AT SEVENTH FALL, THE GOBLIN TRIBES' CASTLE.

CHAPTER : 39 The Return of the Goblin King

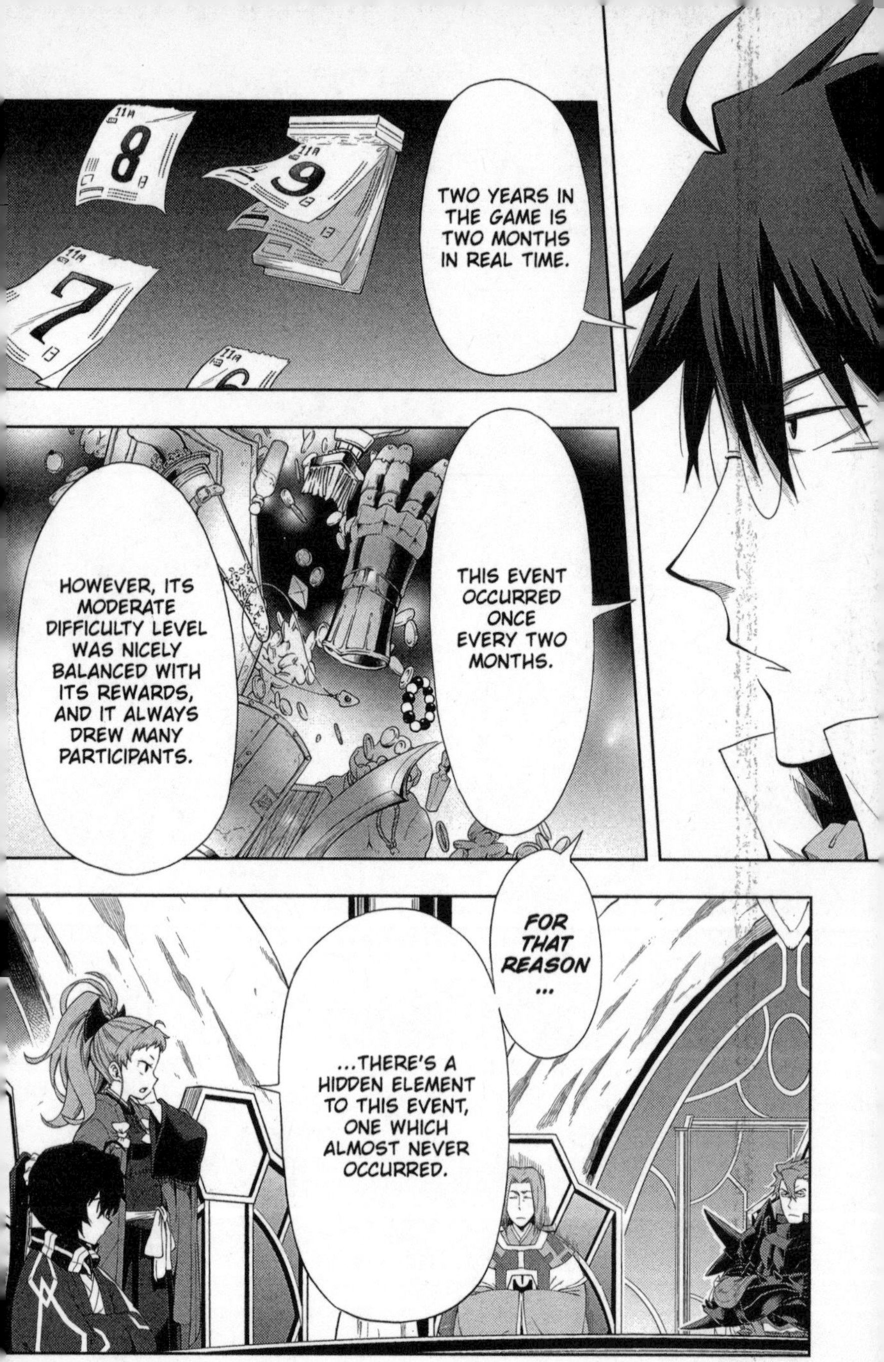
TWO YEARS IN THE GAME IS TWO MONTHS IN REAL TIME.
THIS EVENT OCCURRED ONCE EVERY TWO MONTHS.
HOWEVER, ITS MODERATE DIFFICULTY LEVEL WAS NICELY BALANCED WITH ITS REWARDS, AND IT ALWAYS DREW MANY PARTICIPANTS.
FOR THAT REASON...
...THERE'S A HIDDEN ELEMENT TO THIS EVENT, ONE WHICH ALMOST NEVER OCCURRED.

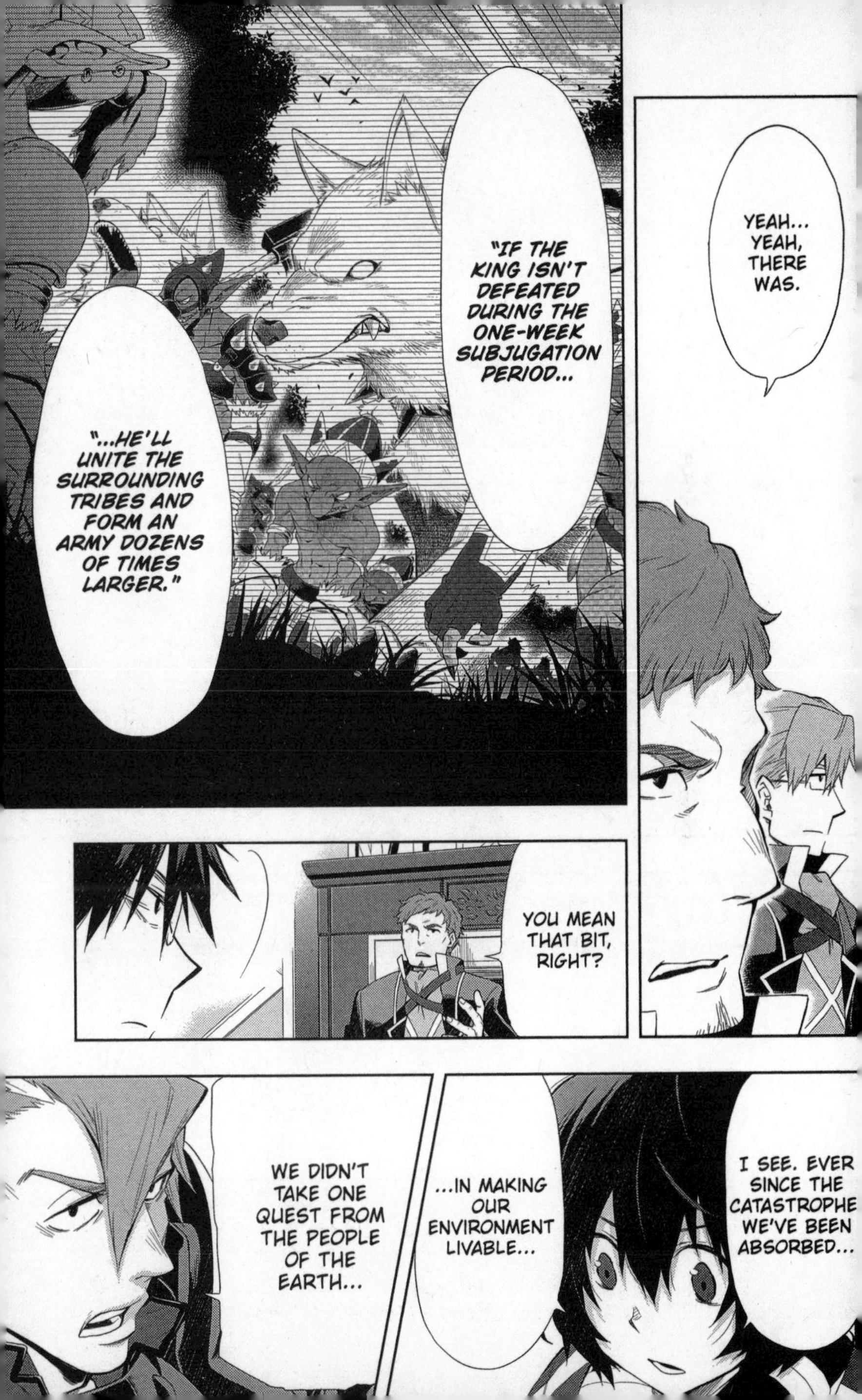
YEAH... YEAH, THERE WAS.
"IF THE KING ISN'T DEFEATED DURING THE ONE-WEEK SUBJUGATION PERIOD...
"...HE'LL UNITE THE SURROUNDING TRIBES AND FORM AN ARMY DOZENS OF TIMES LARGER."
YOU MEAN THAT BIT, RIGHT?
I SEE. EVER SINCE THE CATASTROPHE WE'VE BEEN ABSORBED...
...IN MAKING OUR ENVIRONMENT LIVABLE...
WE DIDN'T TAKE ONE QUEST FROM THE PEOPLE OF THE EARTH...

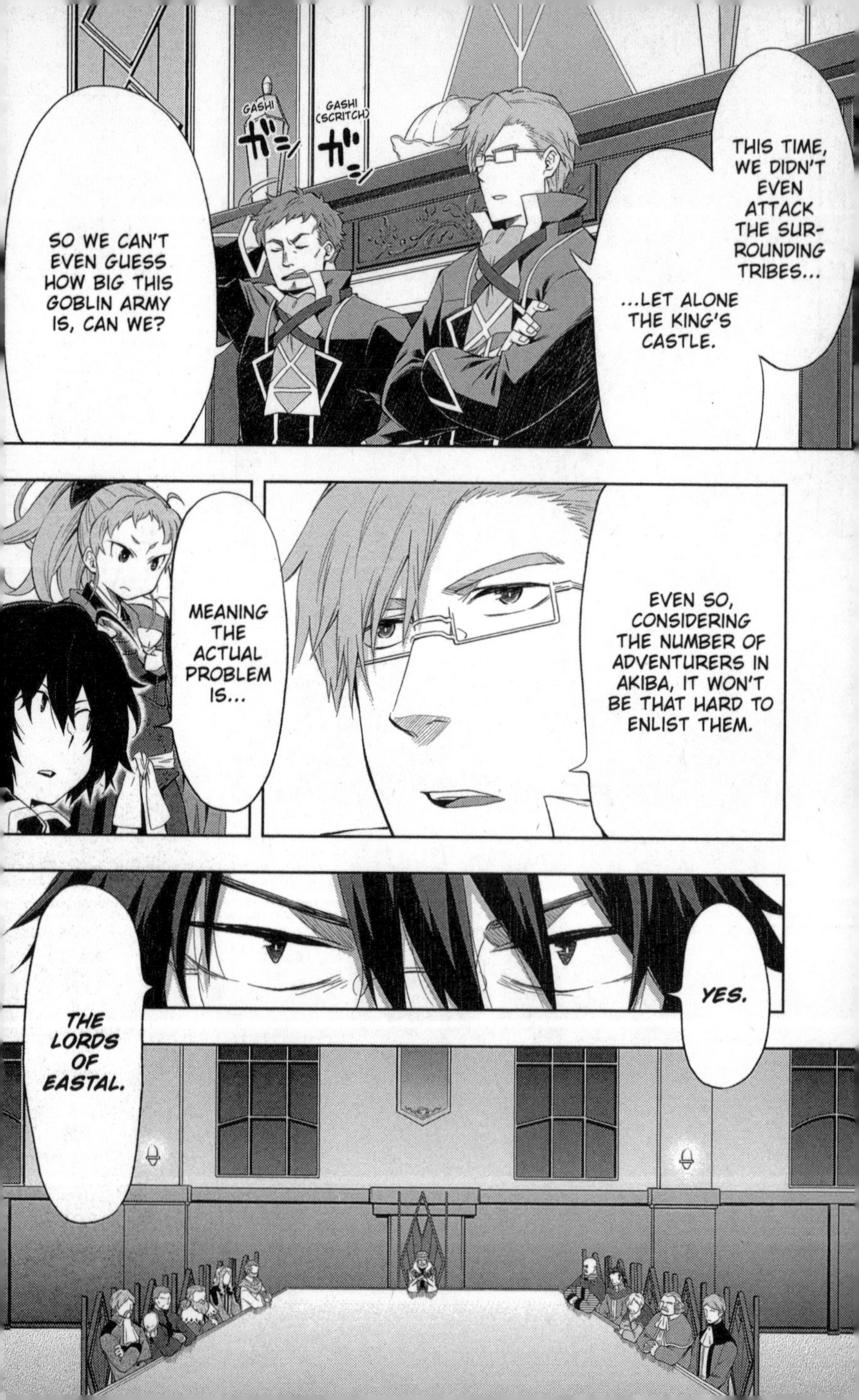
THIS TIME, WE DIDN'T EVEN ATTACK THE SUR-ROUNDING TRIBES...
...LET ALONE THE KING'S CASTLE.
GASHI (SCRITCH)
GASHI
SO WE CAN'T EVEN GUESS HOW BIG THIS GOBLIN ARMY IS, CAN WE?
EVEN SO, CONSIDERING THE NUMBER OF ADVENTURERS IN AKIBA, IT WON'T BE THAT HARD TO ENLIST THEM.
MEANING THE ACTUAL PROBLEM IS...
YES.
THE LORDS OF EASTAL.

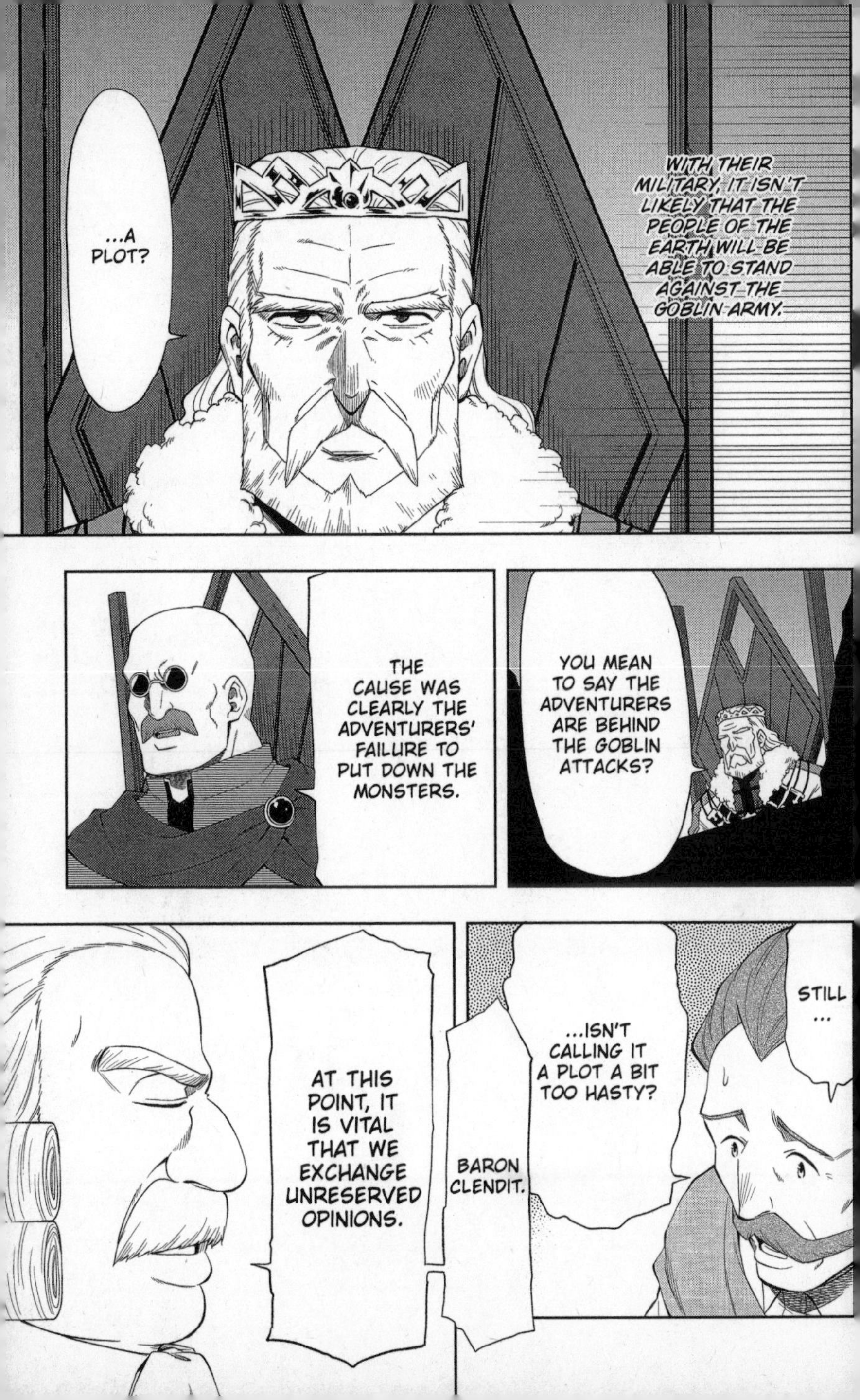
WITH THEIR MILITARY, IT ISN'T LIKELY THAT THE PEOPLE OF THE EARTH WILL BE ABLE TO STAND AGAINST THE GOBLIN ARMY.
...A PLOT?
YOU MEAN TO SAY THE ADVENTURERS ARE BEHIND THE GOBLIN ATTACKS?
THE CAUSE WAS CLEARLY THE ADVENTURERS' FAILURE TO PUT DOWN THE MONSTERS.
STILL...
...ISN'T CALLING IT A PLOT A BIT TOO HASTY?
BARON CLENDIT.
AT THIS POINT, IT IS VITAL THAT WE EXCHANGE UNRESERVED OPINIONS.

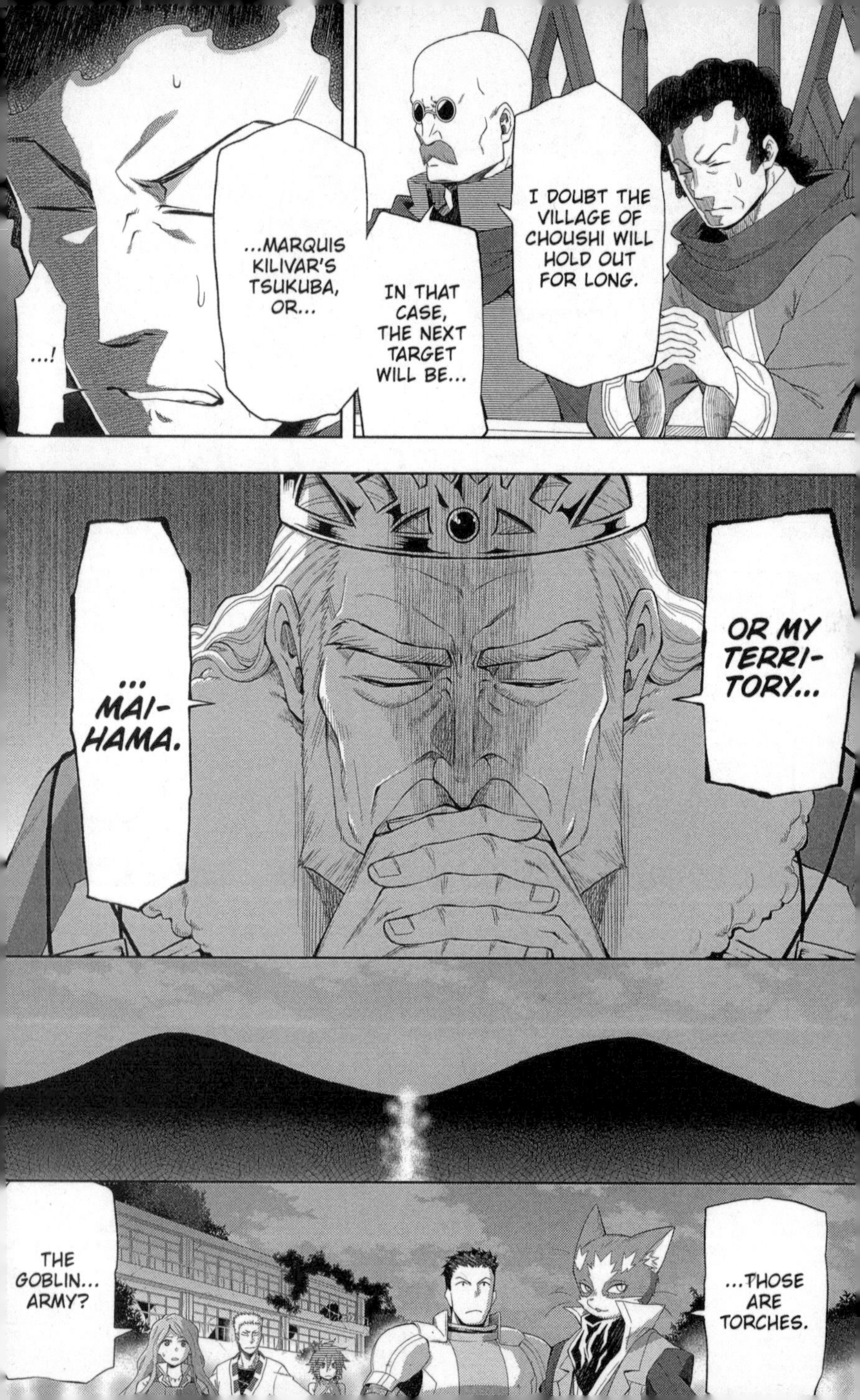
I DOUBT THE VILLAGE OF CHOUSHI WILL HOLD OUT FOR LONG.
IN THAT CASE, THE NEXT TARGET WILL BE...
...MARQUIS KILIVAR'S TSUKUBA, OR...
...!
OR MY TERRI-TORY...
...MAI-HAMA.
...THOSE ARE TORCHES.
THE GOBLIN... ARMY?

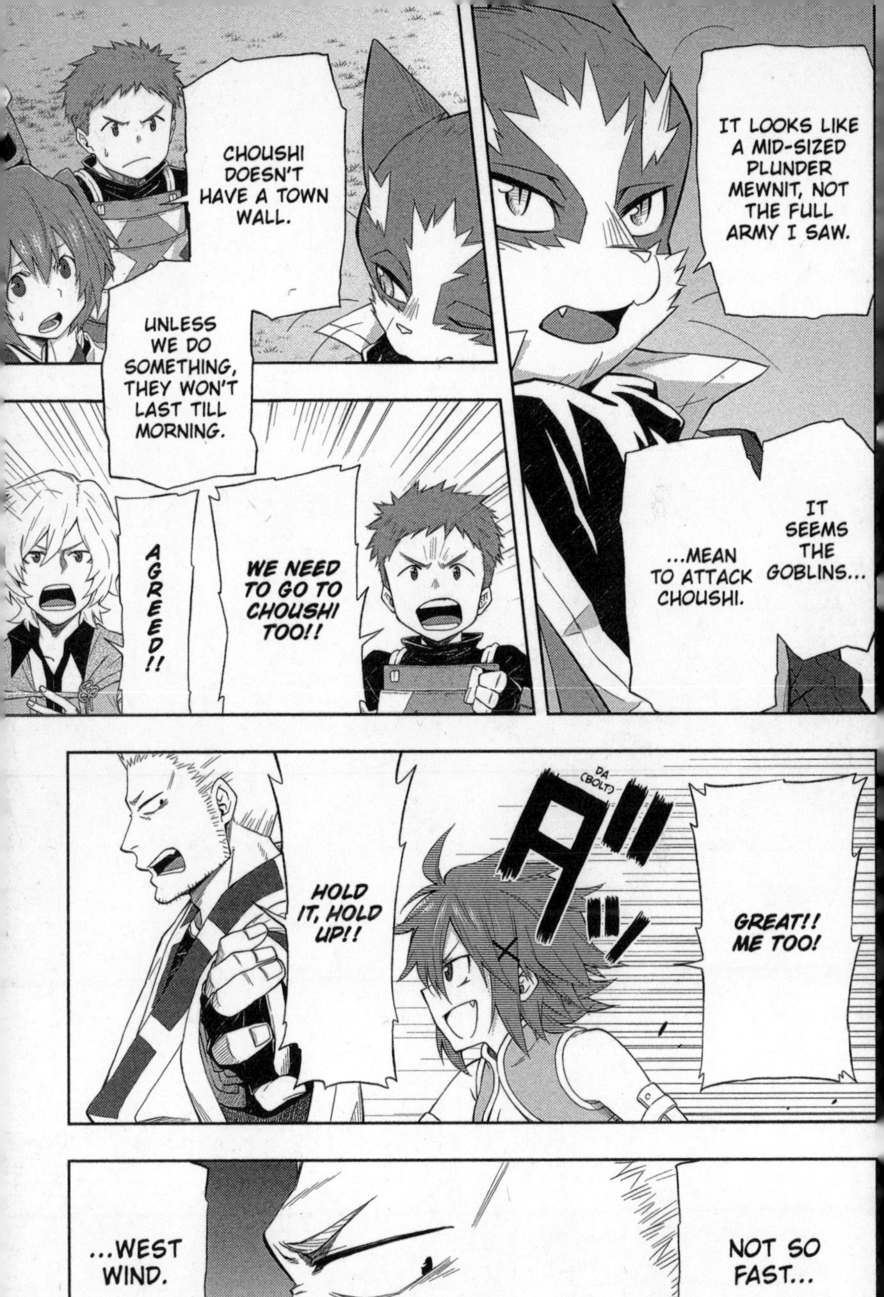

IT LOOKS LIKE A MID-SIZED PLUNDER MEWNIT, NOT THE FULL ARMY I SAW.
IT SEEMS THE GOBLINS...
...MEAN TO ATTACK CHOUSHI.
CHOUSHI DOESN'T HAVE A TOWN WALL.
UNLESS WE DO SOMETHING, THEY WON'T LAST TILL MORNING.
WE NEED TO GO TO CHOUSHI TOO!!
AGREED!!
DA (BOLT)
GREAT!! ME TOO!
HOLD IT, HOLD UP!!
NOT SO FAST...
...WEST WIND.

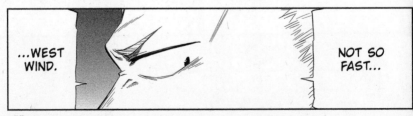

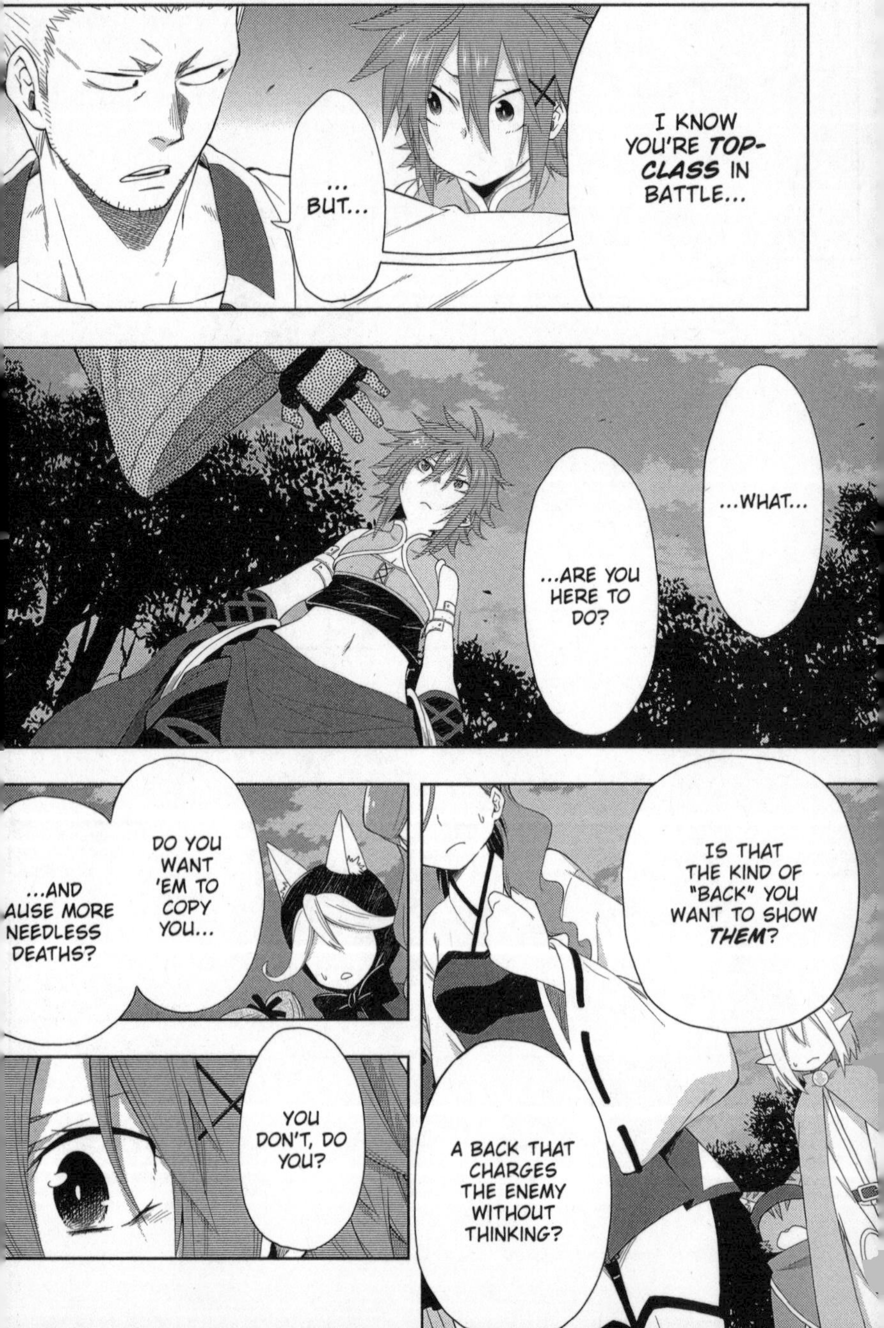
I KNOW YOU'RE ***TOP-CLASS*** IN BATTLE...
... BUT...
...WHAT...
...ARE YOU HERE TO DO?
IS THAT THE KIND OF "BACK" YOU WANT TO SHOW ***THEM***?
A BACK THAT CHARGES THE ENEMY WITHOUT THINKING?
DO YOU WANT 'EM TO COPY YOU...
...AND AUSE MORE NEEDLESS DEATHS?
YOU DON'T, DO YOU?

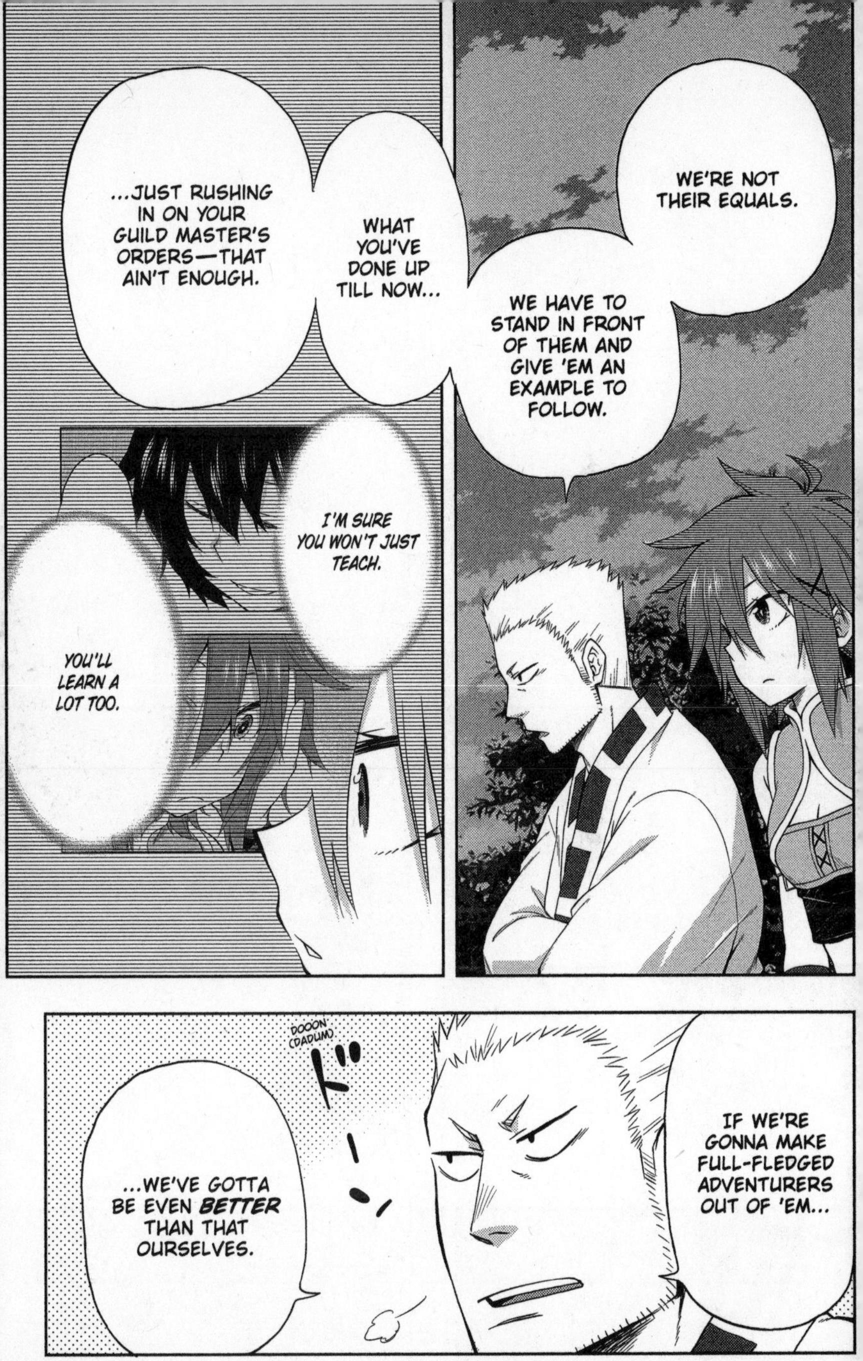
WE'RE NOT THEIR EQUALS.
WE HAVE TO STAND IN FRONT OF THEM AND GIVE 'EM AN EXAMPLE TO FOLLOW.
WHAT YOU'VE DONE UP TILL NOW...
...JUST RUSHING IN ON YOUR GUILD MASTER'S ORDERS—THAT AIN'T ENOUGH.
I'M SURE YOU WON'T JUST TEACH.
YOU'LL LEARN A LOT TOO.
IF WE'RE GONNA MAKE FULL-FLEDGED ADVENTURERS OUT OF 'EM...
DOOON (DADUM)
...WE'VE GOTTA BE EVEN ***BETTER*** THAN THAT OURSELVES.

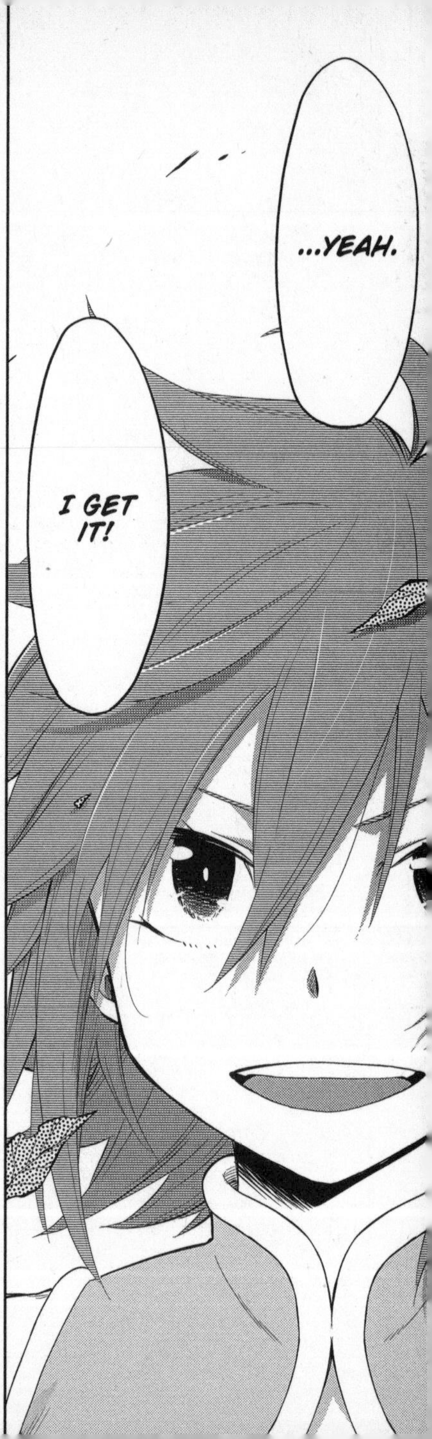
...YEAH.
I GET IT!

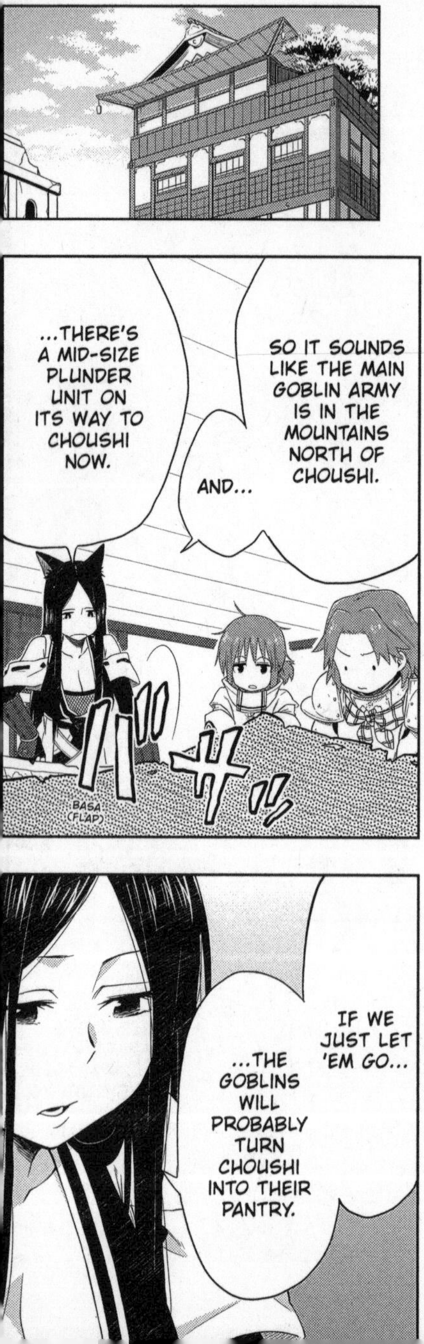
SO IT SOUNDS LIKE THE MAIN GOBLIN ARMY IS IN THE MOUNTAINS NORTH OF CHOUSHI.
AND...
...THERE'S A MID-SIZE PLUNDER UNIT ON ITS WAY TO CHOUSHI NOW.
BASA (FLAP)
IF WE JUST LET 'EM GO...
...THE GOBLINS WILL PROBABLY TURN CHOUSHI INTO THEIR PANTRY.

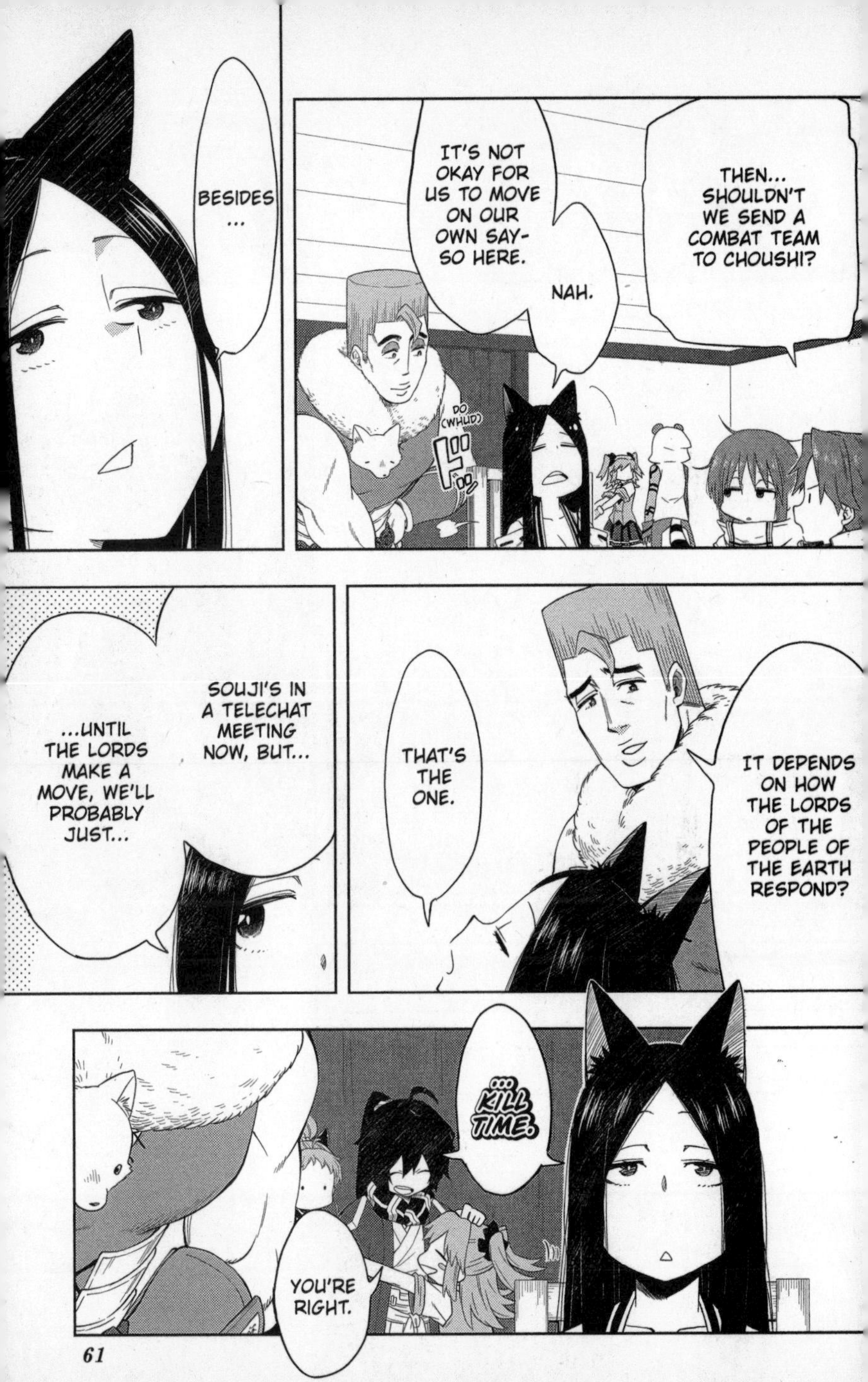
THEN... SHOULDN'T WE SEND A COMBAT TEAM TO CHOUSHI?
NAH.
IT'S NOT OKAY FOR US TO MOVE ON OUR OWN SAY-SO HERE.
DO (WHUD)
BESIDES ...
IT DEPENDS ON HOW THE LORDS OF THE PEOPLE OF THE EARTH RESPOND?
THAT'S THE ONE.
SOUJI'S IN A TELECHAT MEETING NOW, BUT...
...UNTIL THE LORDS MAKE A MOVE, WE'LL PROBABLY JUST...
...KILL TIME.
YOU'RE RIGHT.

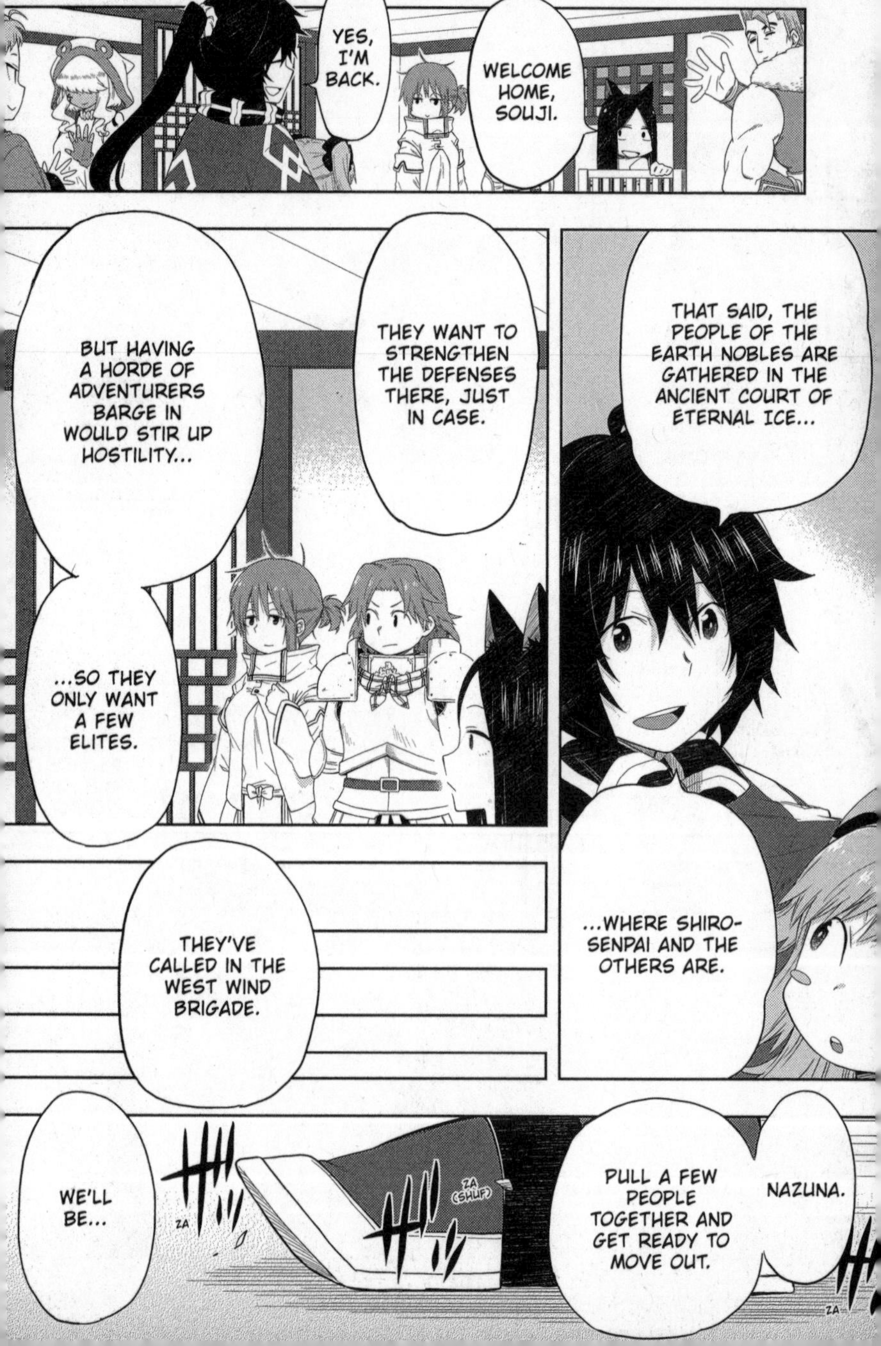
WELCOME HOME, SOUJI.
YES, I'M BACK.
THAT SAID, THE PEOPLE OF THE EARTH NOBLES ARE GATHERED IN THE ANCIENT COURT OF ETERNAL ICE...
...WHERE SHIRO-SENPAI AND THE OTHERS ARE.
THEY WANT TO STRENGTHEN THE DEFENSES THERE, JUST IN CASE.
BUT HAVING A HORDE OF ADVENTURERS BARGE IN WOULD STIR UP HOSTILITY...
...SO THEY ONLY WANT A FEW ELITES.
THEY'VE CALLED IN THE WEST WIND BRIGADE.
NAZUNA.
PULL A FEW PEOPLE TOGETHER AND GET READY TO MOVE OUT.
ZA
ZA (SHUF)
ZA
WE'LL BE...

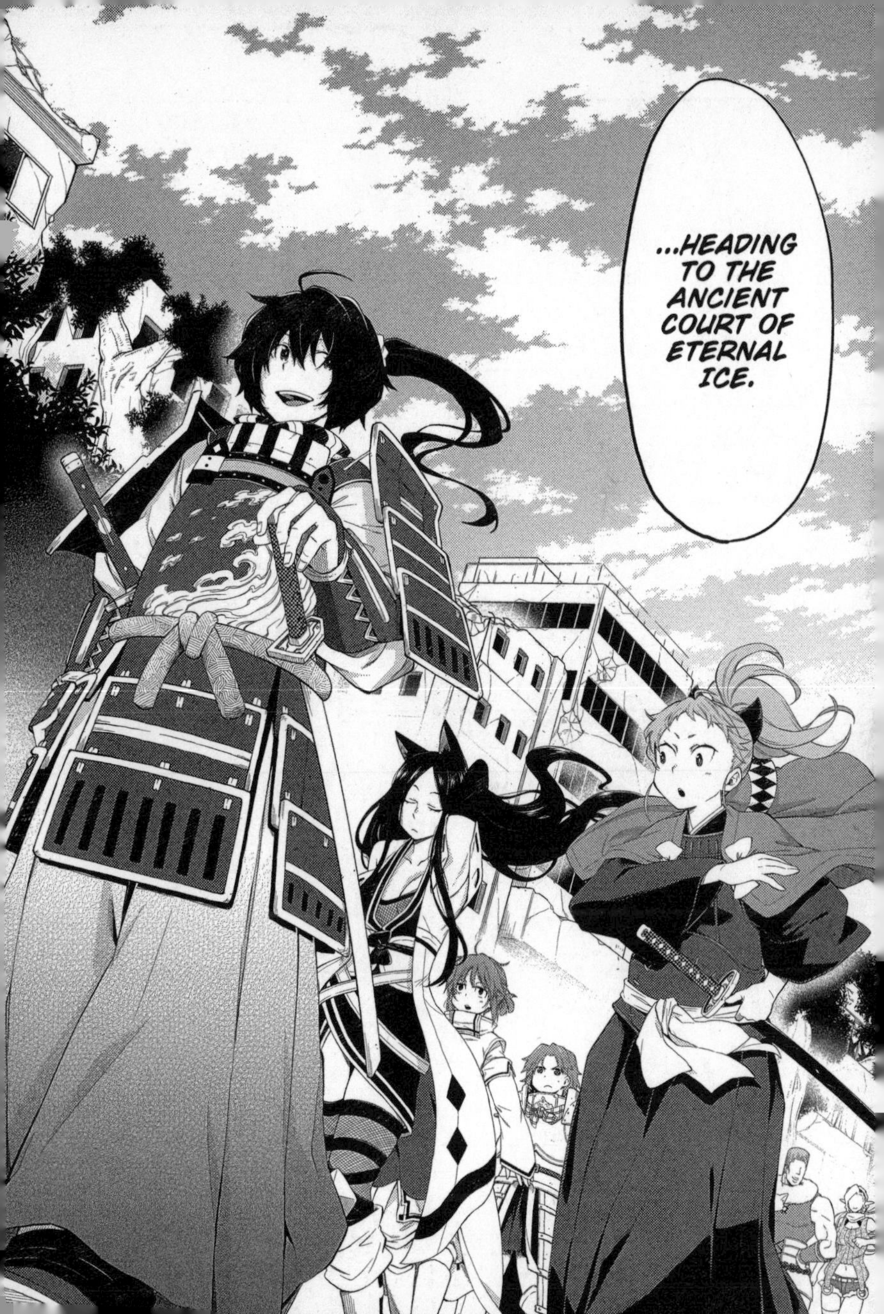
...HEADING TO THE ANCIENT COURT OF ETERNAL ICE.

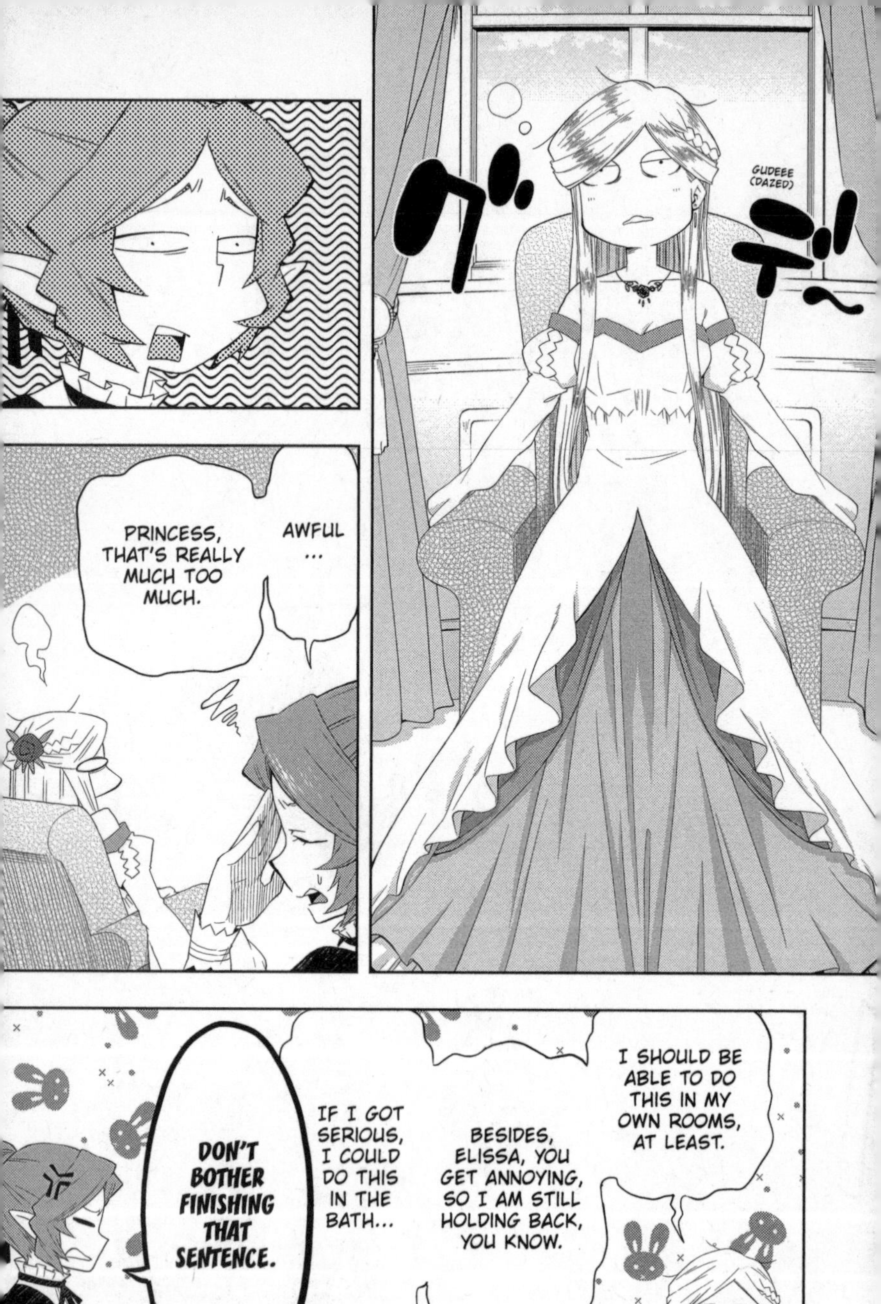

グデ〜
GUDEEE (DAZED)
AWFUL...
PRINCESS, THAT'S REALLY MUCH TOO MUCH.
I SHOULD BE ABLE TO DO THIS IN MY OWN ROOMS, AT LEAST.
BESIDES, ELISSA, YOU GET ANNOYING, SO I AM STILL HOLDING BACK, YOU KNOW.
IF I GOT SERIOUS, I COULD DO THIS IN THE BATH...
DON'T BOTHER FINISHING THAT SENTENCE.

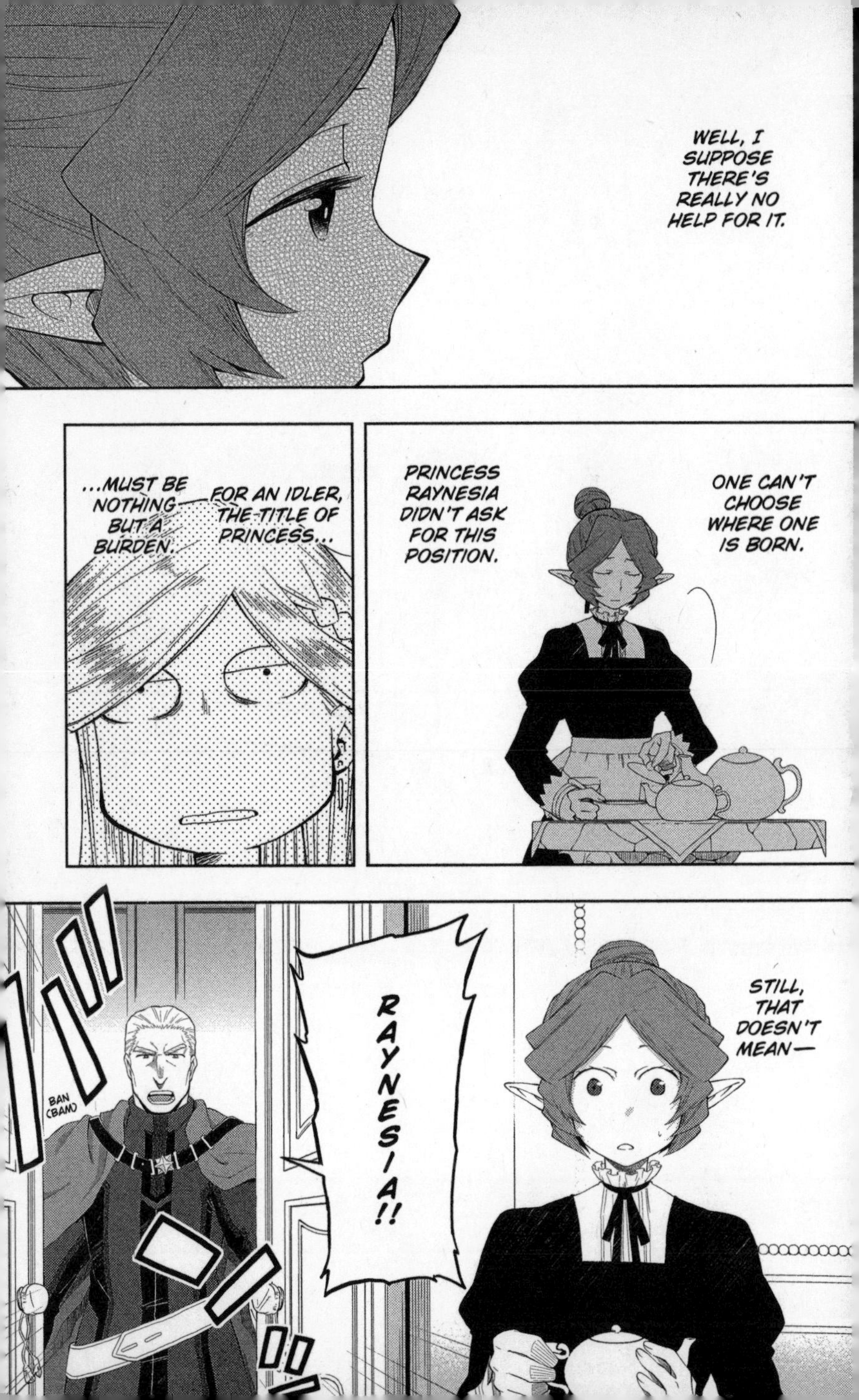
WELL, I SUPPOSE THERE'S REALLY NO HELP FOR IT.
ONE CAN'T CHOOSE WHERE ONE IS BORN.
PRINCESS RAYNESIA DIDN'T ASK FOR THIS POSITION.
FOR AN IDLER, THE TITLE OF PRINCESS...
...MUST BE NOTHING BUT A BURDEN.
STILL, THAT DOESN'T MEAN—
RAYNESIA!!
BAN (BAM)

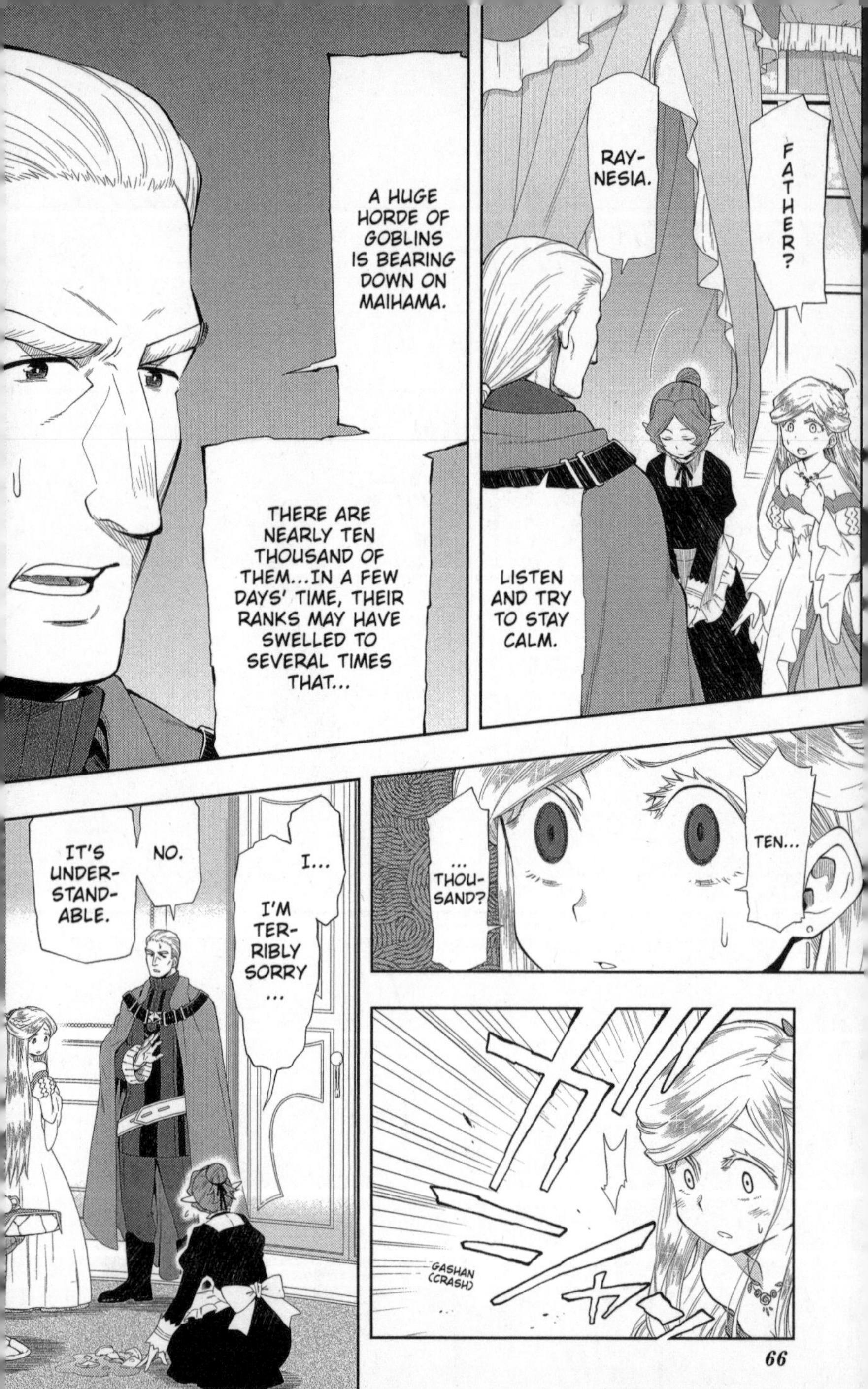
FATHER?
RAY-NESIA.
LISTEN AND TRY TO STAY CALM.
A HUGE HORDE OF GOBLINS IS BEARING DOWN ON MAIHAMA.
THERE ARE NEARLY TEN THOUSAND OF THEM...IN A FEW DAYS' TIME, THEIR RANKS MAY HAVE SWELLED TO SEVERAL TIMES THAT...
TEN...
...THOUSAND?
GASHAN (CRASH)
I...
I'M TERRIBLY SORRY...
NO.
IT'S UNDERSTANDABLE.

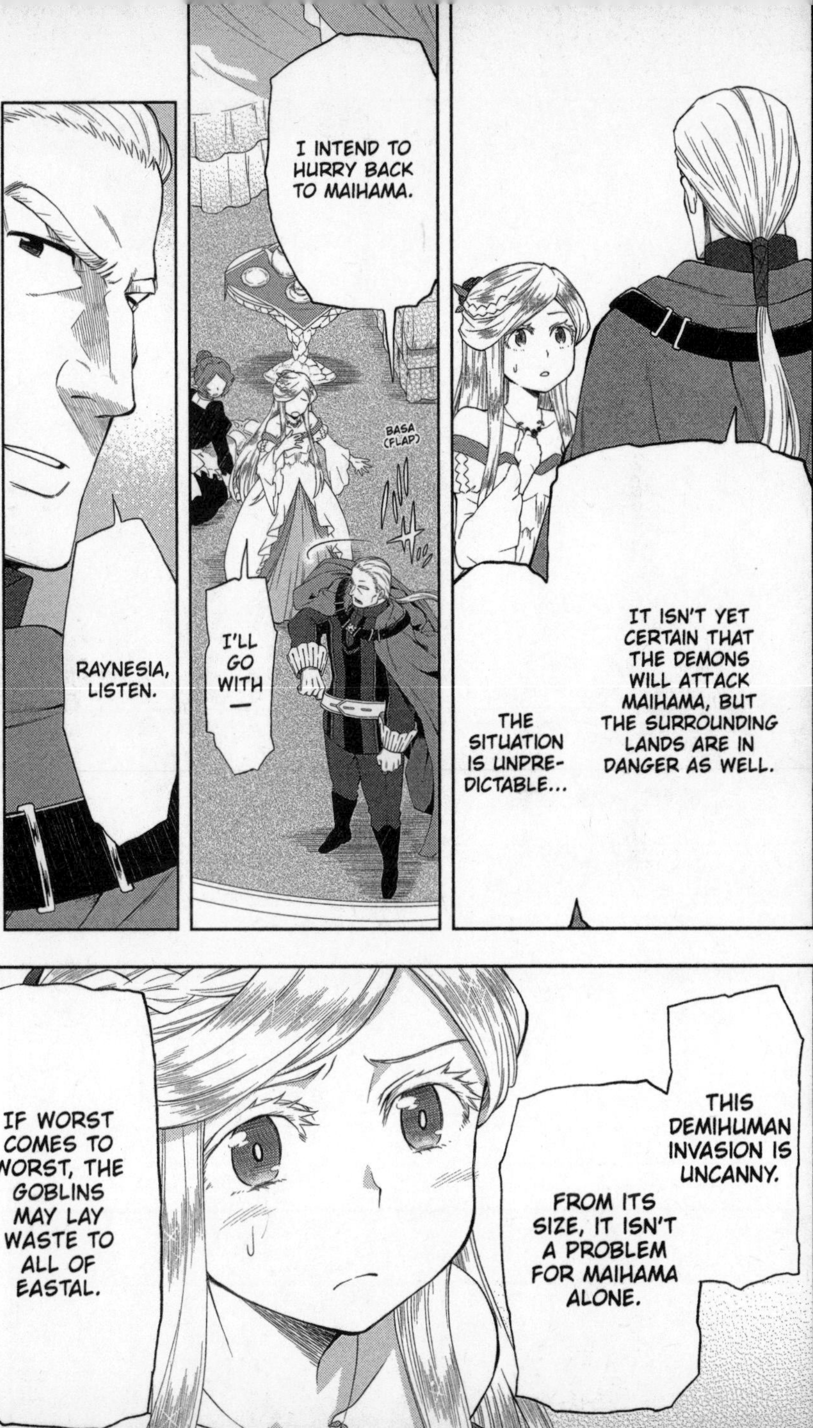
IT ISN'T YET CERTAIN THAT THE DEMONS WILL ATTACK MAIHAMA, BUT THE SURROUNDING LANDS ARE IN DANGER AS WELL.
THE SITUATION IS UNPREDICTABLE...
I INTEND TO HURRY BACK TO MAIHAMA.
BASA (FLAP)
I'LL GO WITH—
RAYNESIA, LISTEN.
THIS DEMIHUMAN INVASION IS UNCANNY.
FROM ITS SIZE, IT ISN'T A PROBLEM FOR MAIHAMA ALONE.
IF WORST COMES TO WORST, THE GOBLINS MAY LAY WASTE TO ALL OF EASTAL.

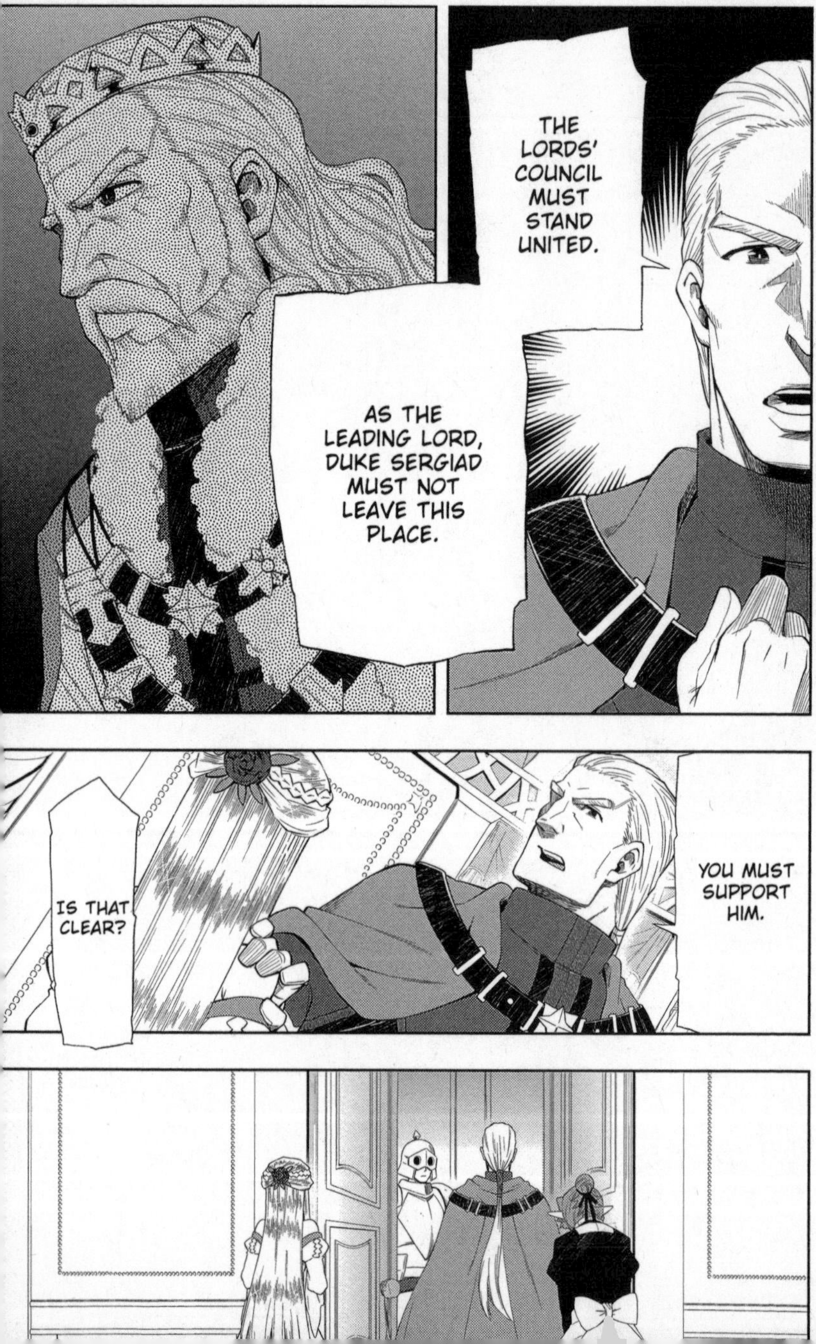
THE LORDS' COUNCIL MUST STAND UNITED.
AS THE LEADING LORD, DUKE SERGIAD MUST NOT LEAVE THIS PLACE.
YOU MUST SUPPORT HIM.
IS THAT CLEAR?

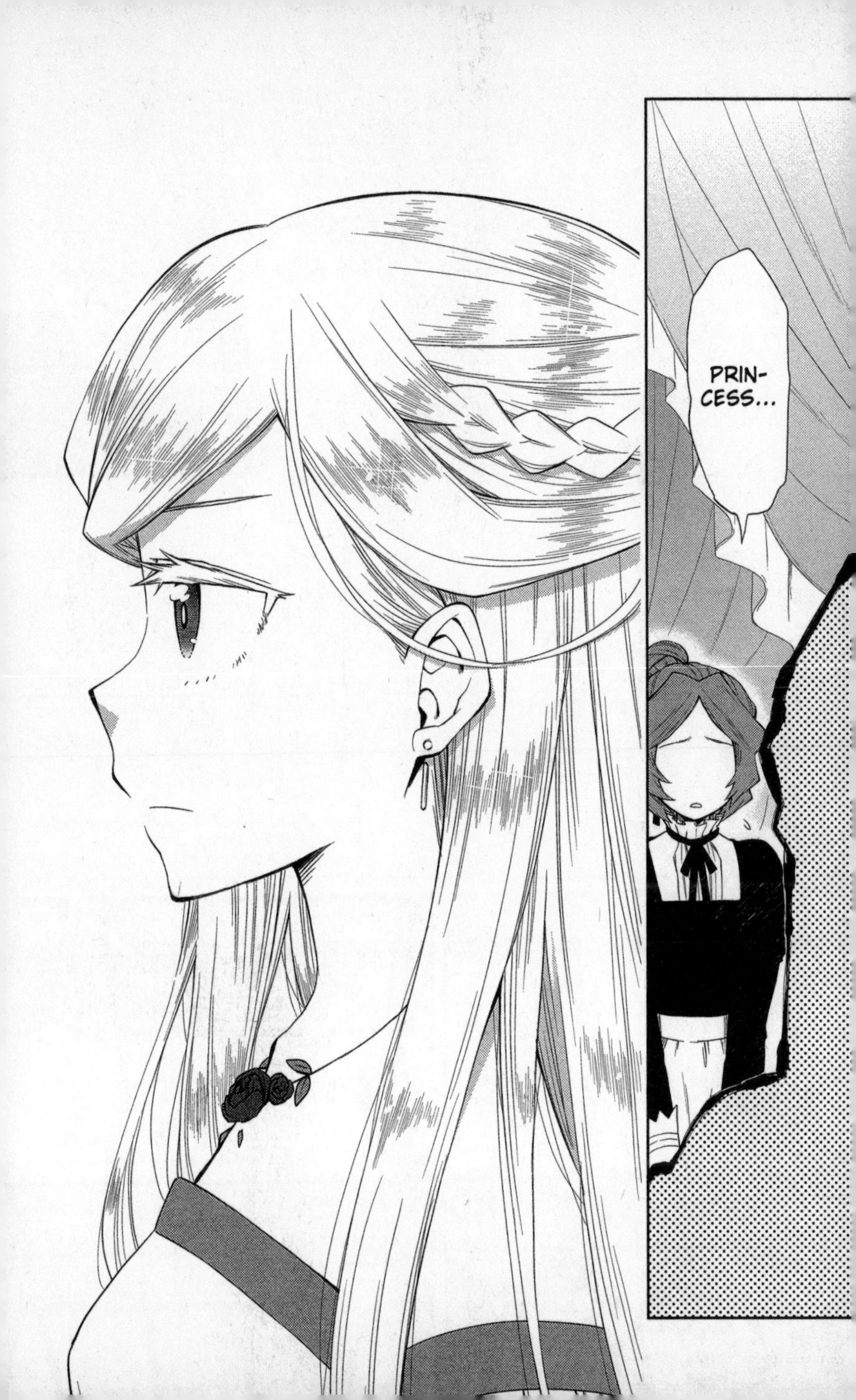
PRIN-
CESS...

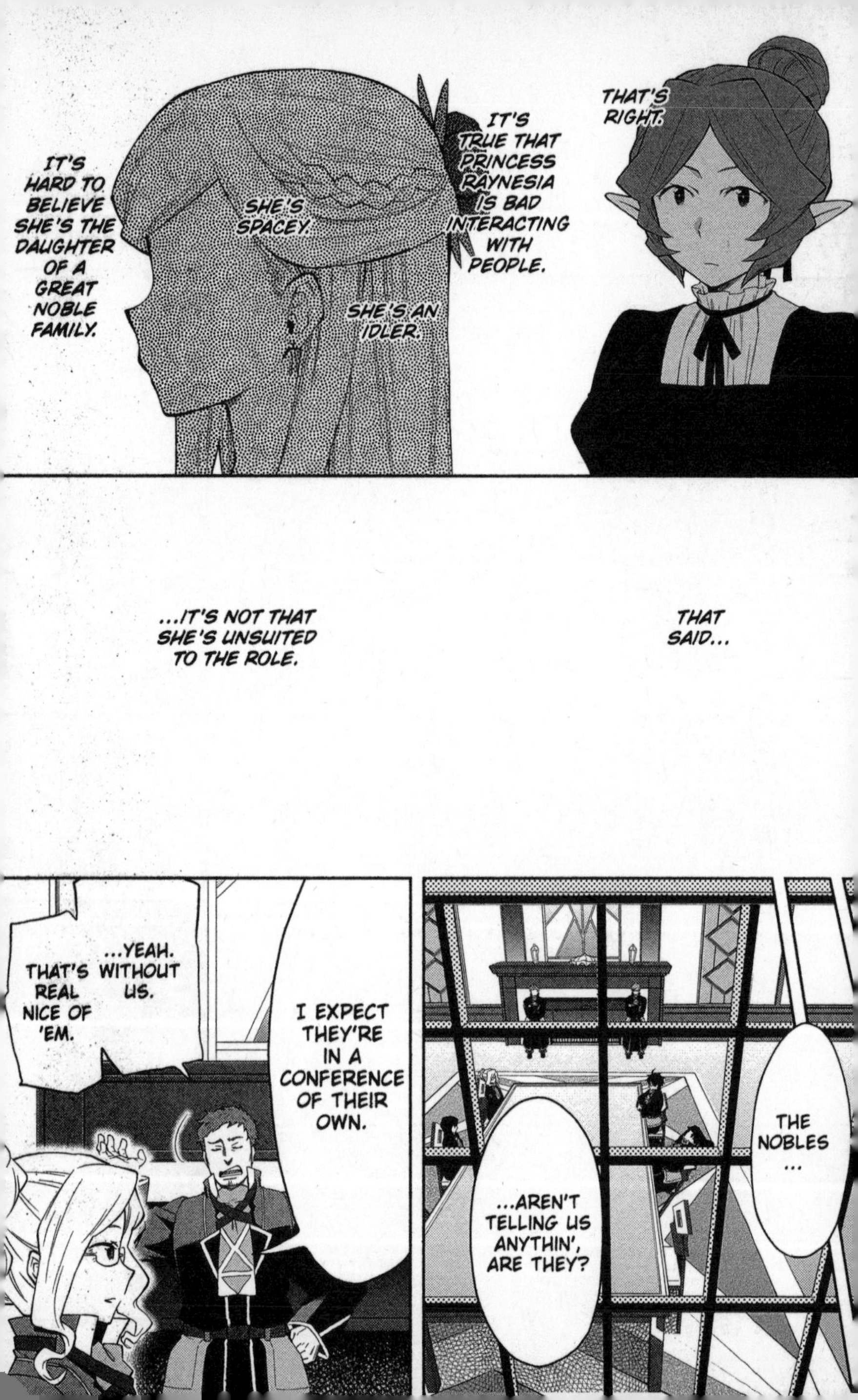
THAT'S RIGHT.
IT'S TRUE THAT PRINCESS RAYNESIA IS BAD INTERACTING WITH PEOPLE.
SHE'S SPACEY.
SHE'S AN IDLER.
IT'S HARD TO BELIEVE SHE'S THE DAUGHTER OF A GREAT NOBLE FAMILY.
THAT SAID...
...IT'S NOT THAT SHE'S UNSUITED TO THE ROLE.
THE NOBLES...
...AREN'T TELLING US ANYTHIN', ARE THEY?
I EXPECT THEY'RE IN A CONFERENCE OF THEIR OWN.
...YEAH. WITHOUT US.
THAT'S REAL NICE OF 'EM.

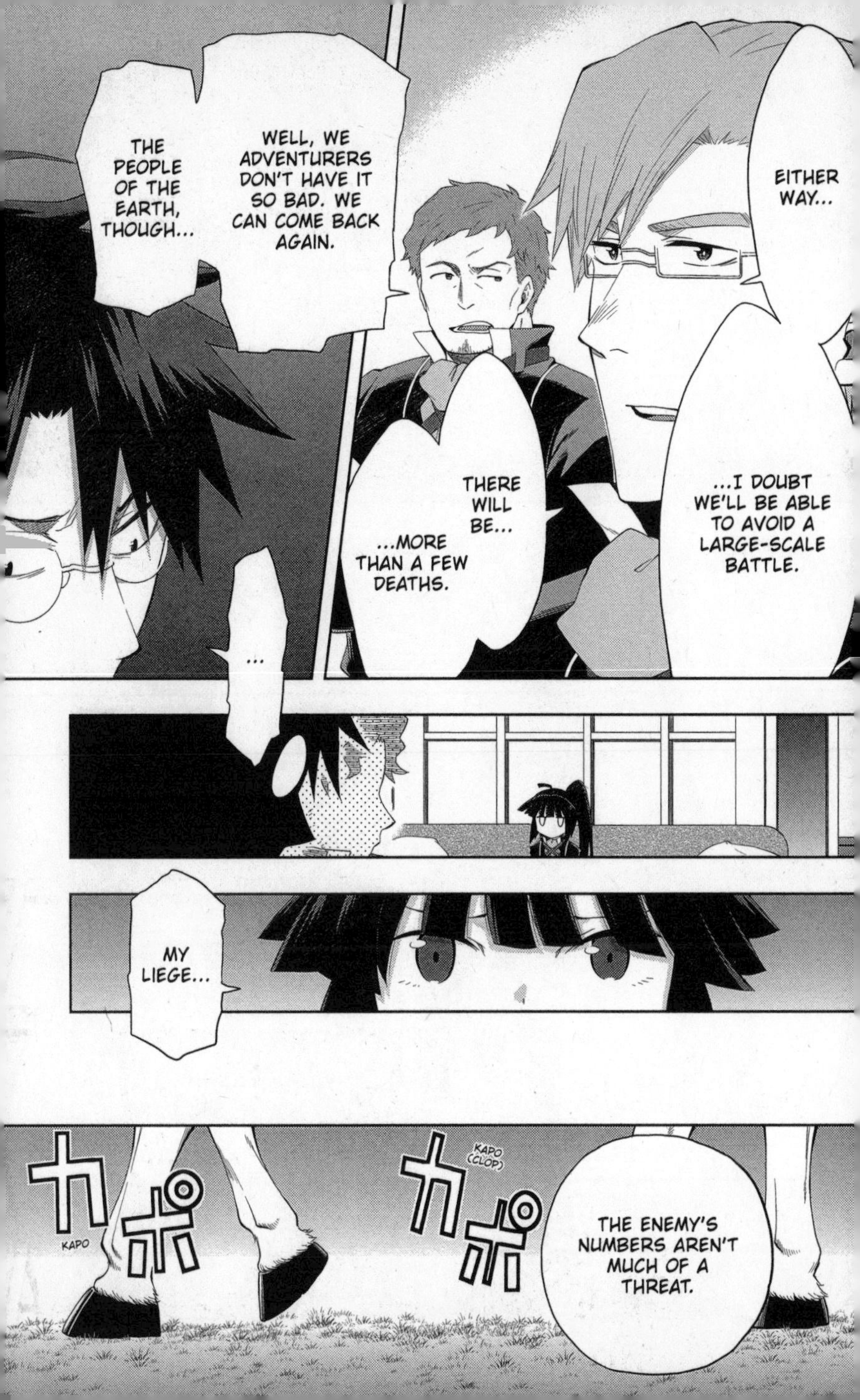
EITHER WAY...
...I DOUBT WE'LL BE ABLE TO AVOID A LARGE-SCALE BATTLE.
WELL, WE ADVENTURERS DON'T HAVE IT SO BAD. WE CAN COME BACK AGAIN.
THE PEOPLE OF THE EARTH, THOUGH...
THERE WILL BE...
...MORE THAN A FEW DEATHS.
...
MY LIEGE...
THE ENEMY'S NUMBERS AREN'T MUCH OF A THREAT.
カポ
KAPO (CLOP)
カポ
KAPO

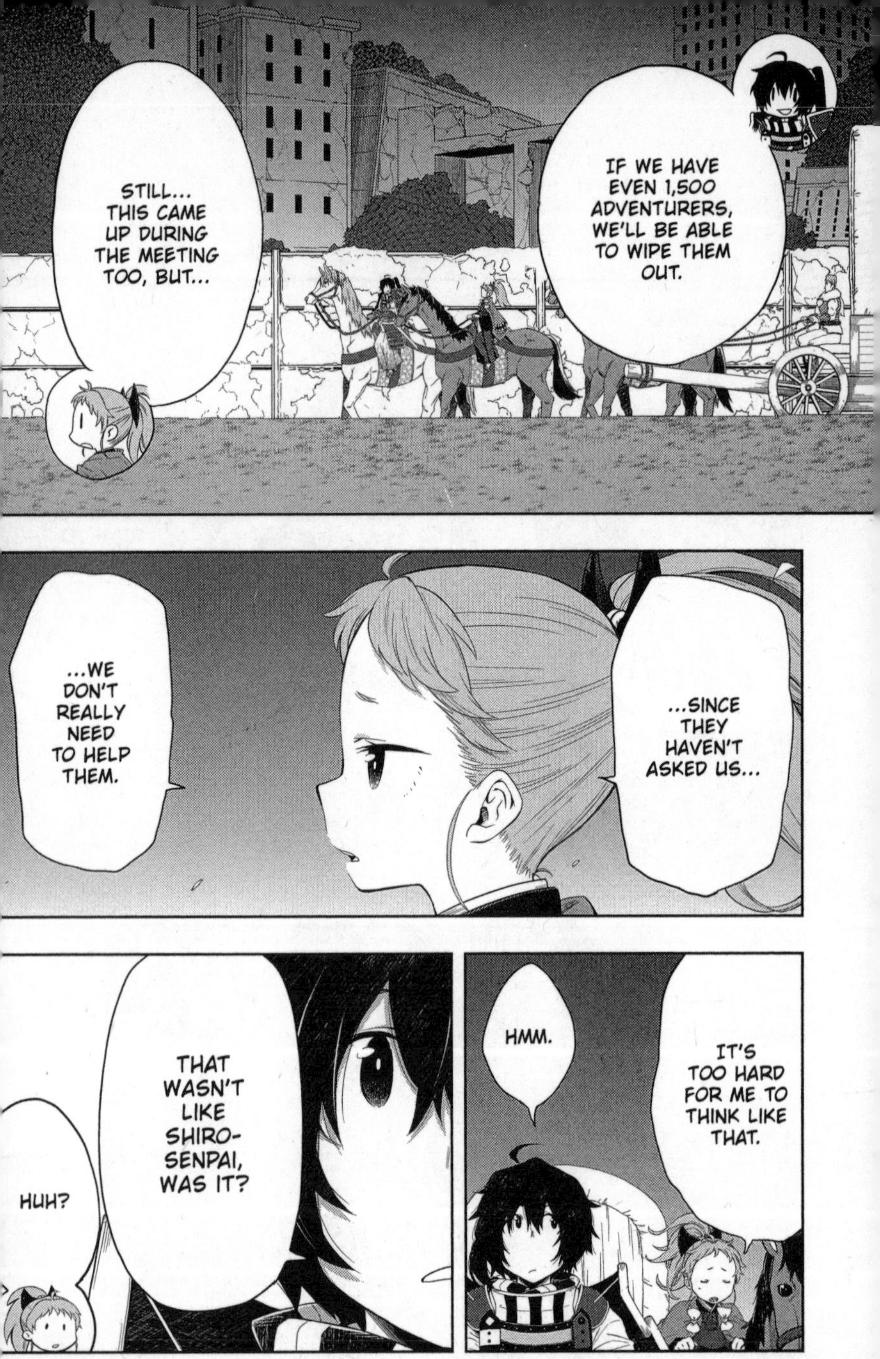
IF WE HAVE EVEN 1,500 ADVENTURERS, WE'LL BE ABLE TO WIPE THEM OUT.
STILL... THIS CAME UP DURING THE MEETING TOO, BUT...
...SINCE THEY HAVEN'T ASKED US...
...WE DON'T REALLY NEED TO HELP THEM.
IT'S TOO HARD FOR ME TO THINK LIKE THAT.
HMM.
THAT WASN'T LIKE SHIRO-SENPAI, WAS IT?
HUH?

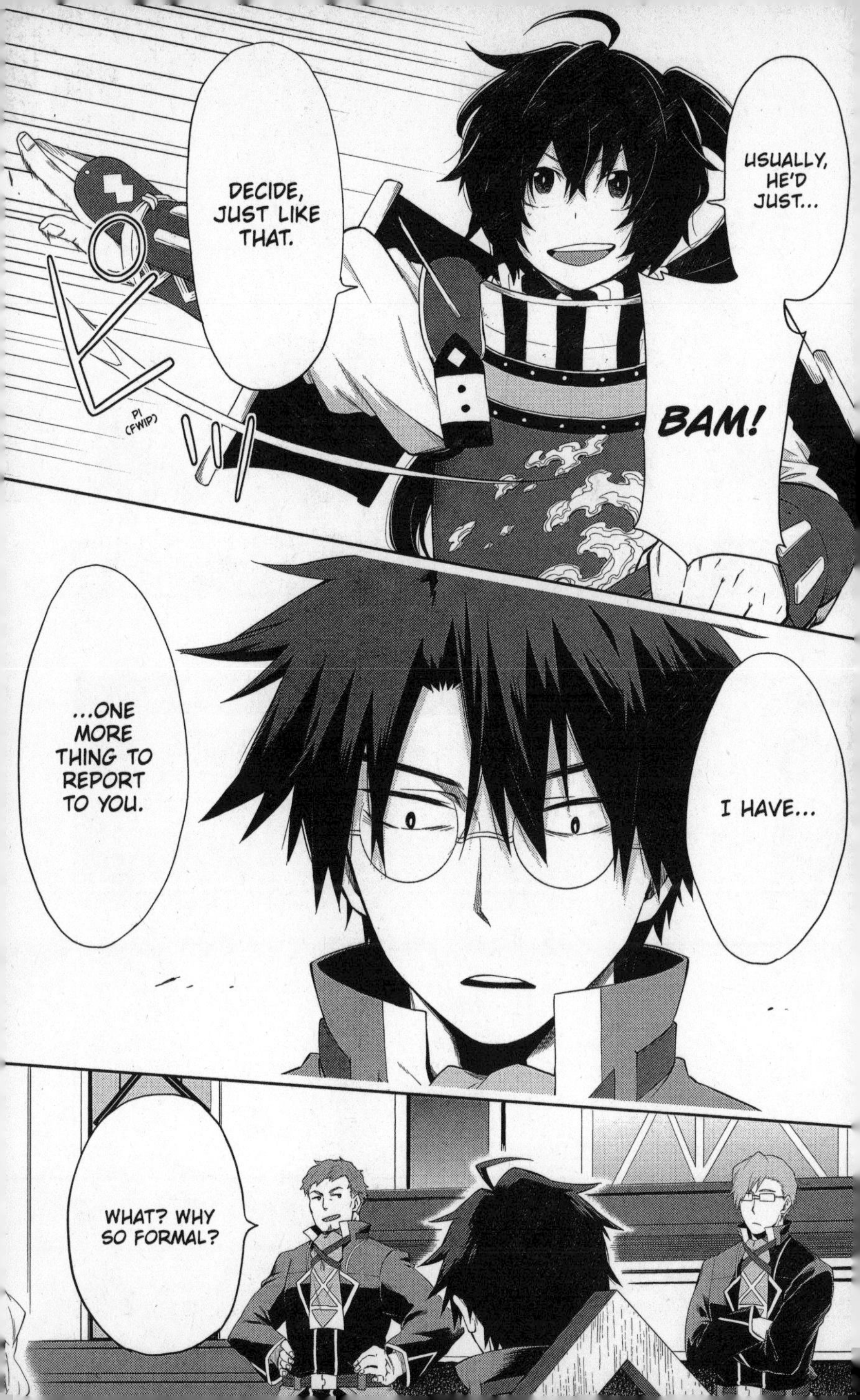
USUALLY, HE'D JUST...
DECIDE, JUST LIKE THAT.
BAM!
PI (FWIP)
I HAVE...
...ONE MORE THING TO REPORT TO YOU.
WHAT? WHY SO FORMAL?

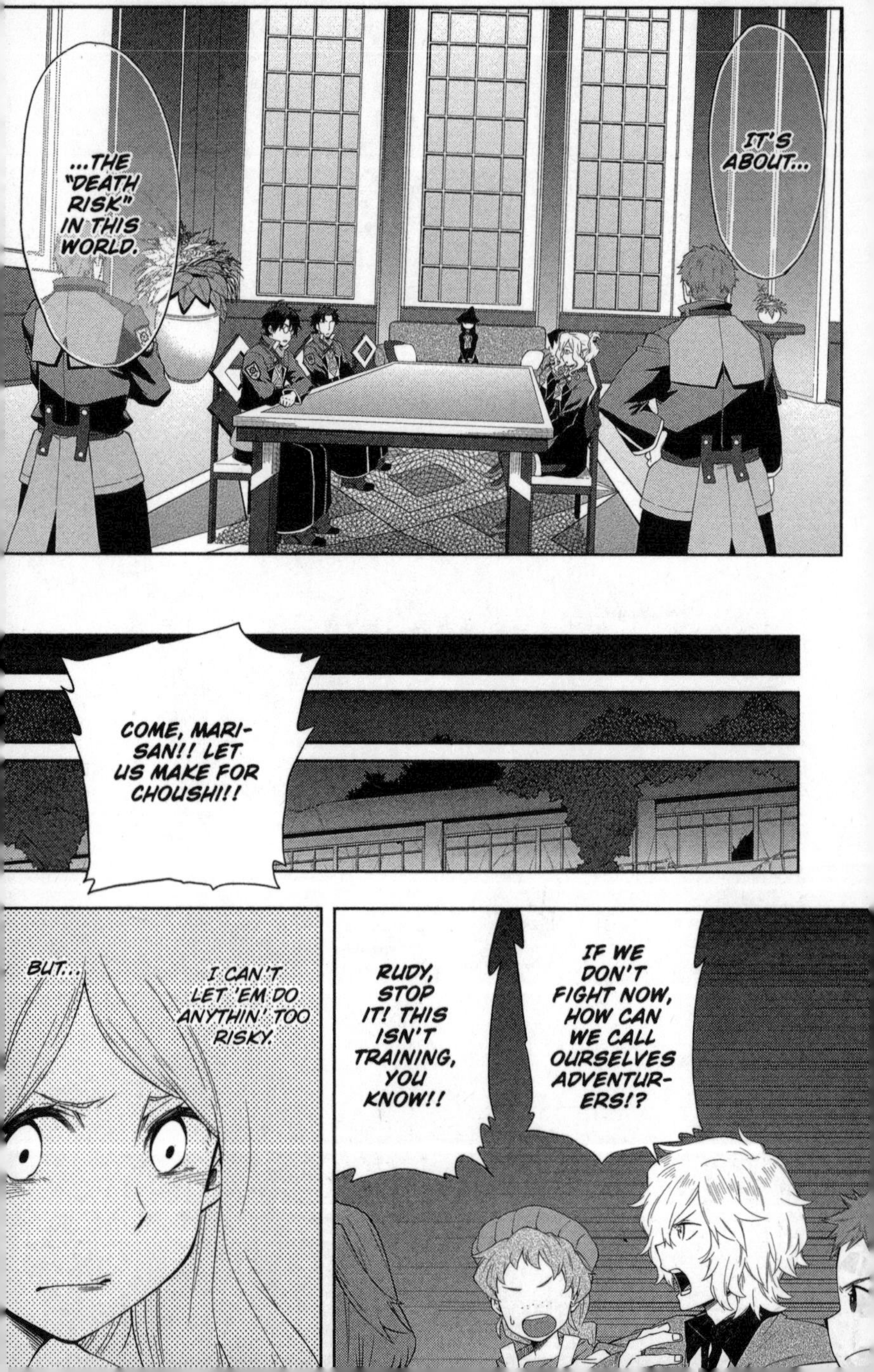
IT'S ABOUT...
...THE "DEATH RISK" IN THIS WORLD.
COME, MARI-SAN!! LET US MAKE FOR CHOUSHI!!
IF WE DON'T FIGHT NOW, HOW CAN WE CALL OURSELVES ADVENTURERS!?
RUDY, STOP IT! THIS ISN'T TRAINING, YOU KNOW!!
BUT...
I CAN'T LET 'EM DO ANYTHIN' TOO RISKY.

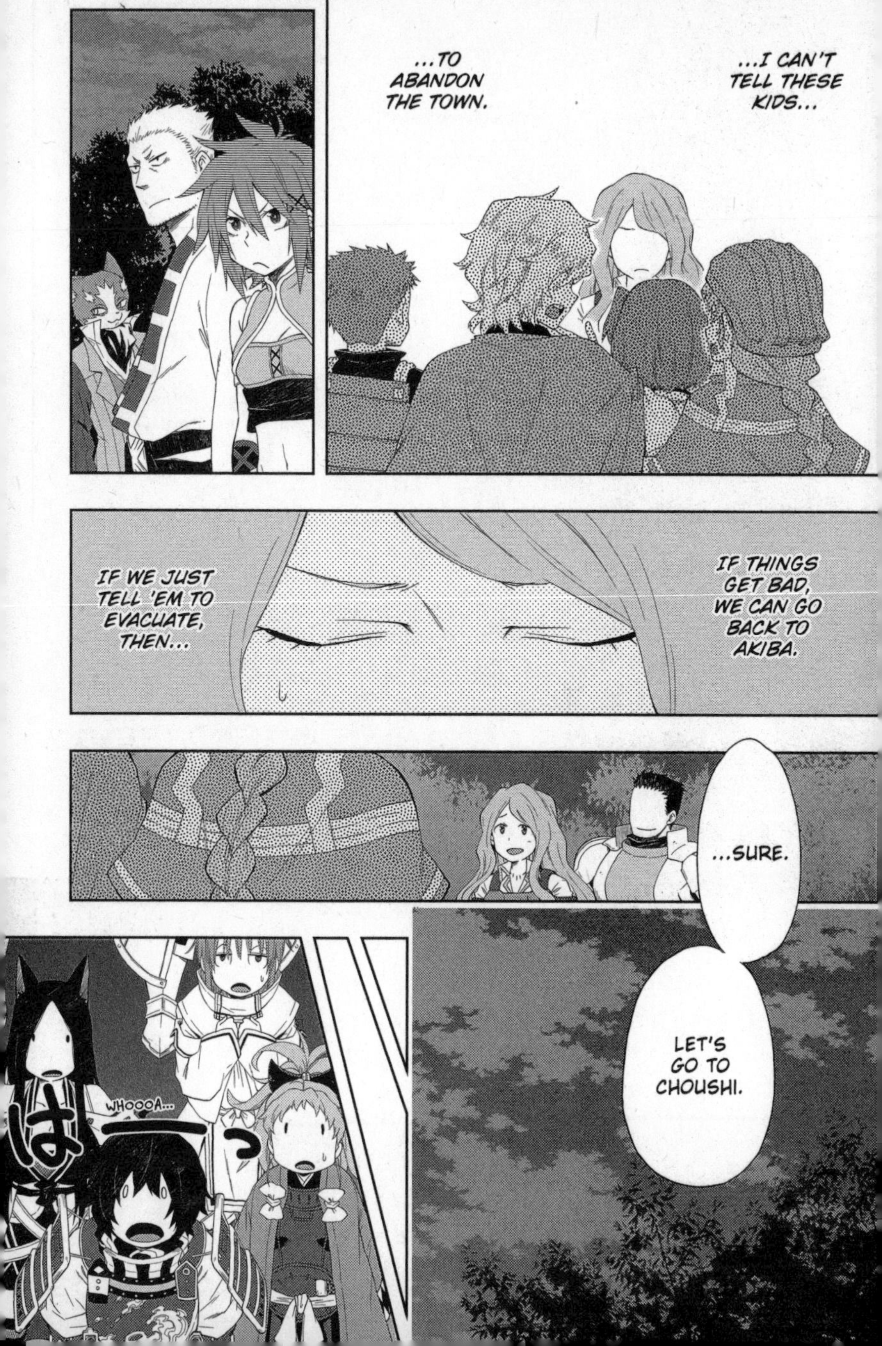
...I CAN'T TELL THESE KIDS...
...TO ABANDON THE TOWN.
IF THINGS GET BAD, WE CAN GO BACK TO AKIBA.
IF WE JUST TELL 'EM TO EVACUATE, THEN...
...SURE.
LET'S GO TO CHOUSHI.
WHOOOA...
はーーっ

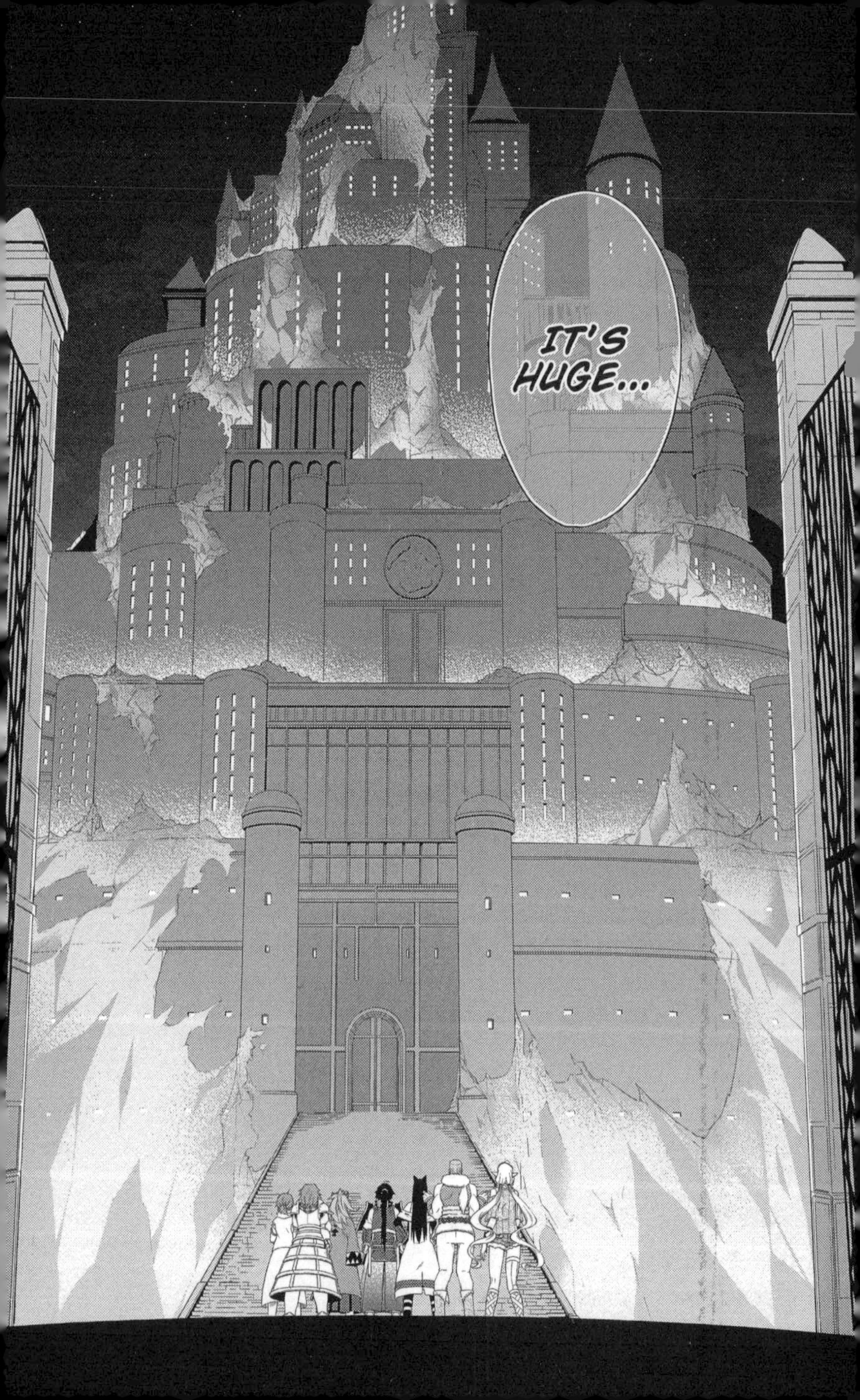
IT'S HUGE...

LOG HORIZON
THE WEST WIND BRIGADE

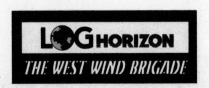

LOG HORIZON
THE WEST WIND BRIGADE

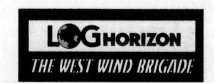

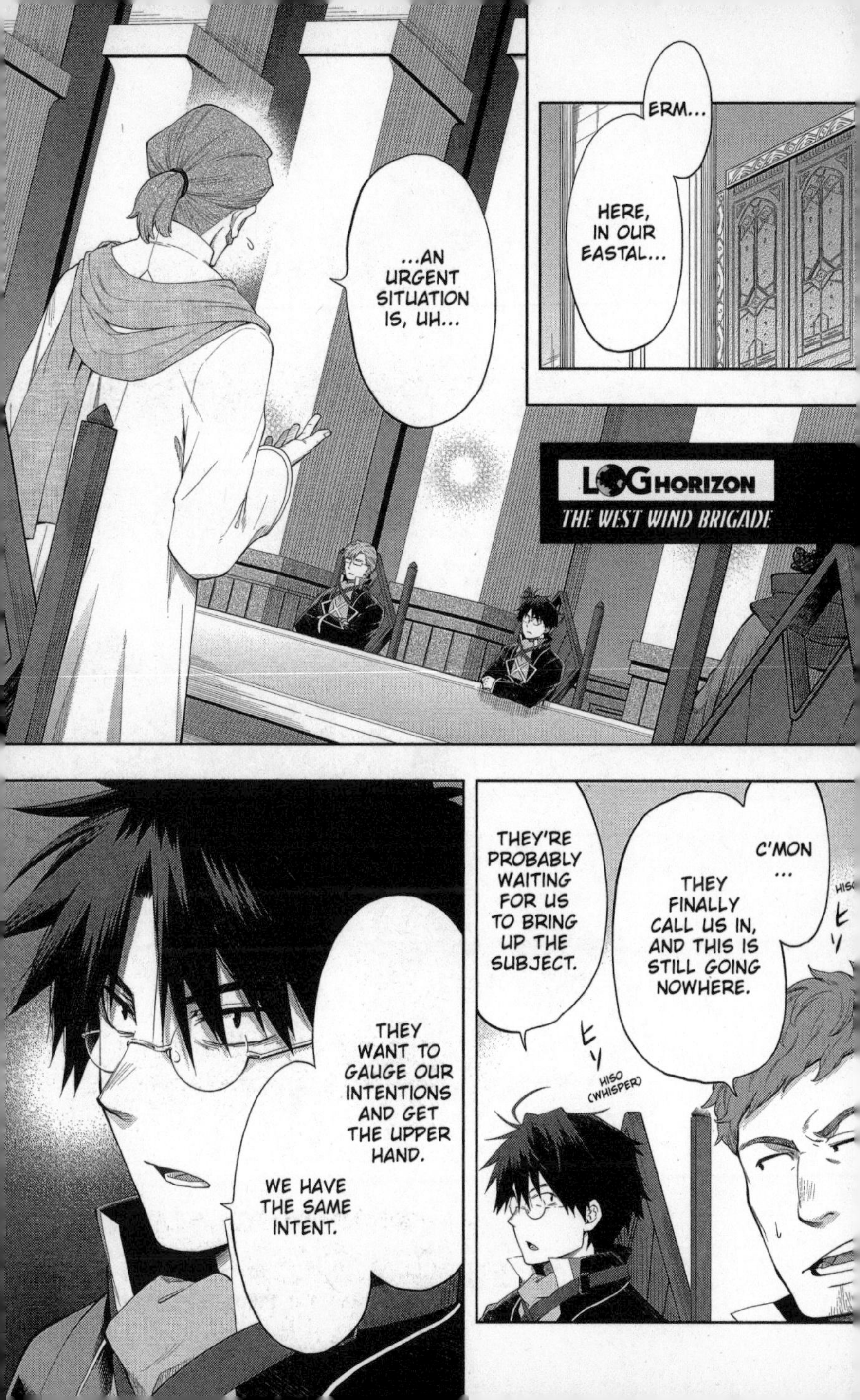
ERM...
HERE, IN OUR EASTAL...
...AN URGENT SITUATION IS, UH...
LOG HORIZON
THE WEST WIND BRIGADE
C'MON ...
THEY FINALLY CALL US IN, AND THIS IS STILL GOING NOWHERE.
ヒソ
THEY'RE PROBABLY WAITING FOR US TO BRING UP THE SUBJECT.
ヒソ
HISO (WHISPER)
THEY WANT TO GAUGE OUR INTENTIONS AND GET THE UPPER HAND.
WE HAVE THE SAME INTENT.

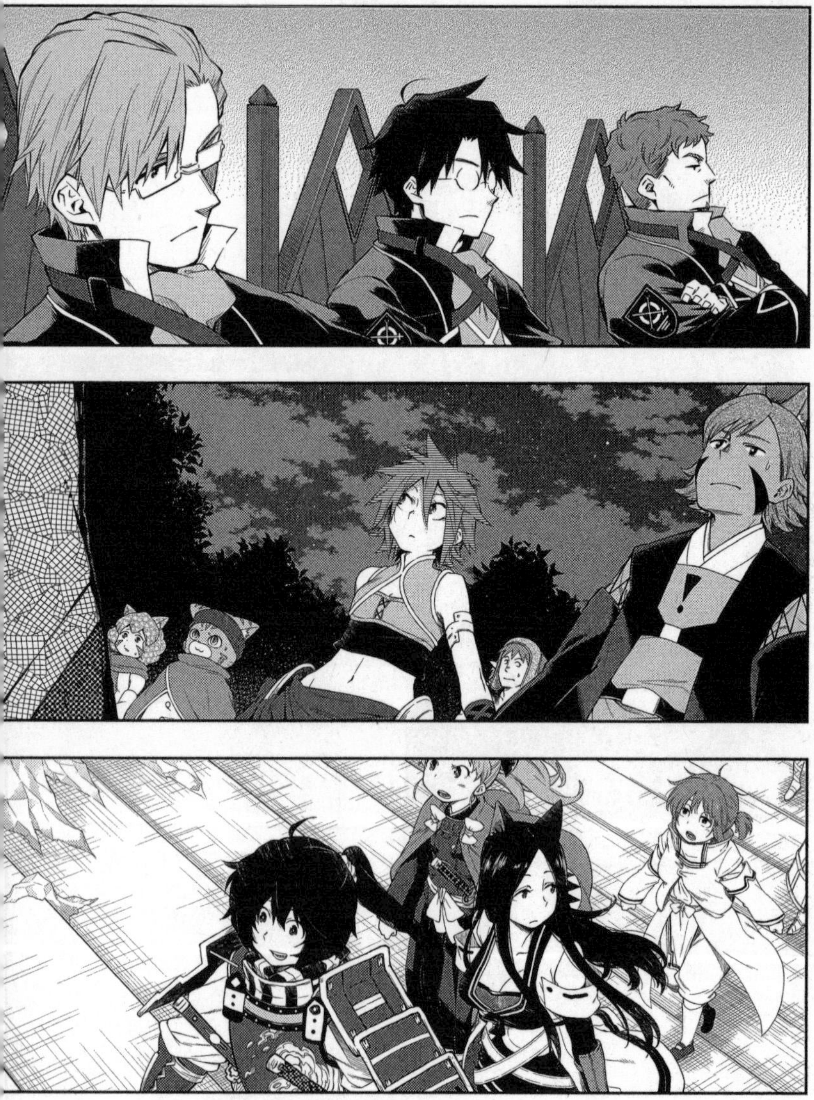

CHAPTER : 40 Separate Battles

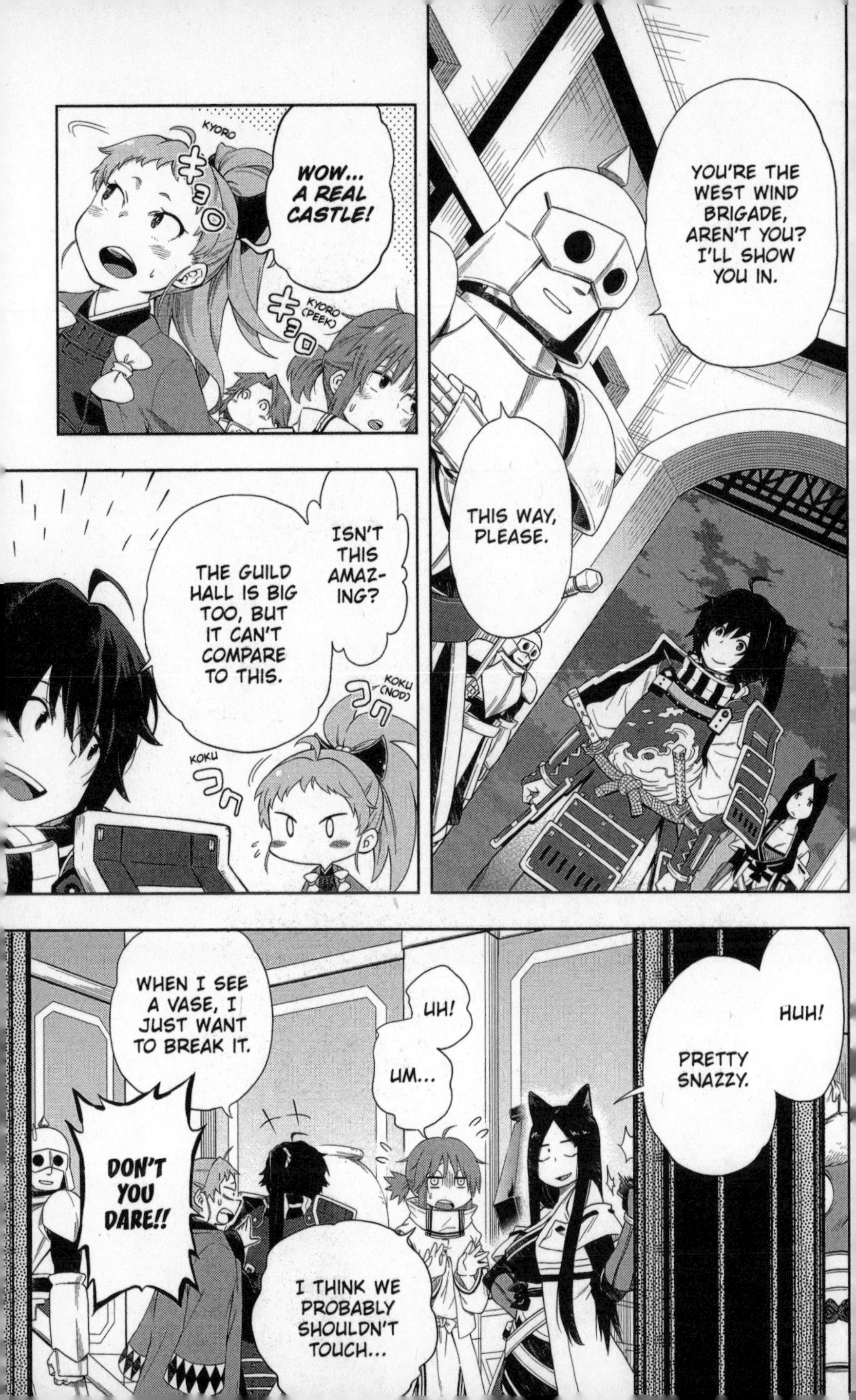
YOU'RE THE WEST WIND BRIGADE, AREN'T YOU? I'LL SHOW YOU IN.
THIS WAY, PLEASE.
KYORO
キョロ
WOW... A REAL CASTLE!
KYORO (PEEK)
キョロ
ISN'T THIS AMAZ-ING?
THE GUILD HALL IS BIG TOO, BUT IT CAN'T COMPARE TO THIS.
KOKU (NOD)
コク
KOKU
コク
HUH!
PRETTY SNAZZY.
UH!
UM...
WHEN I SEE A VASE, I JUST WANT TO BREAK IT.
DON'T YOU DARE!!
I THINK WE PROBABLY SHOULDN'T TOUCH...

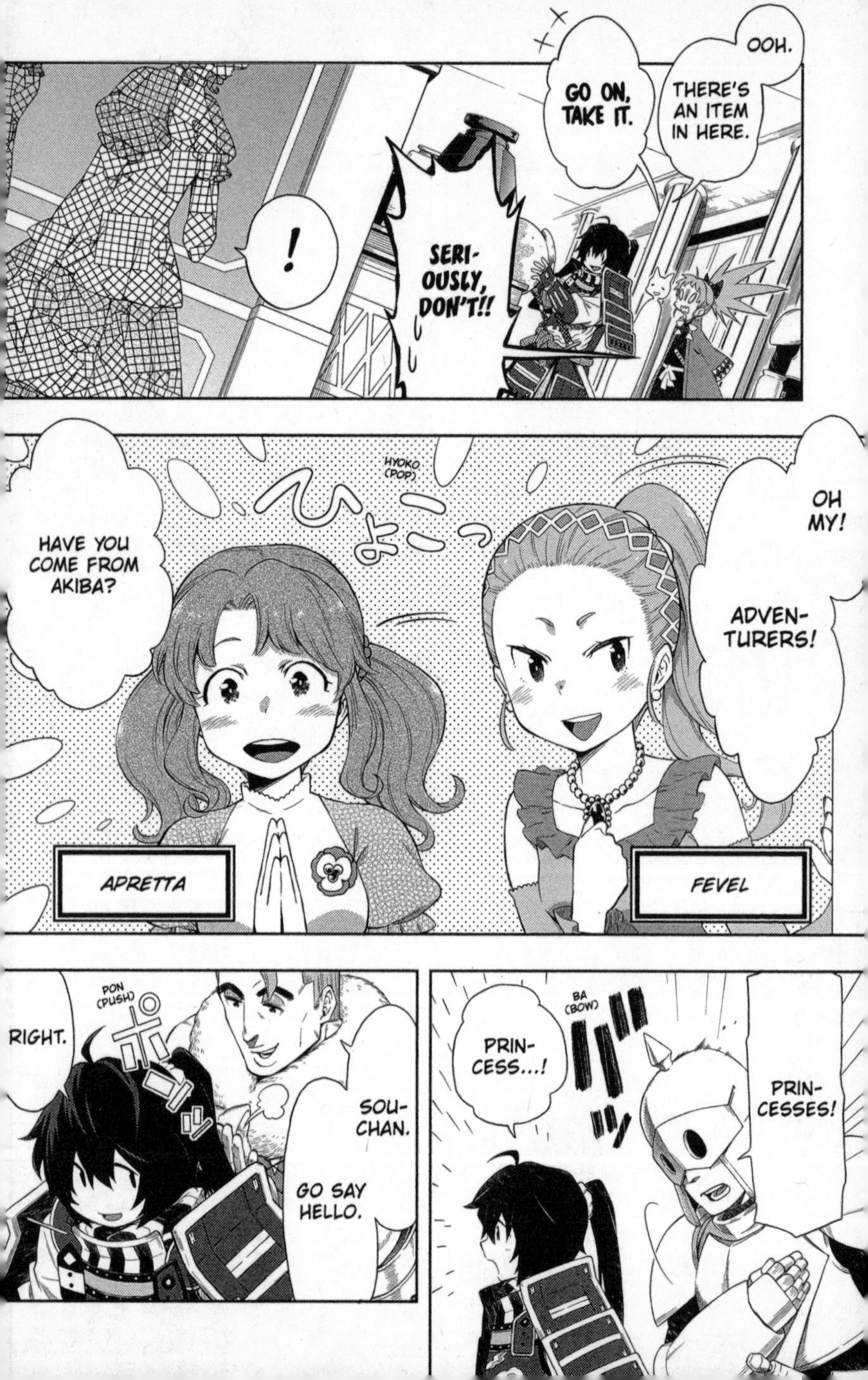
OOH.
THERE'S AN ITEM IN HERE.
GO ON, TAKE IT.
SERI-OUSLY, DON'T!!
!
OH MY!
ADVEN-TURERS!
HYOKO (POP)
HAVE YOU COME FROM AKIBA?
FEVEL
APRETTA
PRIN-CESSES!
BA (BOW)
PRIN-CESS...!
SOU-CHAN.
GO SAY HELLO.
PON (PUSH)
RIGHT.

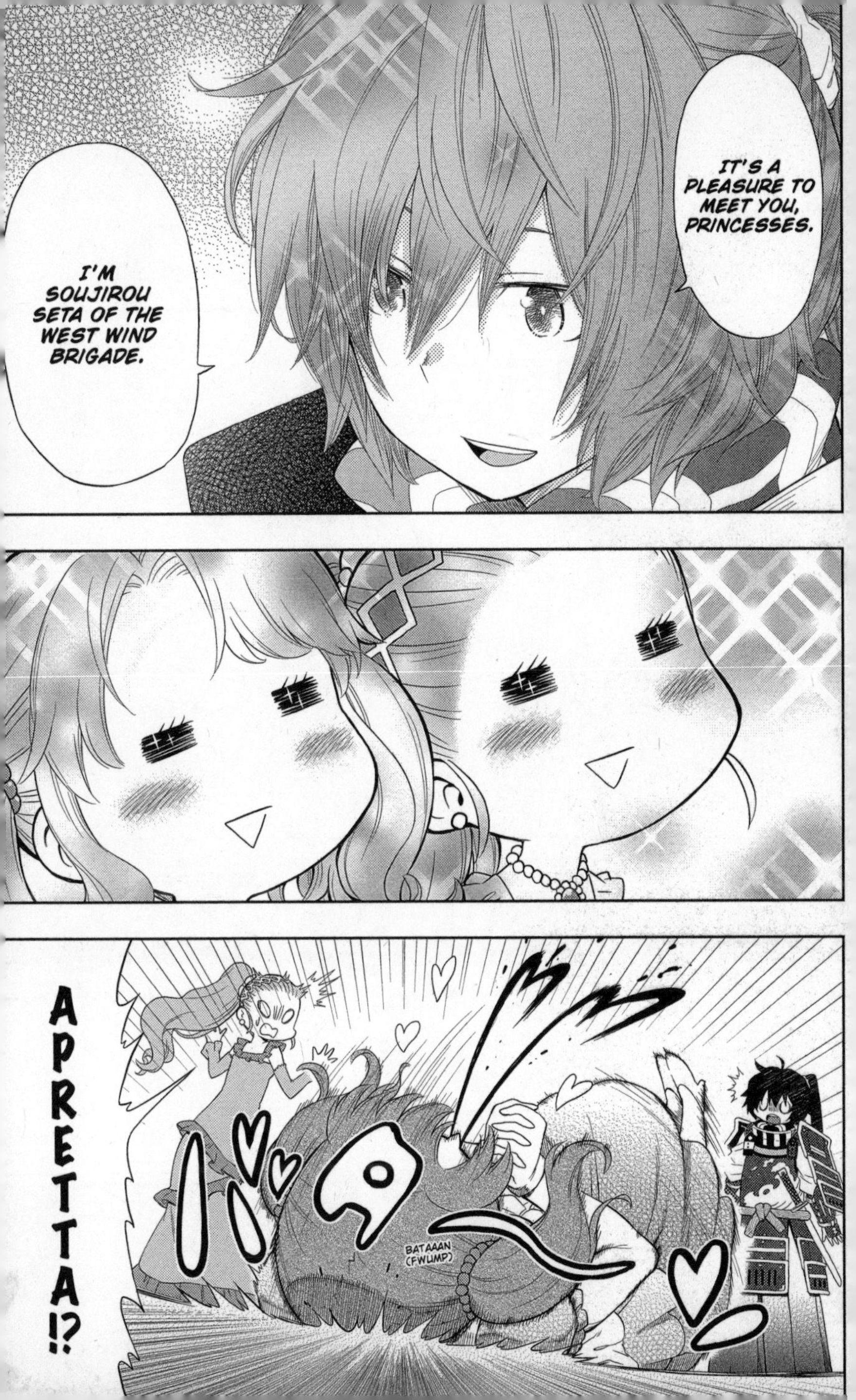
IT'S A PLEASURE TO MEET YOU, PRINCESSES.
I'M SOUJIROU SETA OF THE WEST WIND BRIGADE.
BATAAAN (FWUMP)
APRETTA!?

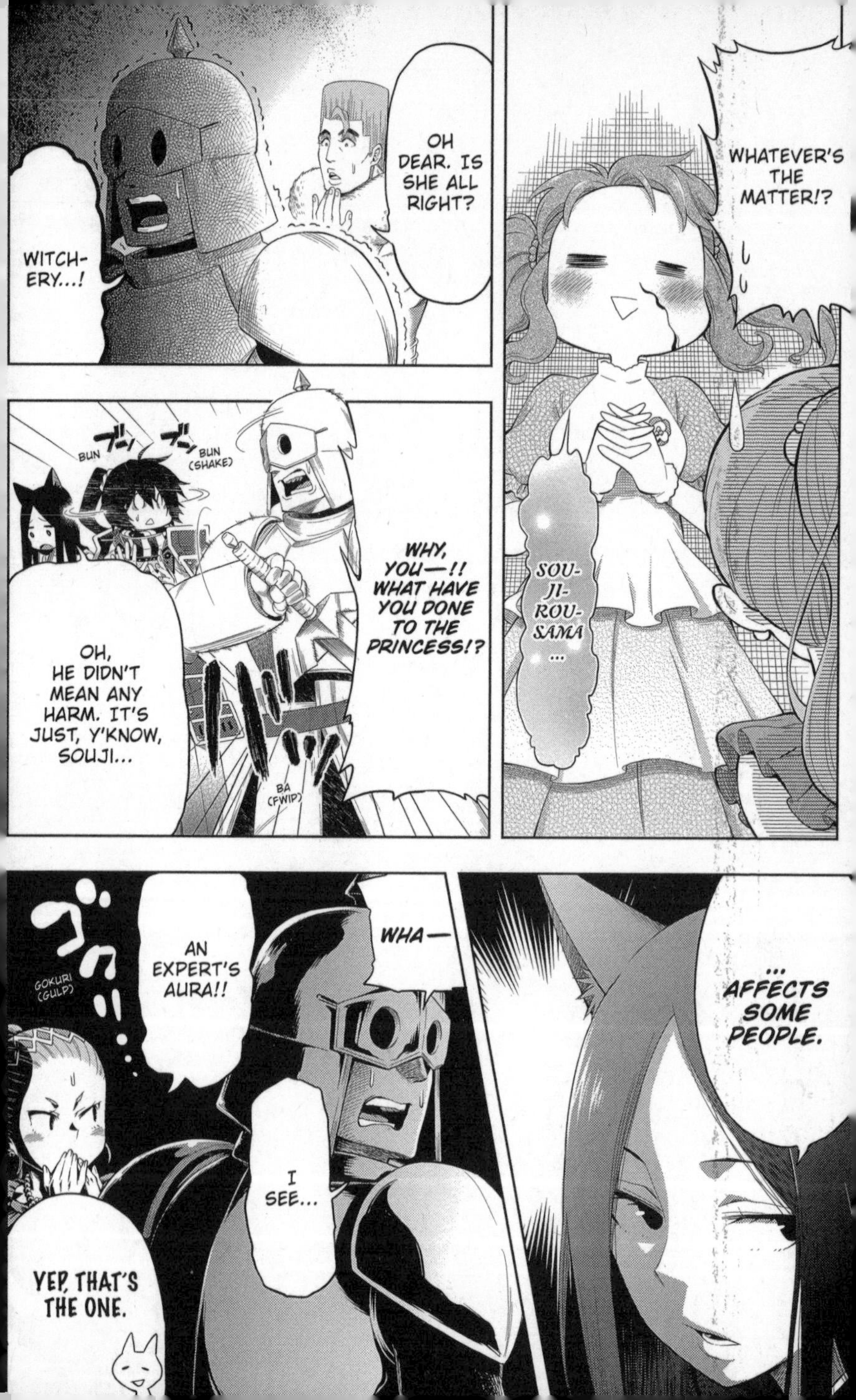

WHATEVER'S THE MATTER!?
SOUJIROU-SAMA...
OH DEAR. IS SHE ALL RIGHT?
WITCHERY...!
WHY, YOU—!! WHAT HAVE YOU DONE TO THE PRINCESS!?
BUN BUN (SHAKE)
OH, HE DIDN'T MEAN ANY HARM. IT'S JUST, Y'KNOW, SOUJI...
BA (FWIP)
...AFFECTS SOME PEOPLE.
WHA—
AN EXPERT'S AURA!!
GOKURI (GULP)
I SEE...
YEP, THAT'S THE ONE.

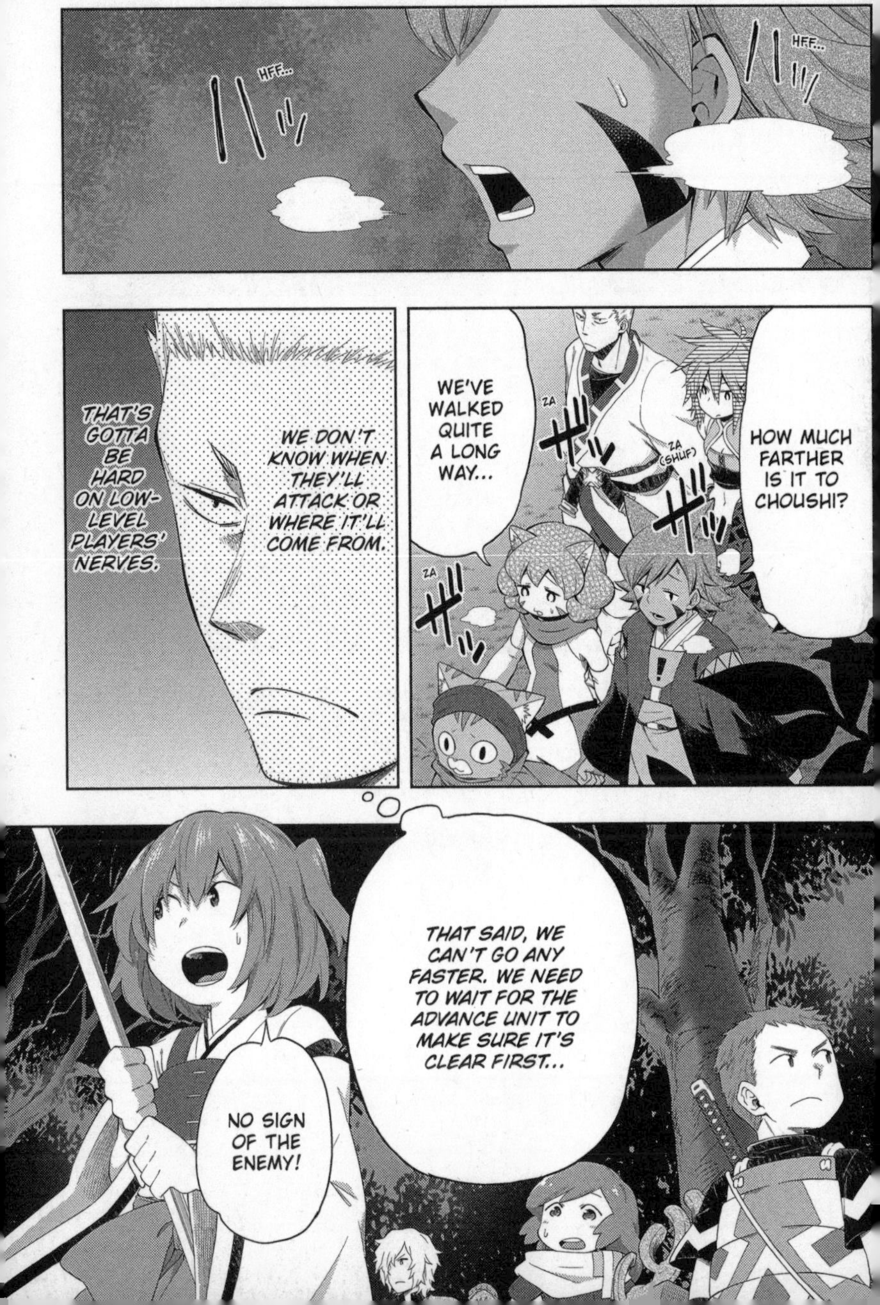
HFF...
HFF...
HOW MUCH FARTHER IS IT TO CHOUSHI?
ZA
ZA (SHUF)
WE'VE WALKED QUITE A LONG WAY...
ZA
WE DON'T KNOW WHEN THEY'LL ATTACK OR WHERE IT'LL COME FROM.
THAT'S GOTTA BE HARD ON LOW-LEVEL PLAYERS' NERVES.
THAT SAID, WE CAN'T GO ANY FASTER. WE NEED TO WAIT FOR THE ADVANCE UNIT TO MAKE SURE IT'S CLEAR FIRST...
NO SIGN OF THE ENEMY!

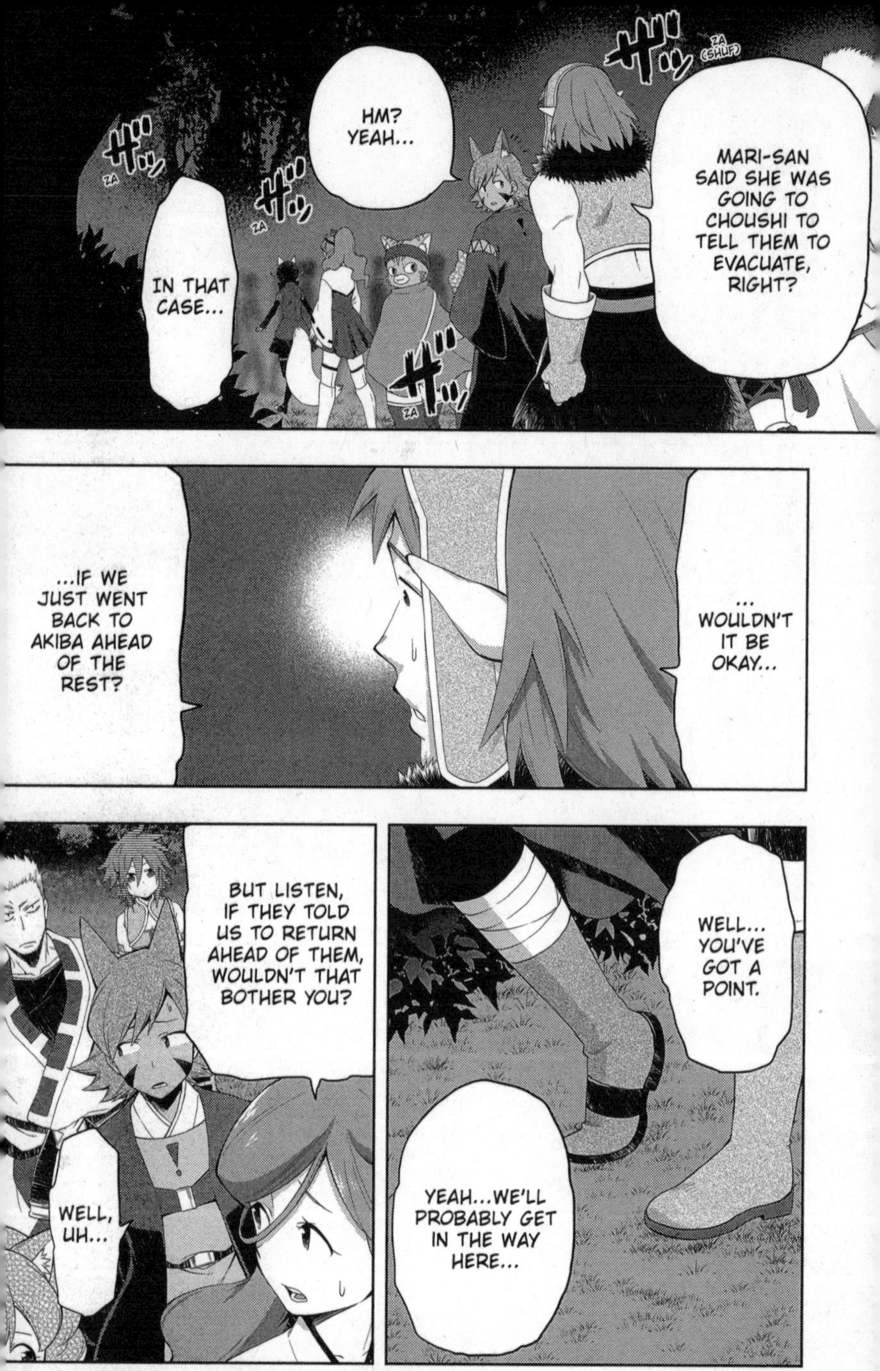
ZA (SHUF)
MARI-SAN SAID SHE WAS GOING TO CHOUSHI TO TELL THEM TO EVACUATE, RIGHT?
HM? YEAH...
ZA
ZA
IN THAT CASE...
ZA
...
WOULDN'T IT BE OKAY...
...IF WE JUST WENT BACK TO AKIBA AHEAD OF THE REST?
WELL... YOU'VE GOT A POINT.
YEAH...WE'LL PROBABLY GET IN THE WAY HERE...
BUT LISTEN, IF THEY TOLD US TO RETURN AHEAD OF THEM, WOULDN'T THAT BOTHER YOU?
WELL, UH...

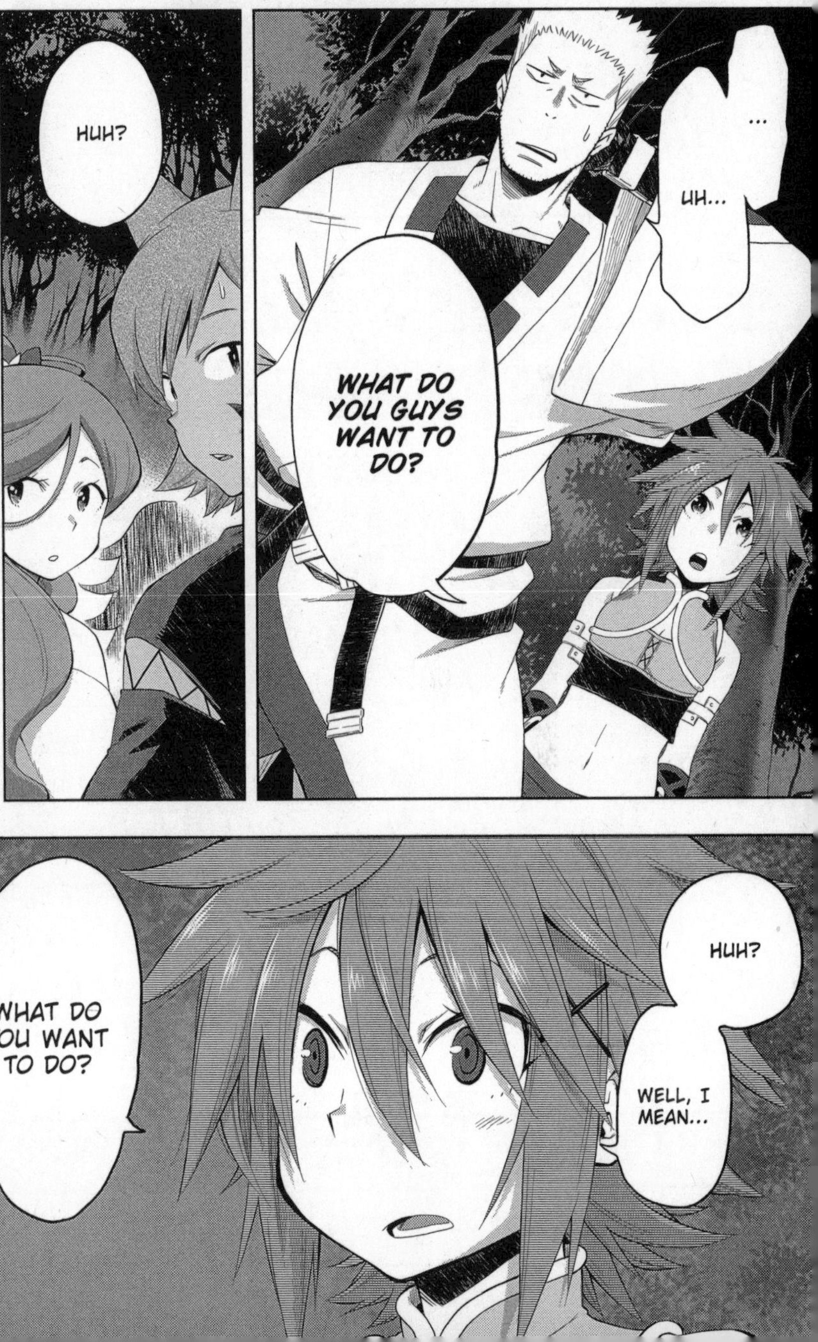
...
UH...
WHAT DO YOU GUYS WANT TO DO?
HUH?
HUH?
WHAT DO YOU WANT TO DO?
WELL, I MEAN...

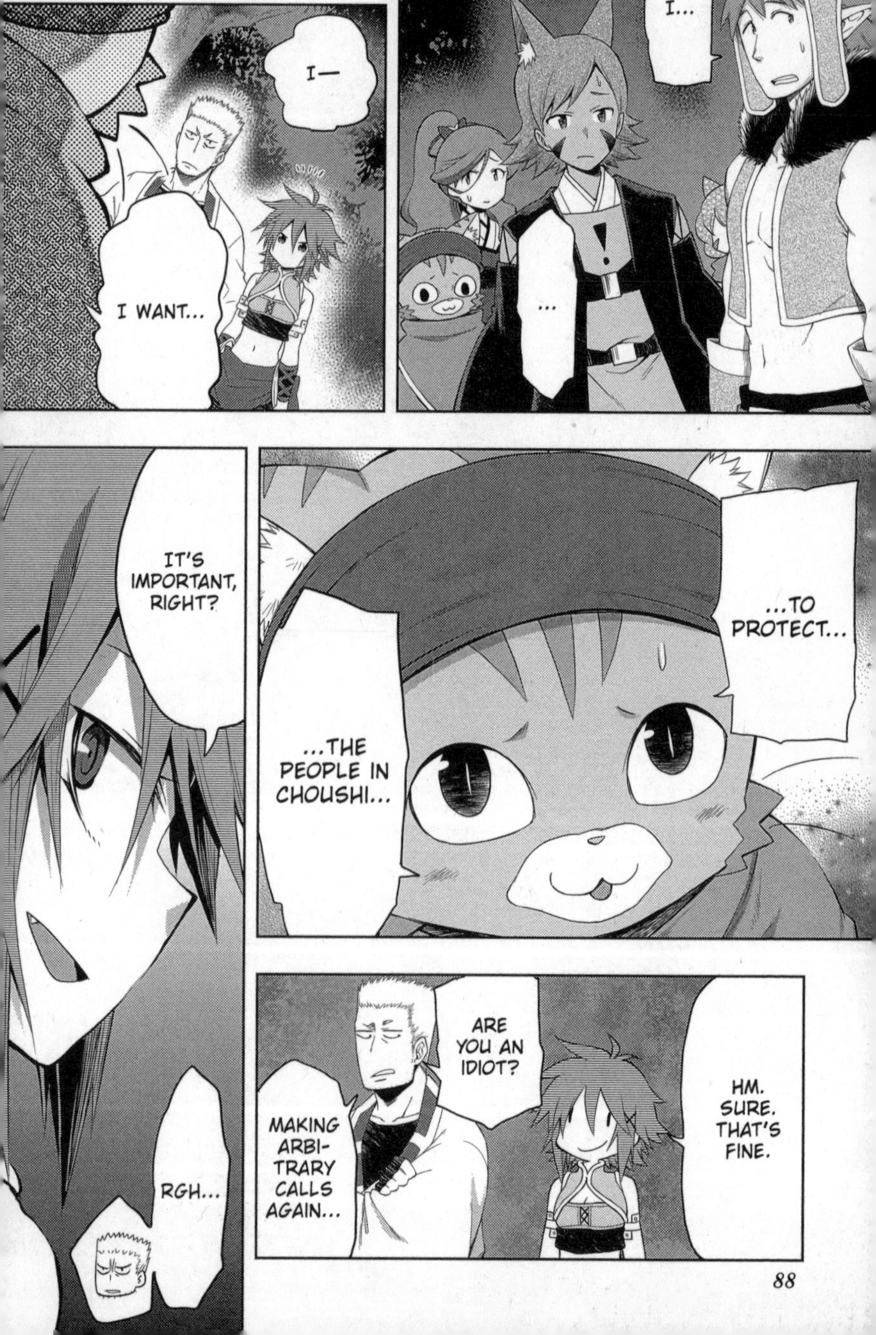
I...
...
I—
I WANT...
...TO PROTECT...
...THE PEOPLE IN CHOUSHI...
HM. SURE. THAT'S FINE.
ARE YOU AN IDIOT?
MAKING ARBI-TRARY CALLS AGAIN...
IT'S IMPORTANT, RIGHT?
RGH...

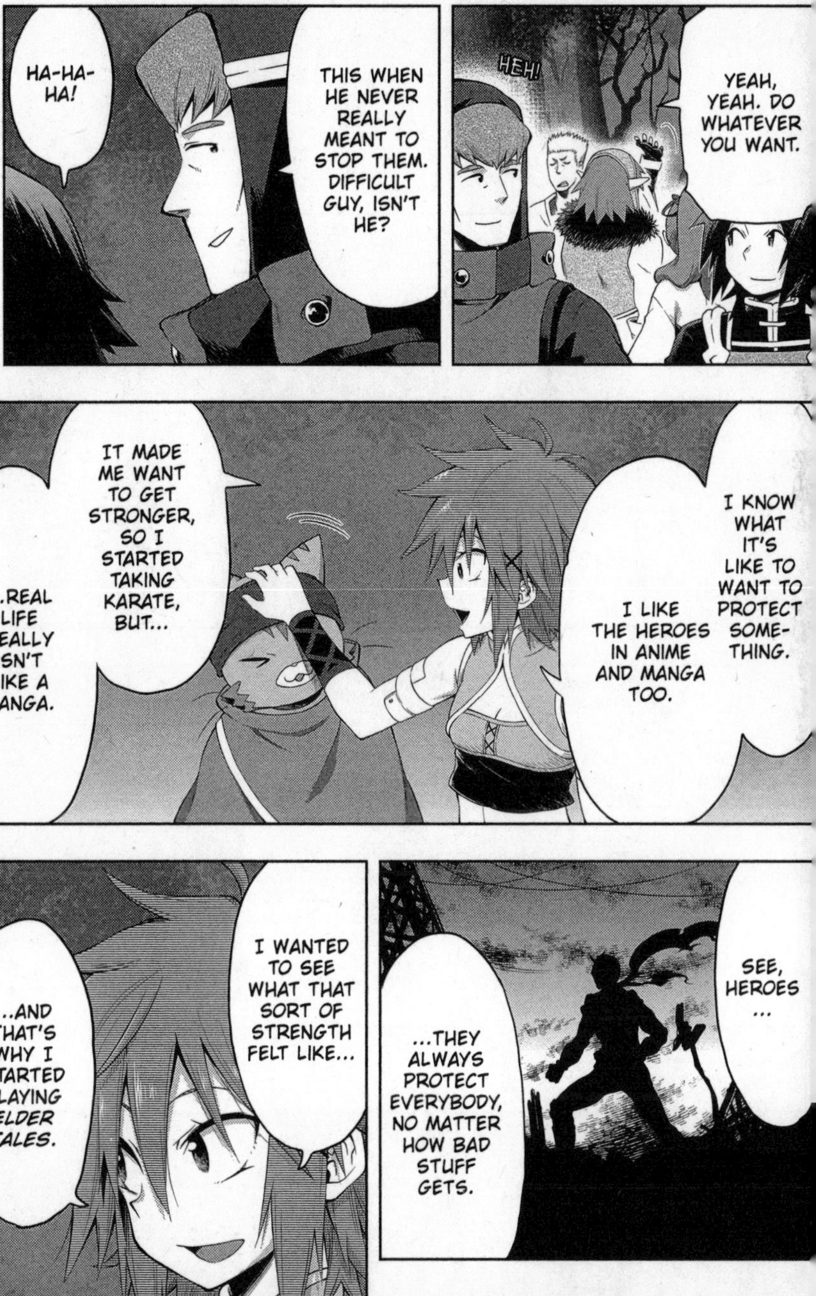
HEH!
YEAH, YEAH. DO WHATEVER YOU WANT.
THIS WHEN HE NEVER REALLY MEANT TO STOP THEM. DIFFICULT GUY, ISN'T HE?
HA-HA-HA!
I KNOW WHAT IT'S LIKE TO WANT TO PROTECT SOME-THING.
I LIKE THE HEROES IN ANIME AND MANGA TOO.
IT MADE ME WANT TO GET STRONGER, SO I STARTED TAKING KARATE, BUT...
...REAL LIFE REALLY ISN'T LIKE A MANGA.
SEE, HEROES ...
...THEY ALWAYS PROTECT EVERYBODY, NO MATTER HOW BAD STUFF GETS.
I WANTED TO SEE WHAT THAT SORT OF STRENGTH FELT LIKE...
...AND THAT'S WHY I STARTED PLAYING *ELDER TALES*.

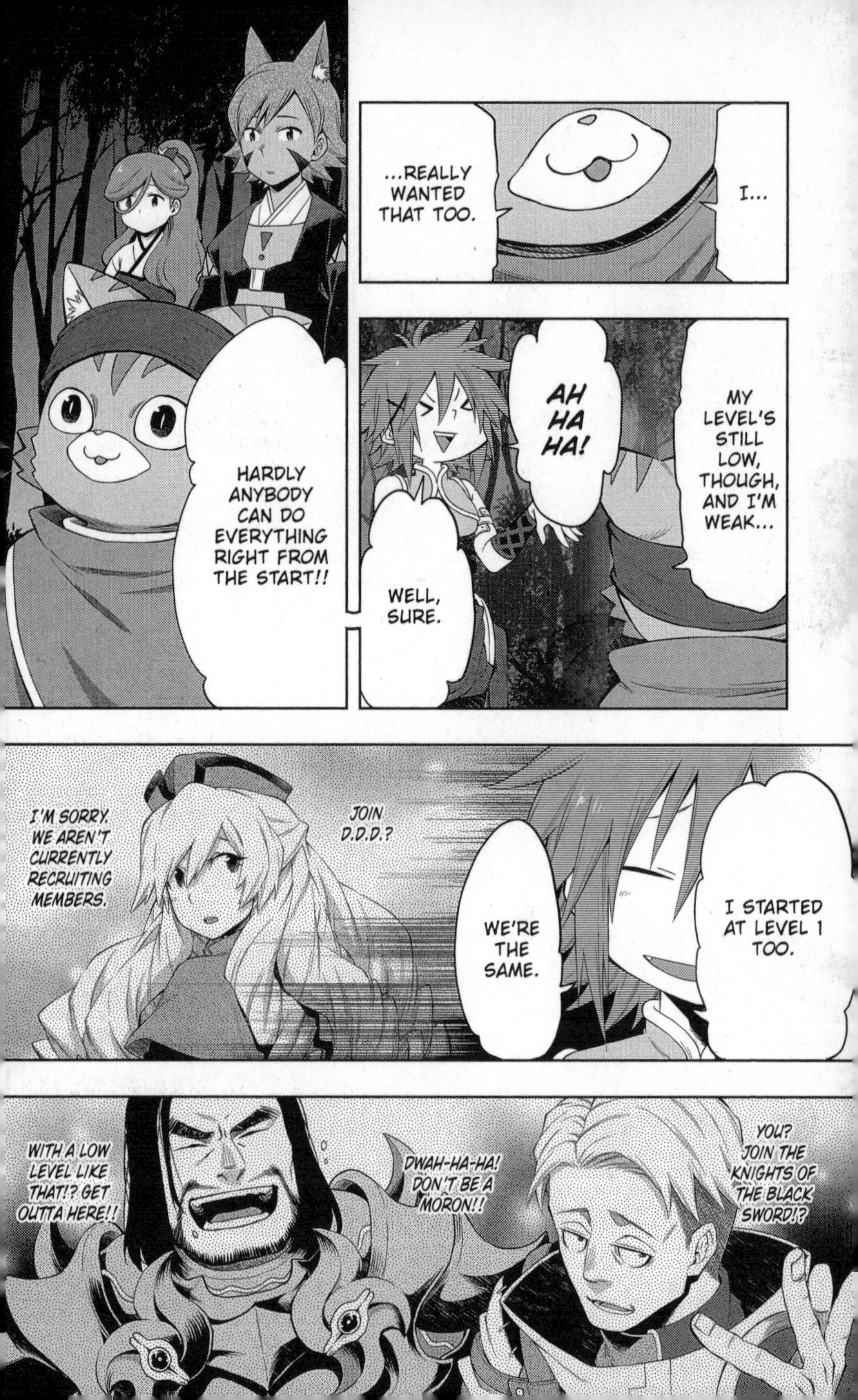
I...
...REALLY WANTED THAT TOO.
MY LEVEL'S STILL LOW, THOUGH, AND I'M WEAK...
AH HA HA!
WELL, SURE.
HARDLY ANYBODY CAN DO EVERYTHING RIGHT FROM THE START!!
I STARTED AT LEVEL 1 TOO.
WE'RE THE SAME.
JOIN D.D.D.?
I'M SORRY. WE AREN'T CURRENTLY RECRUITING MEMBERS.
YOU? JOIN THE KNIGHTS OF THE BLACK SWORD!?
DWAH-HA-HA! DON'T BE A MORON!!
WITH A LOW LEVEL LIKE THAT!? GET OUTTA HERE!!

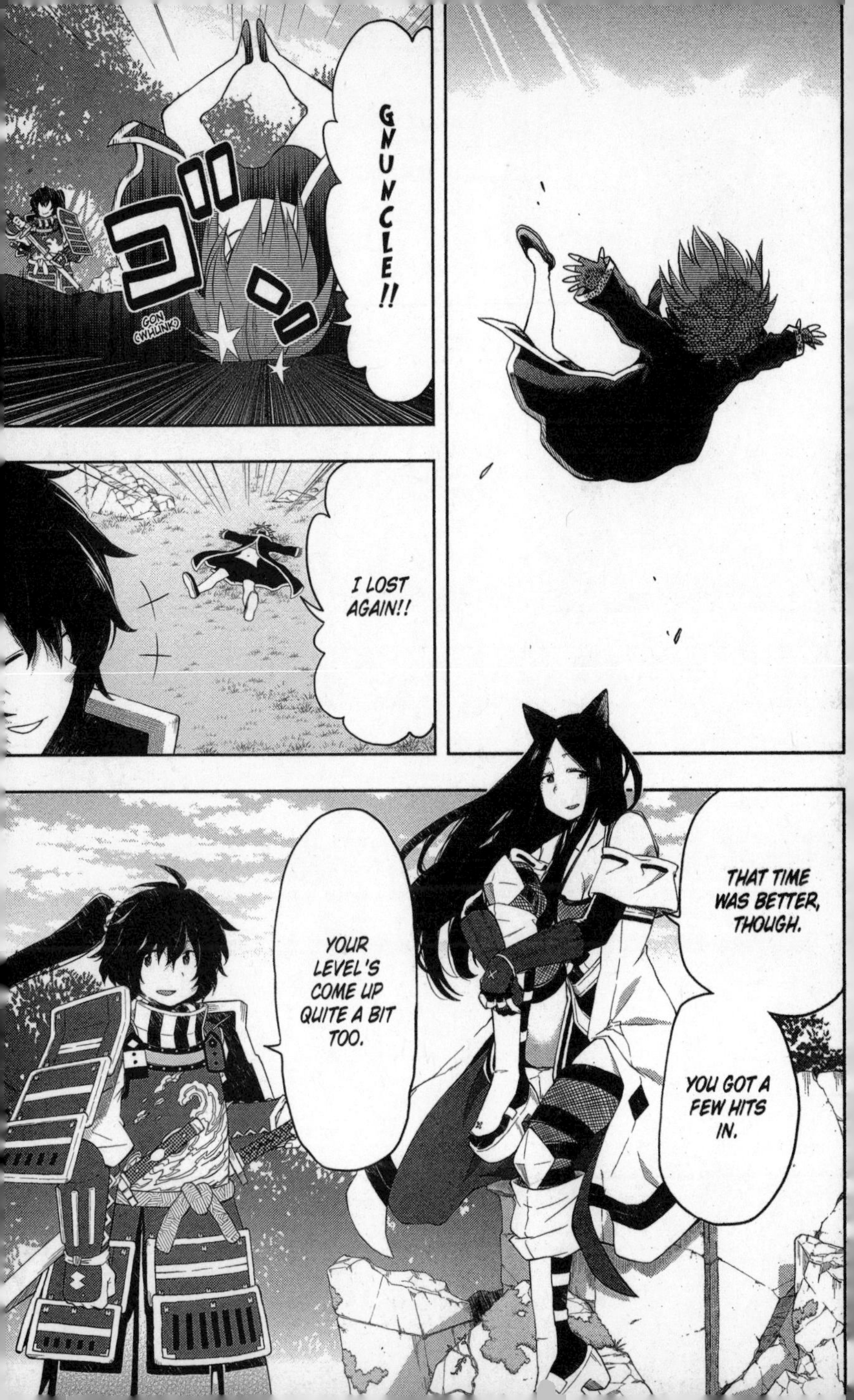
GNUNCLE!!
GON (WHUNK)
I LOST AGAIN!!
THAT TIME WAS BETTER, THOUGH.
YOU GOT A FEW HITS IN.
YOUR LEVEL'S COME UP QUITE A BIT TOO.

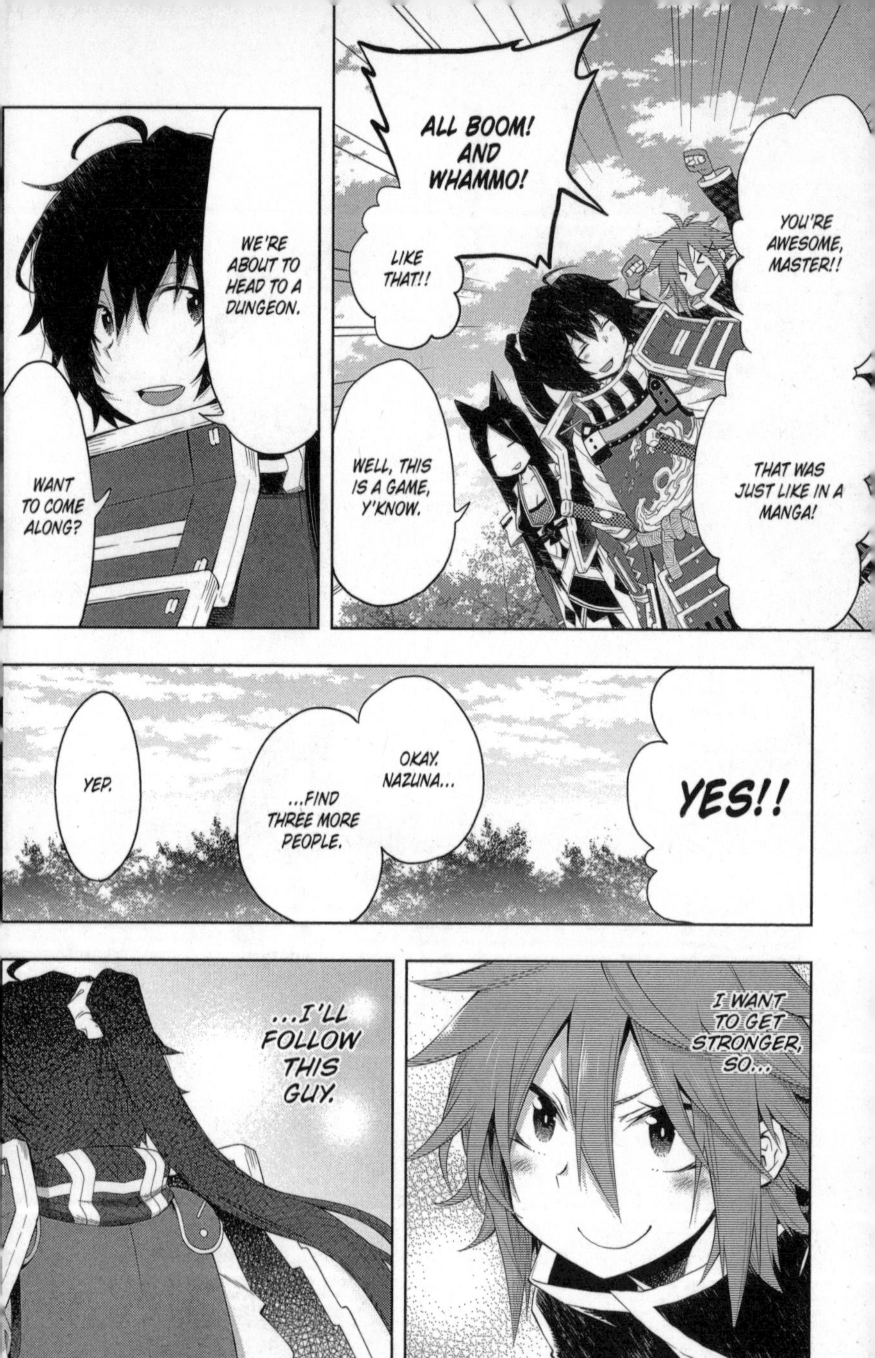
ALL BOOM! AND WHAMMO!
LIKE THAT!!
YOU'RE AWESOME, MASTER!!
THAT WAS JUST LIKE IN A MANGA!
WELL, THIS IS A GAME, Y'KNOW.
WE'RE ABOUT TO HEAD TO A DUNGEON.
WANT TO COME ALONG?
YES!!
OKAY. NAZUNA...
...FIND THREE MORE PEOPLE.
YEP.
I WANT TO GET STRONGER, SO...
...I'LL FOLLOW THIS GUY.

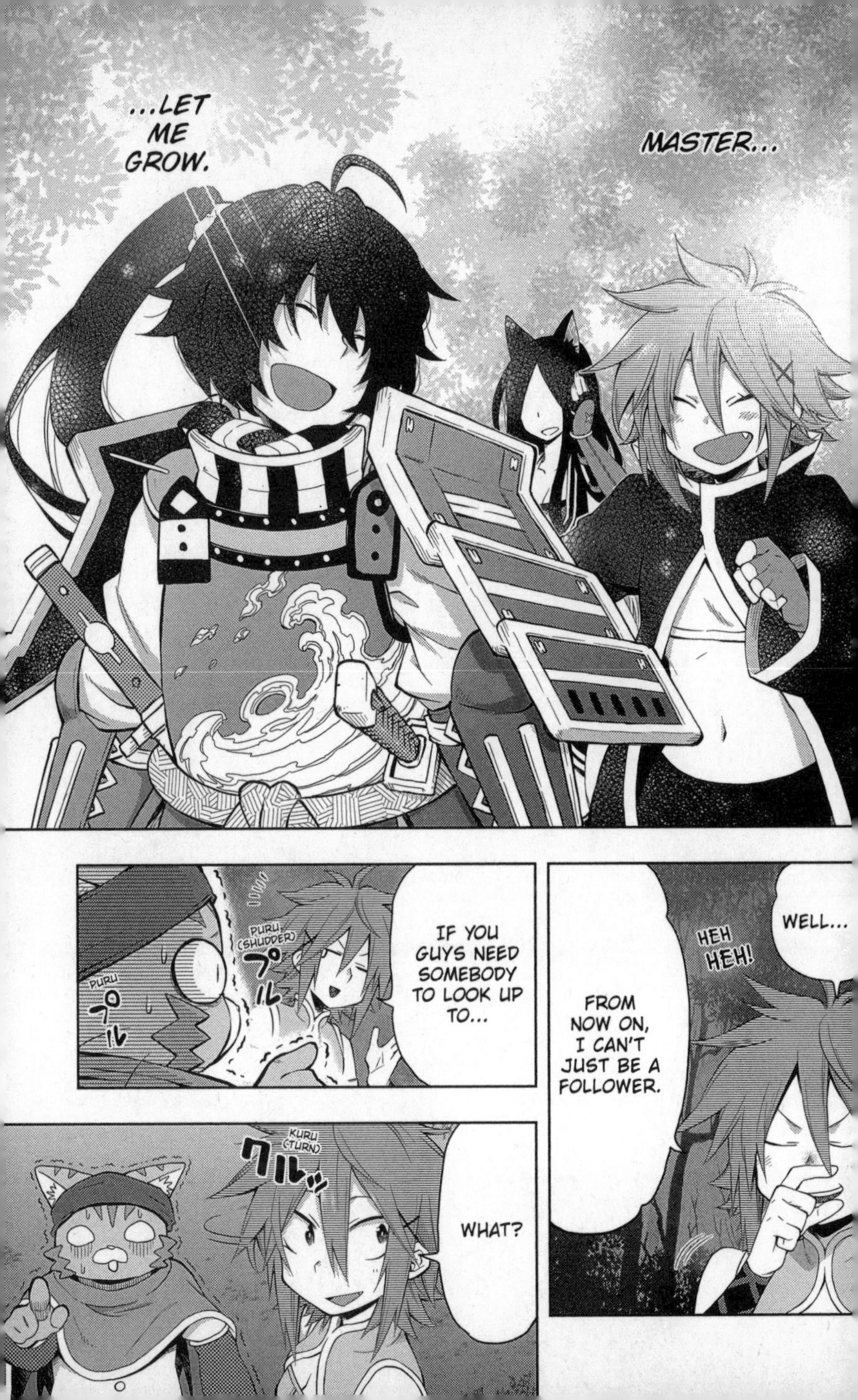
MASTER...
...LET ME GROW.
WELL...
HEH HEH!
FROM NOW ON, I CAN'T JUST BE A FOLLOWER.
IF YOU GUYS NEED SOMEBODY TO LOOK UP TO...
PURU (SHUDDER) プル
PURU プル
WHAT?
KURU (TURN) クルッ

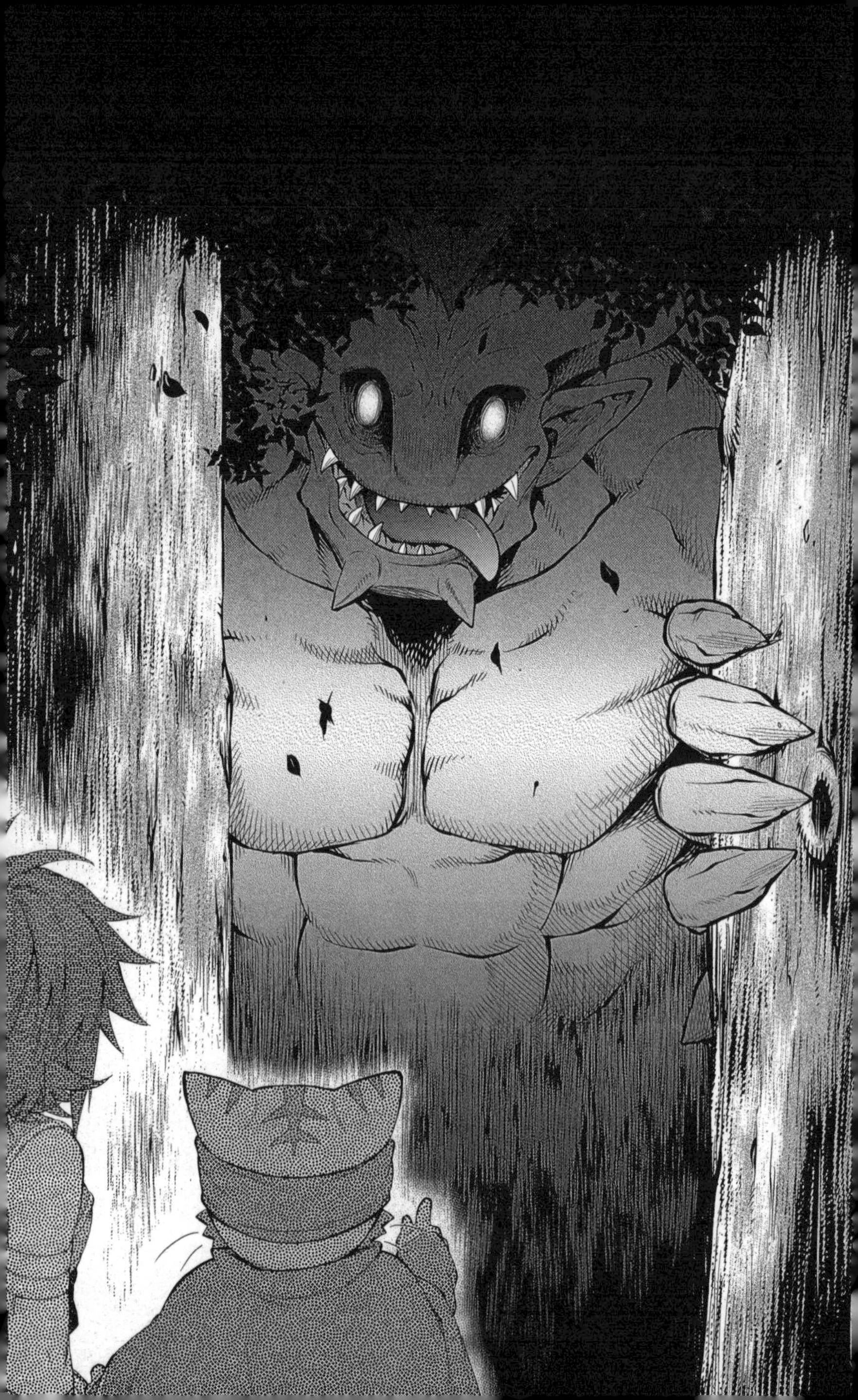

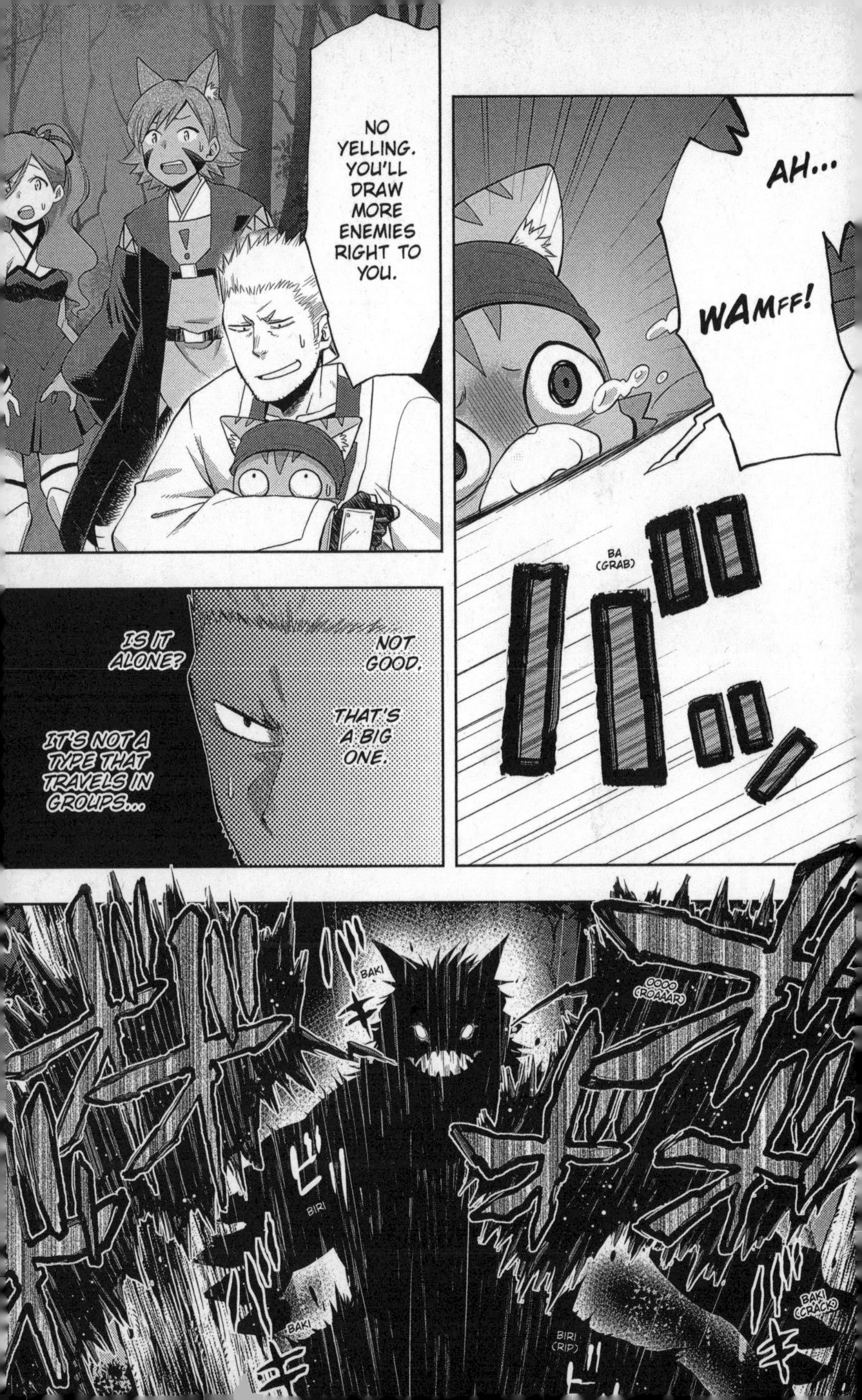
AH...
WAMFF!
BA (GRAB)
NO YELLING. YOU'LL DRAW MORE ENEMIES RIGHT TO YOU.
NOT GOOD.
THAT'S A BIG ONE.
IS IT ALONE?
IT'S NOT A TYPE THAT TRAVELS IN GROUPS...
OOOO (ROAAAR)
BAKI
BIRI
BAKI (CRACK)
BIRI (RIP)
BAKI

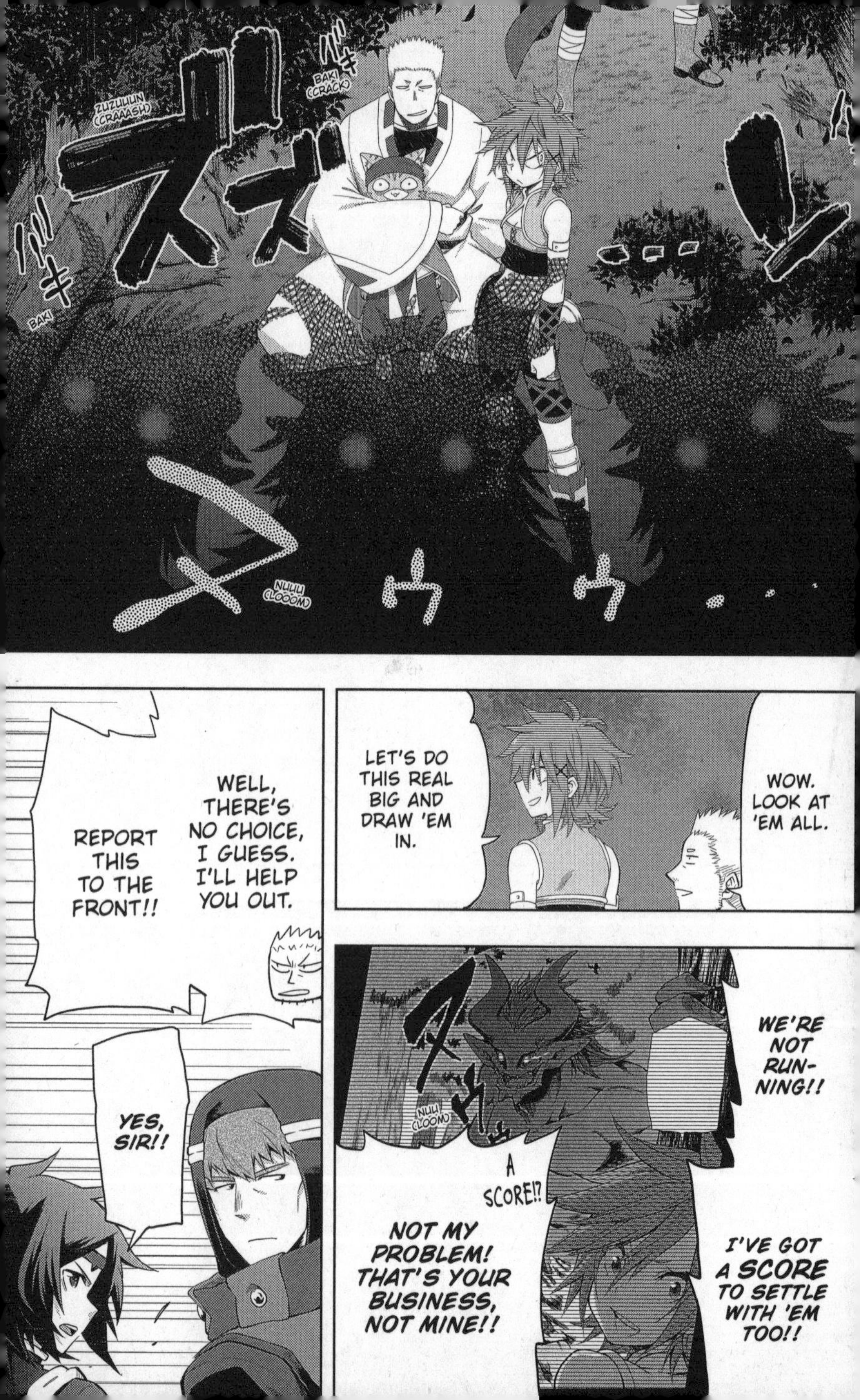
BAKI (CRACK)
ZUZULUUN (CRAAASH)
BAKI
NUUU (LOOOM)
WOW. LOOK AT 'EM ALL.
LET'S DO THIS REAL BIG AND DRAW 'EM IN.
WE'RE NOT RUN-NING!!
NUU (LOOM)
A SCORE!?
I'VE GOT A SCORE TO SETTLE WITH 'EM TOO!!
NOT MY PROBLEM! THAT'S YOUR BUSINESS, NOT MINE!!
WELL, THERE'S NO CHOICE, I GUESS. I'LL HELP YOU OUT.
REPORT THIS TO THE FRONT!!
YES, SIR!!

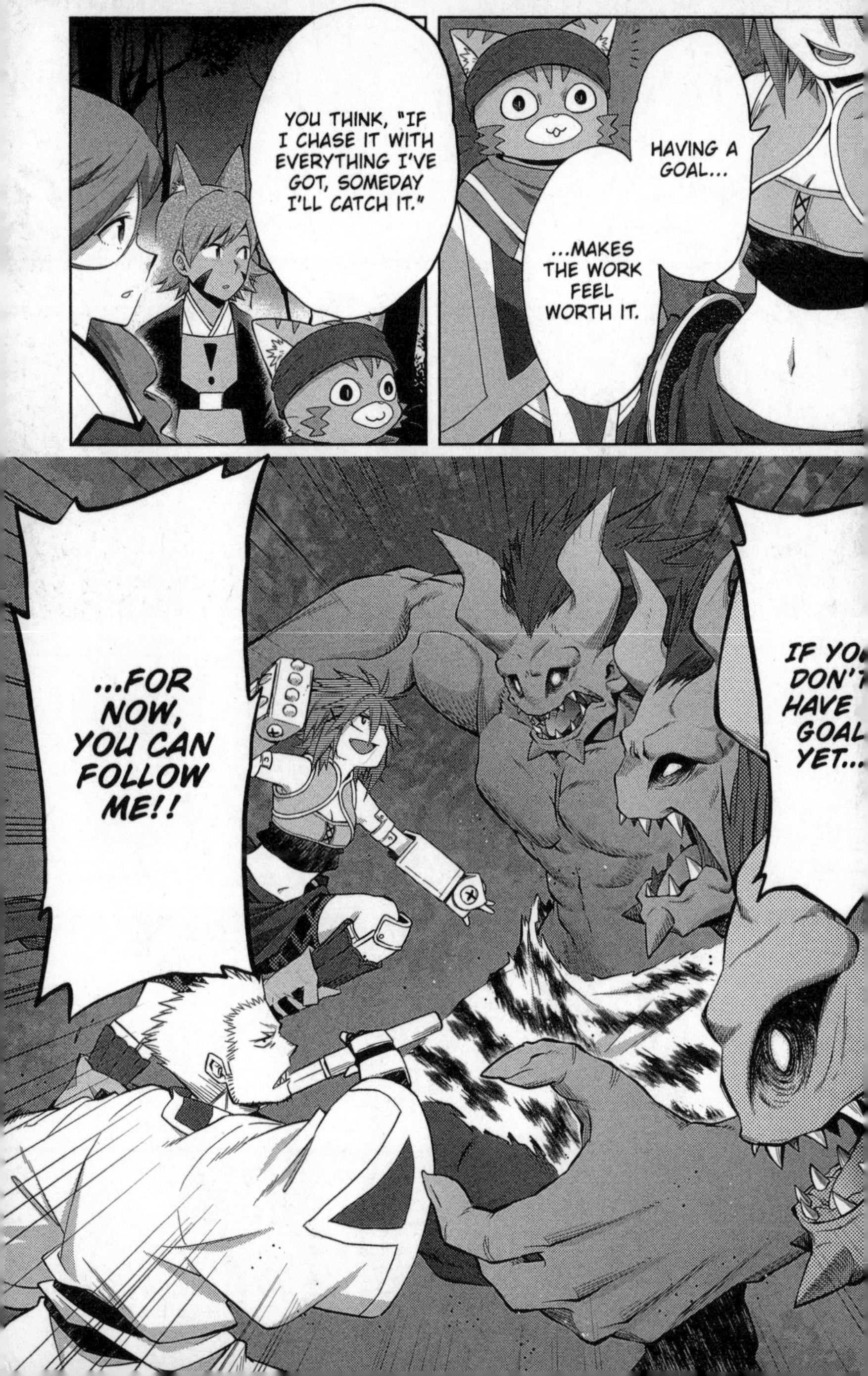
HAVING A GOAL...
...MAKES THE WORK FEEL WORTH IT.
YOU THINK, "IF I CHASE IT WITH EVERYTHING I'VE GOT, SOMEDAY I'LL CATCH IT."
IF YO DON'T HAVE GOAL YET...
...FOR NOW, YOU CAN FOLLOW ME!!

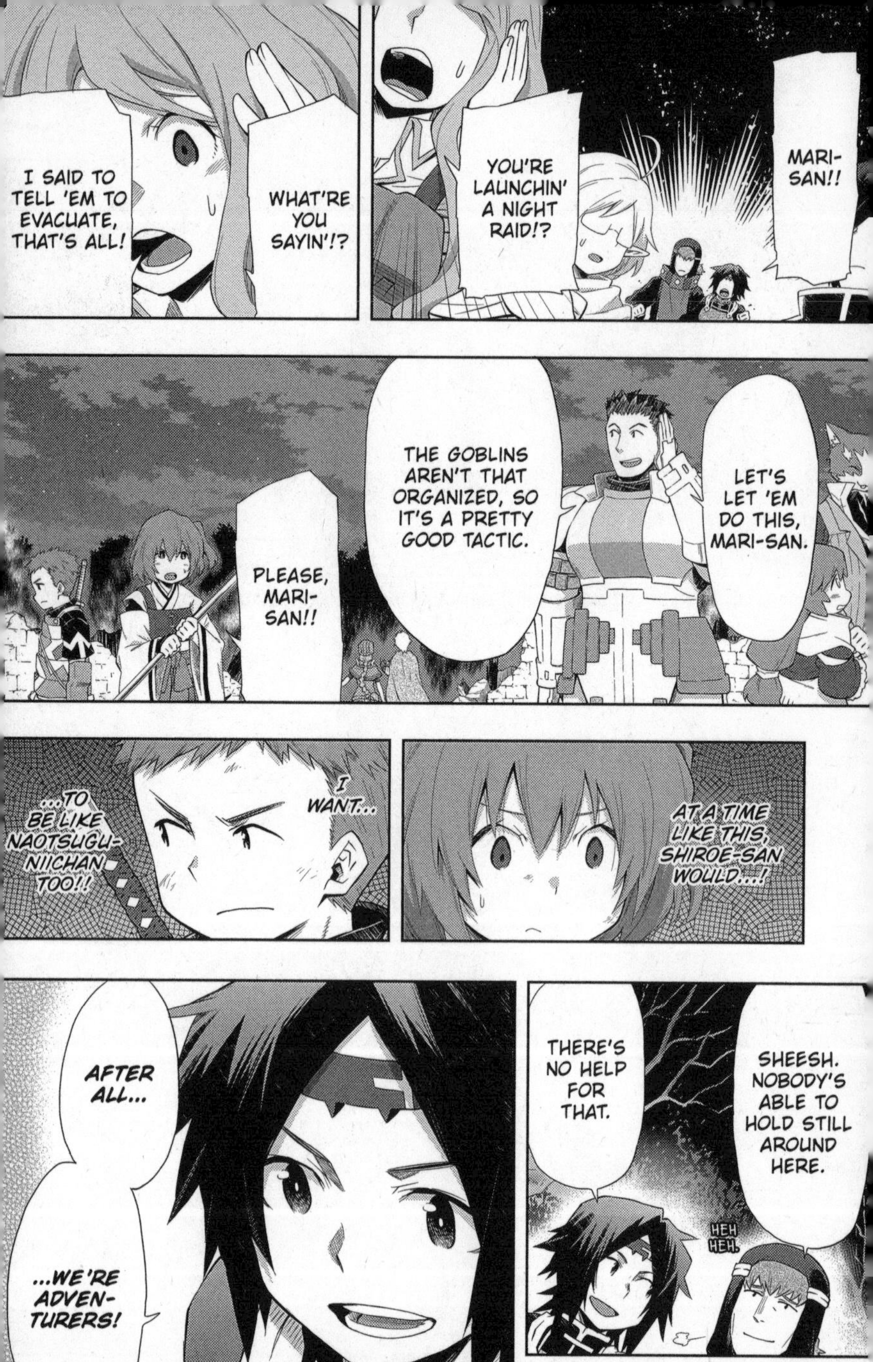
MARI-SAN!!
YOU'RE LAUNCHIN' A NIGHT RAID!?
WHAT'RE YOU SAYIN'!?
I SAID TO TELL 'EM TO EVACUATE, THAT'S ALL!
LET'S LET 'EM DO THIS, MARI-SAN.
THE GOBLINS AREN'T THAT ORGANIZED, SO IT'S A PRETTY GOOD TACTIC.
PLEASE, MARI-SAN!!
AT A TIME LIKE THIS, SHIROE-SAN WOULD...!
I WANT...
...TO BE LIKE NAOTSUGU-NIICHAN TOO!!
SHEESH. NOBODY'S ABLE TO HOLD STILL AROUND HERE.
HEH HEH.
THERE'S NO HELP FOR THAT.
AFTER ALL...
...WE'RE ADVENTURERS!

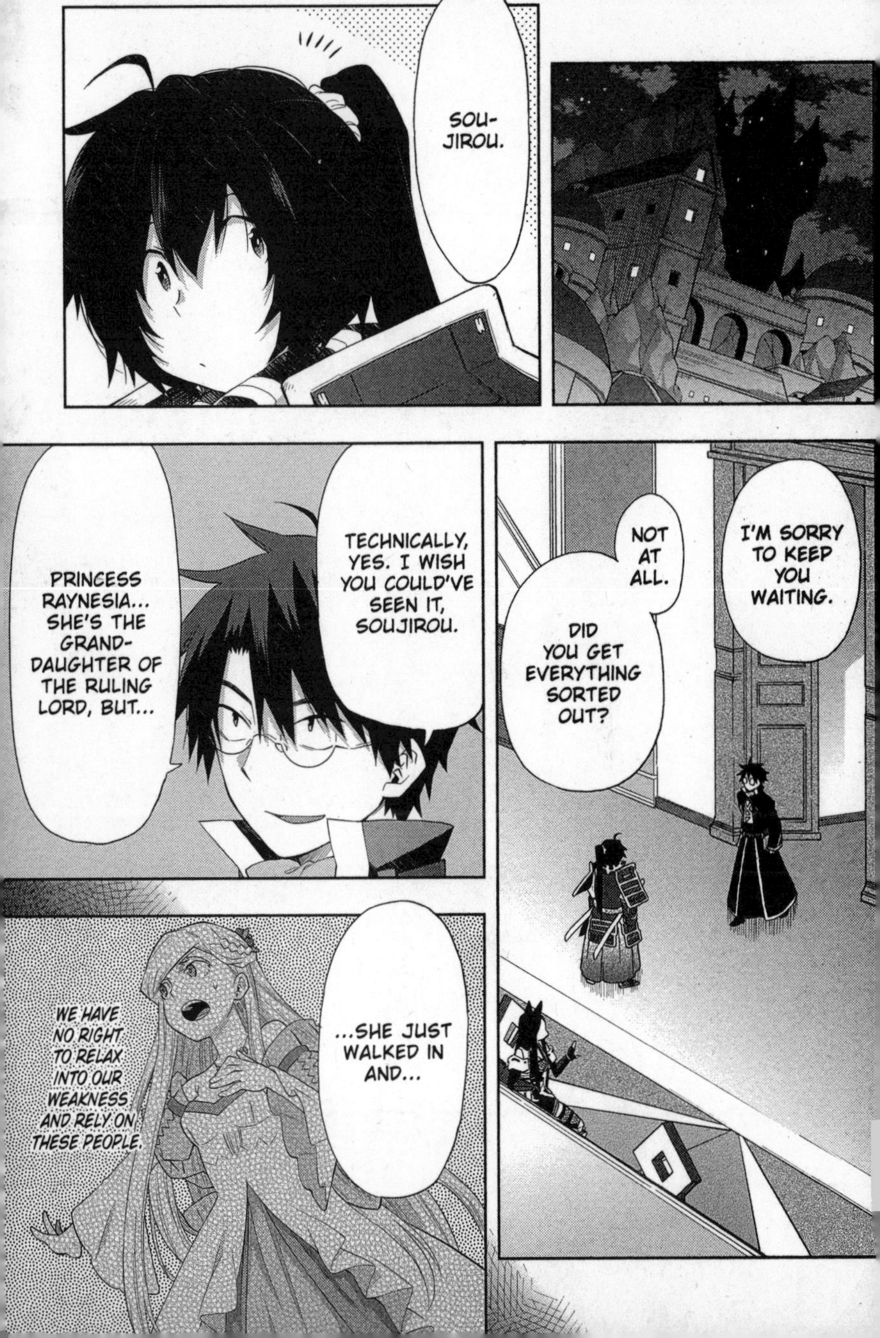
SOU-JIROU.
I'M SORRY TO KEEP YOU WAITING.
NOT AT ALL.
DID YOU GET EVERYTHING SORTED OUT?
TECHNICALLY, YES. I WISH YOU COULD'VE SEEN IT, SOUJIROU.
PRINCESS RAYNESIA... SHE'S THE GRAND-DAUGHTER OF THE RULING LORD, BUT...
...SHE JUST WALKED IN AND...
WE HAVE NO RIGHT TO RELAX INTO OUR WEAKNESS AND RELY ON THESE PEOPLE.

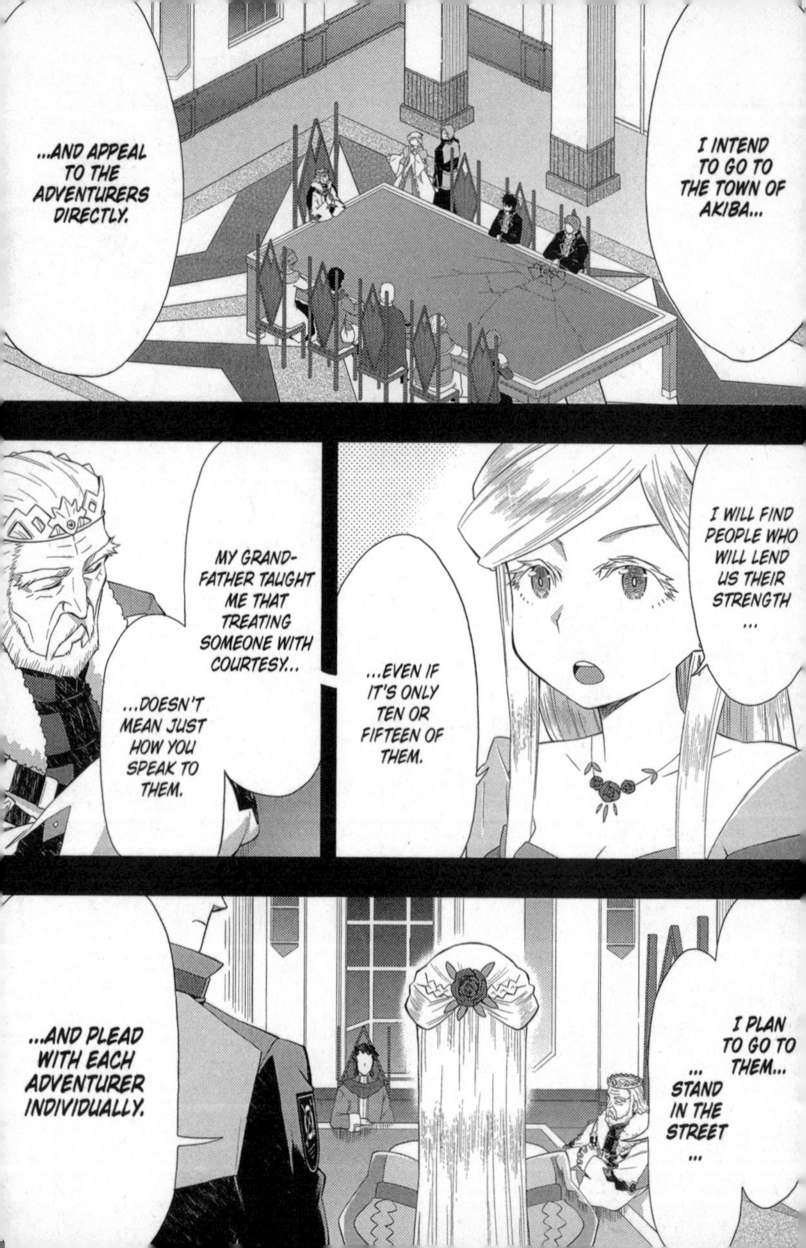
I INTEND TO GO TO THE TOWN OF AKIBA...
...AND APPEAL TO THE ADVENTURERS DIRECTLY.
I WILL FIND PEOPLE WHO WILL LEND US THEIR STRENGTH ...
...EVEN IF IT'S ONLY TEN OR FIFTEEN OF THEM.
MY GRAND-FATHER TAUGHT ME THAT TREATING SOMEONE WITH COURTESY...
...DOESN'T MEAN JUST HOW YOU SPEAK TO THEM.
I PLAN TO GO TO THEM...
... STAND IN THE STREET ...
...AND PLEAD WITH EACH ADVENTURER INDIVIDUALLY.

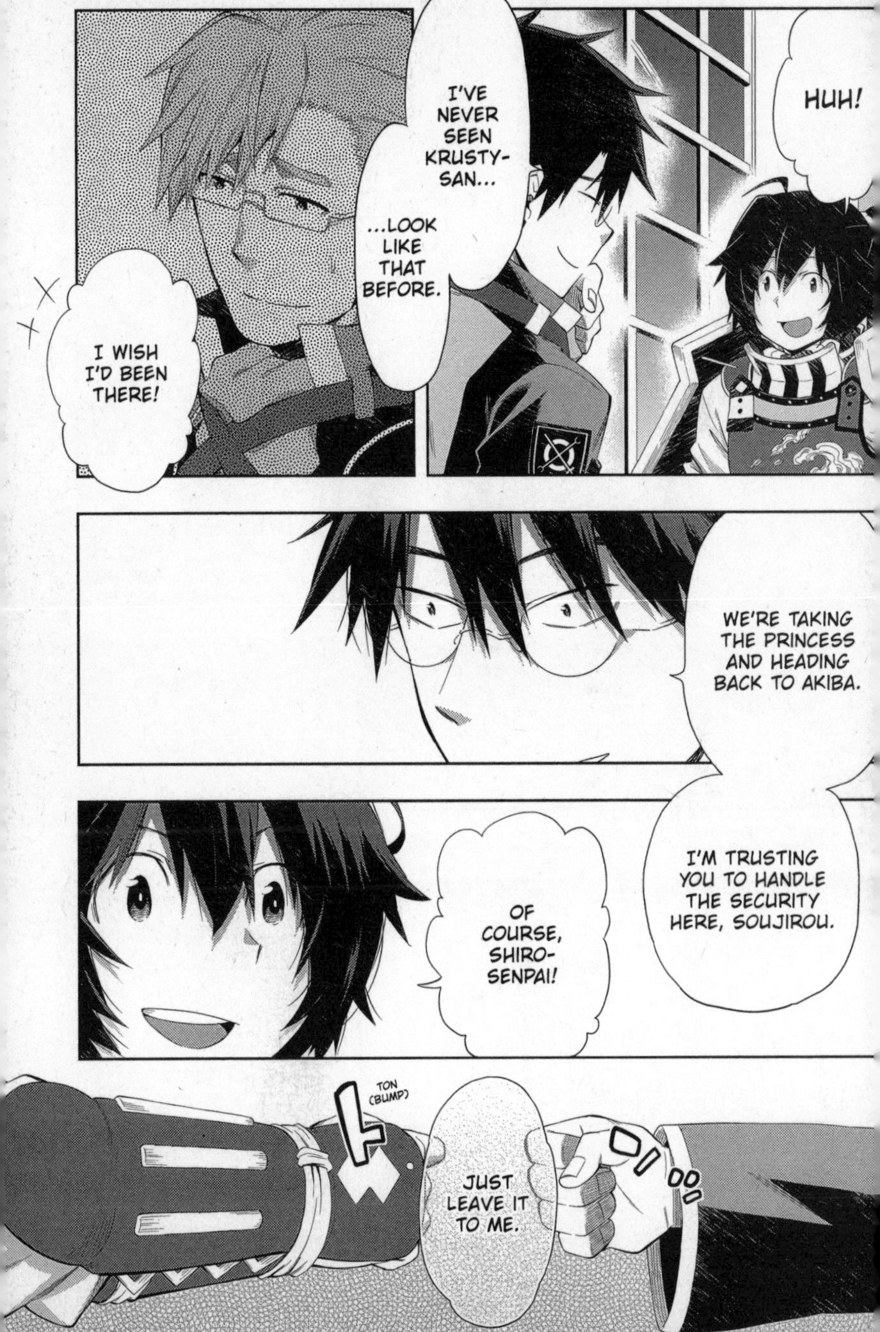
HUH!
I'VE NEVER SEEN KRUSTY-SAN...
...LOOK LIKE THAT BEFORE.
I WISH I'D BEEN THERE!
WE'RE TAKING THE PRINCESS AND HEADING BACK TO AKIBA.
I'M TRUSTING YOU TO HANDLE THE SECURITY HERE, SOUJIROU.
OF COURSE, SHIRO-SENPAI!
TON (BUMP)
JUST LEAVE IT TO ME.

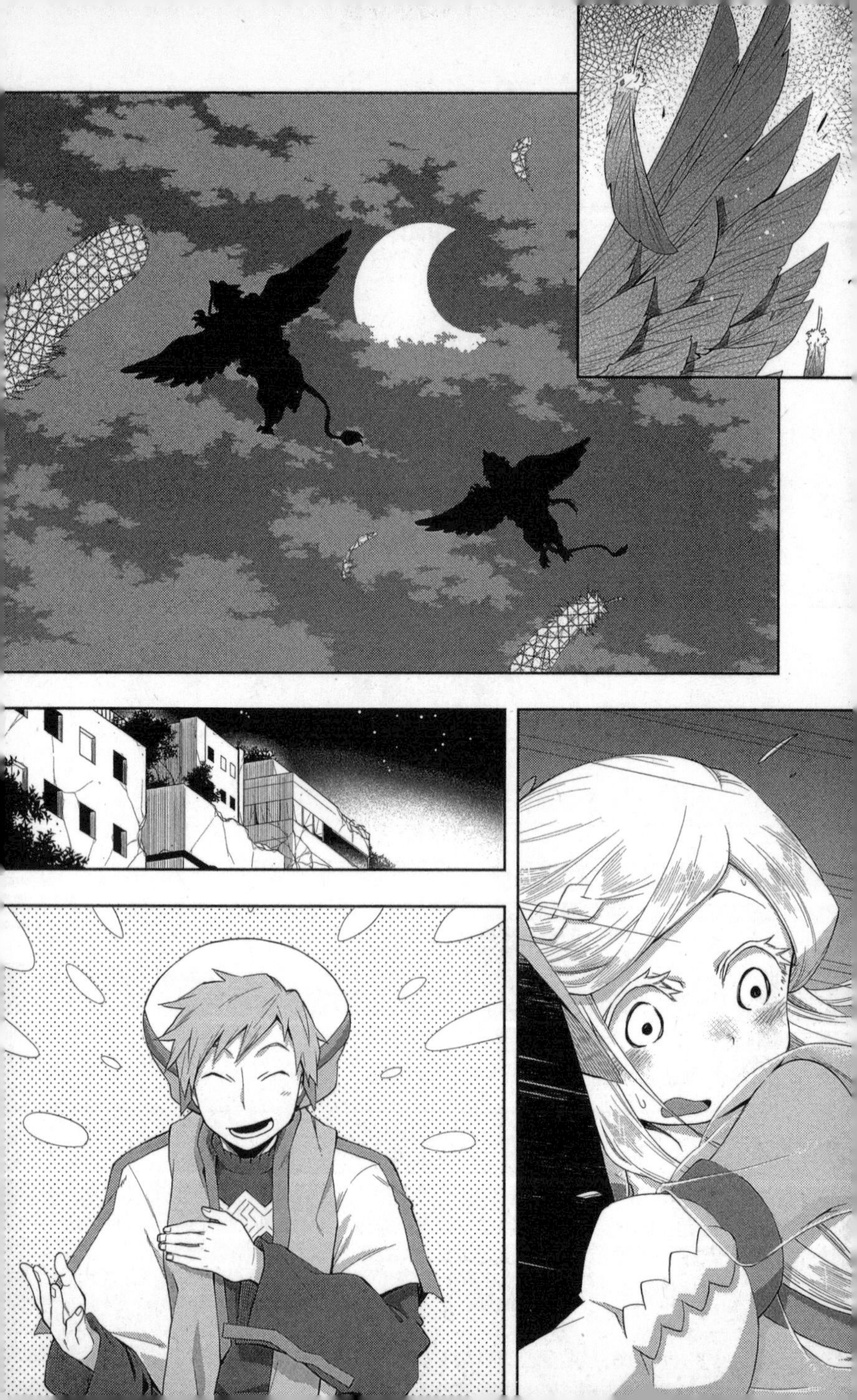

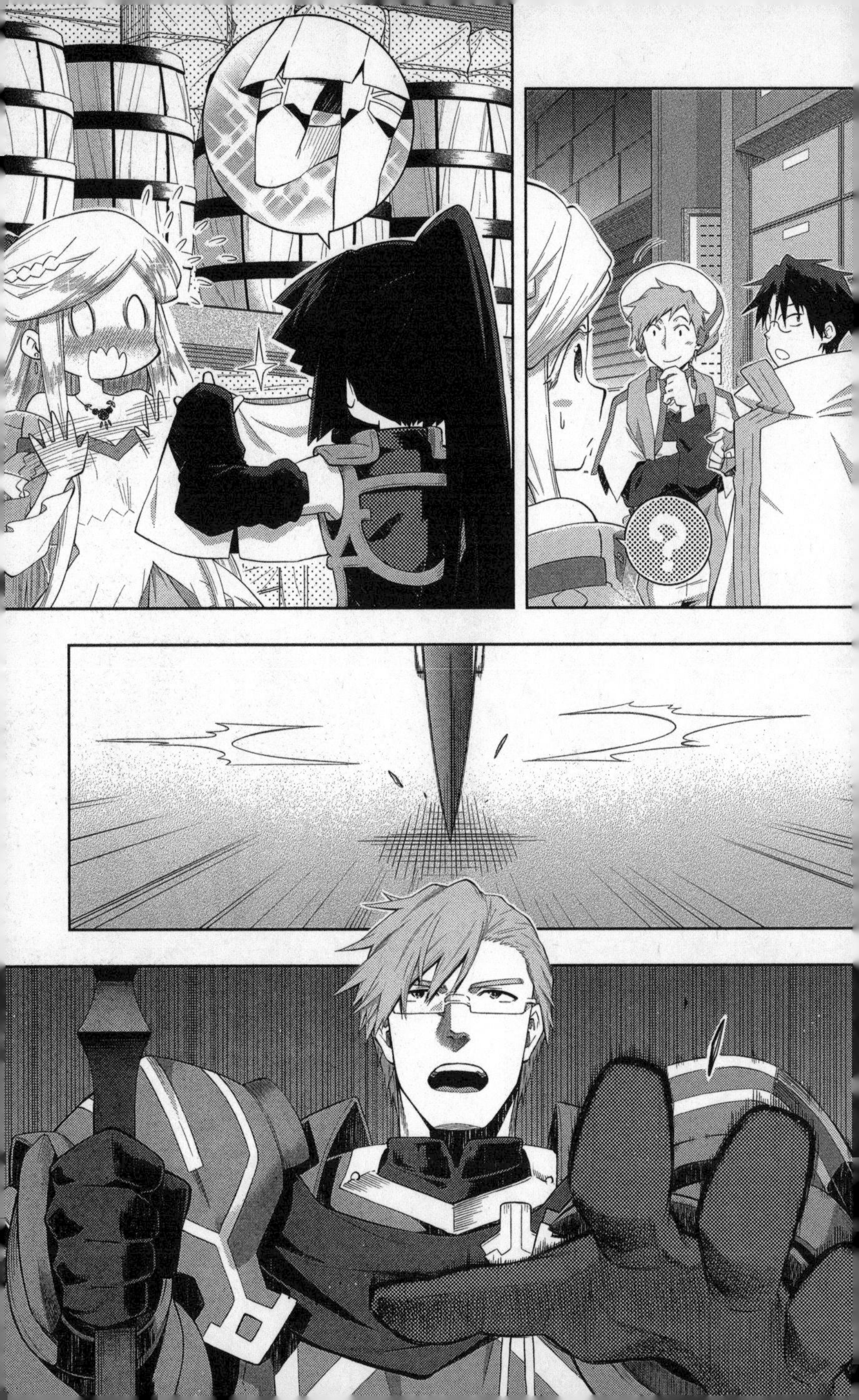
?

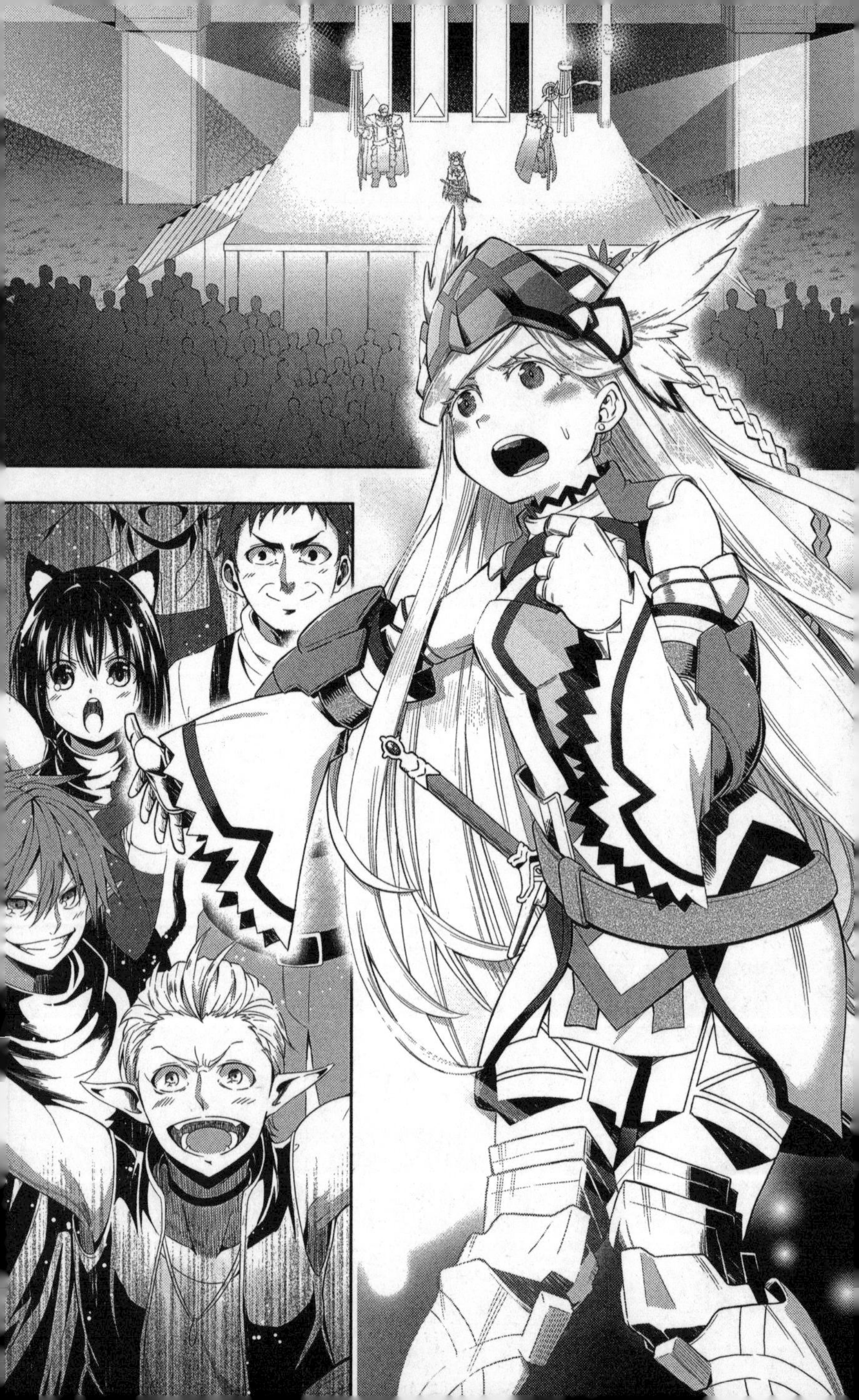

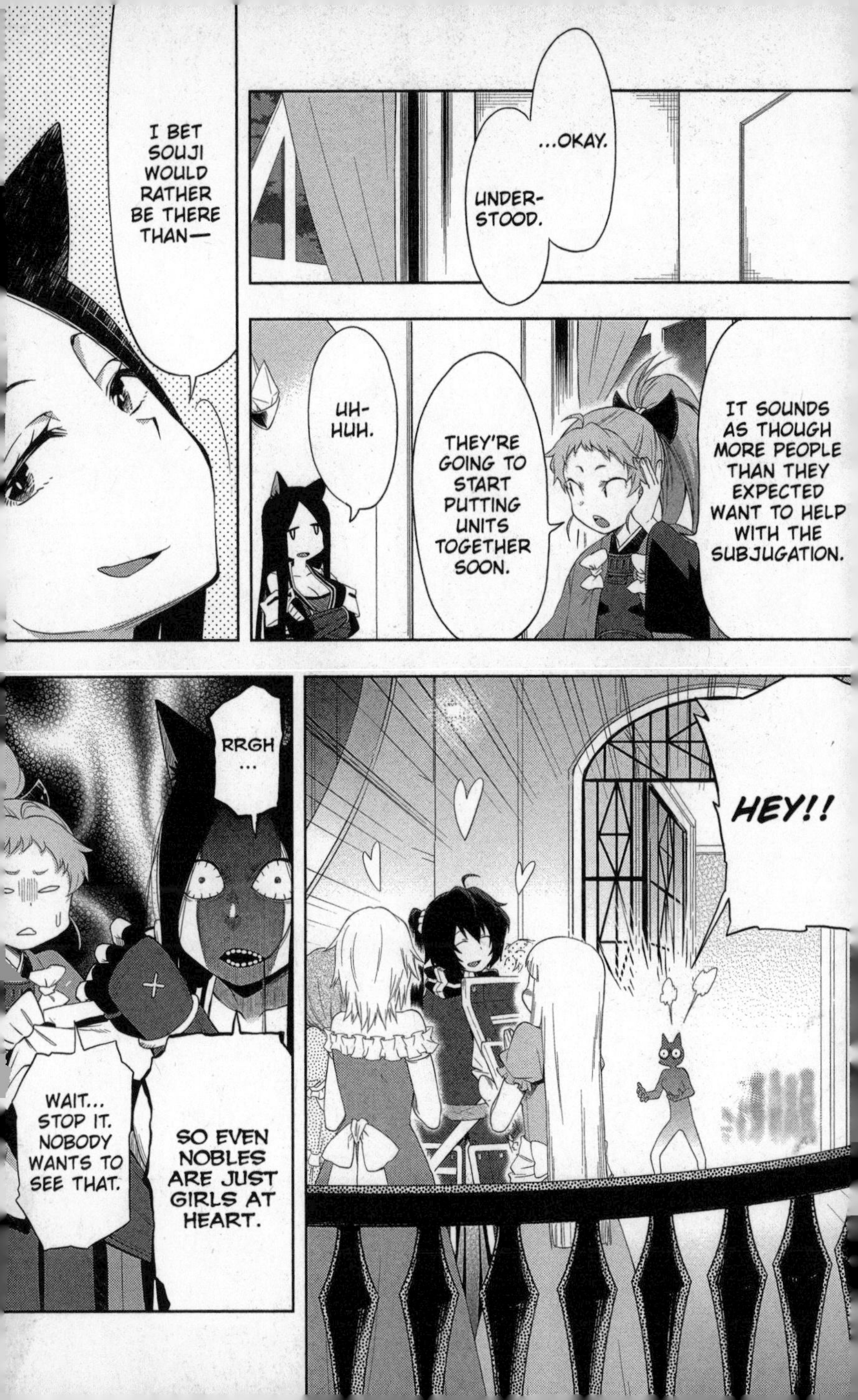
...OKAY.
UNDER-STOOD.
IT SOUNDS AS THOUGH MORE PEOPLE THAN THEY EXPECTED WANT TO HELP WITH THE SUBJUGATION.
THEY'RE GOING TO START PUTTING UNITS TOGETHER SOON.
UH-HUH.
I BET SOUJI WOULD RATHER BE THERE THAN—
HEY!!
RRGH ...
SO EVEN NOBLES ARE JUST GIRLS AT HEART.
WAIT... STOP IT. NOBODY WANTS TO SEE THAT.

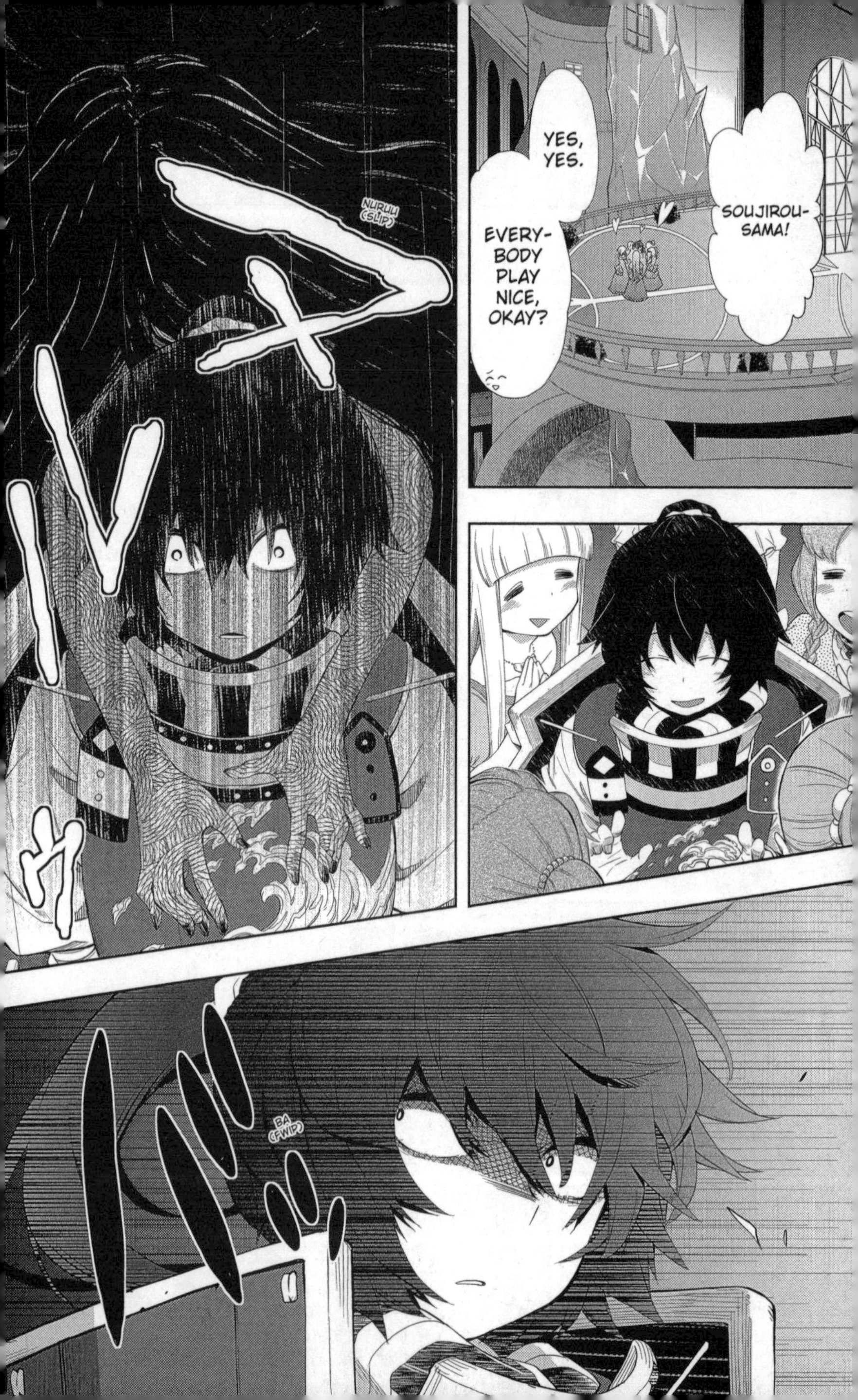
SOUJIROU-SAMA!
YES, YES.
EVERY-BODY PLAY NICE, OKAY?
NURUU (SLIP)
BA (FWIP)

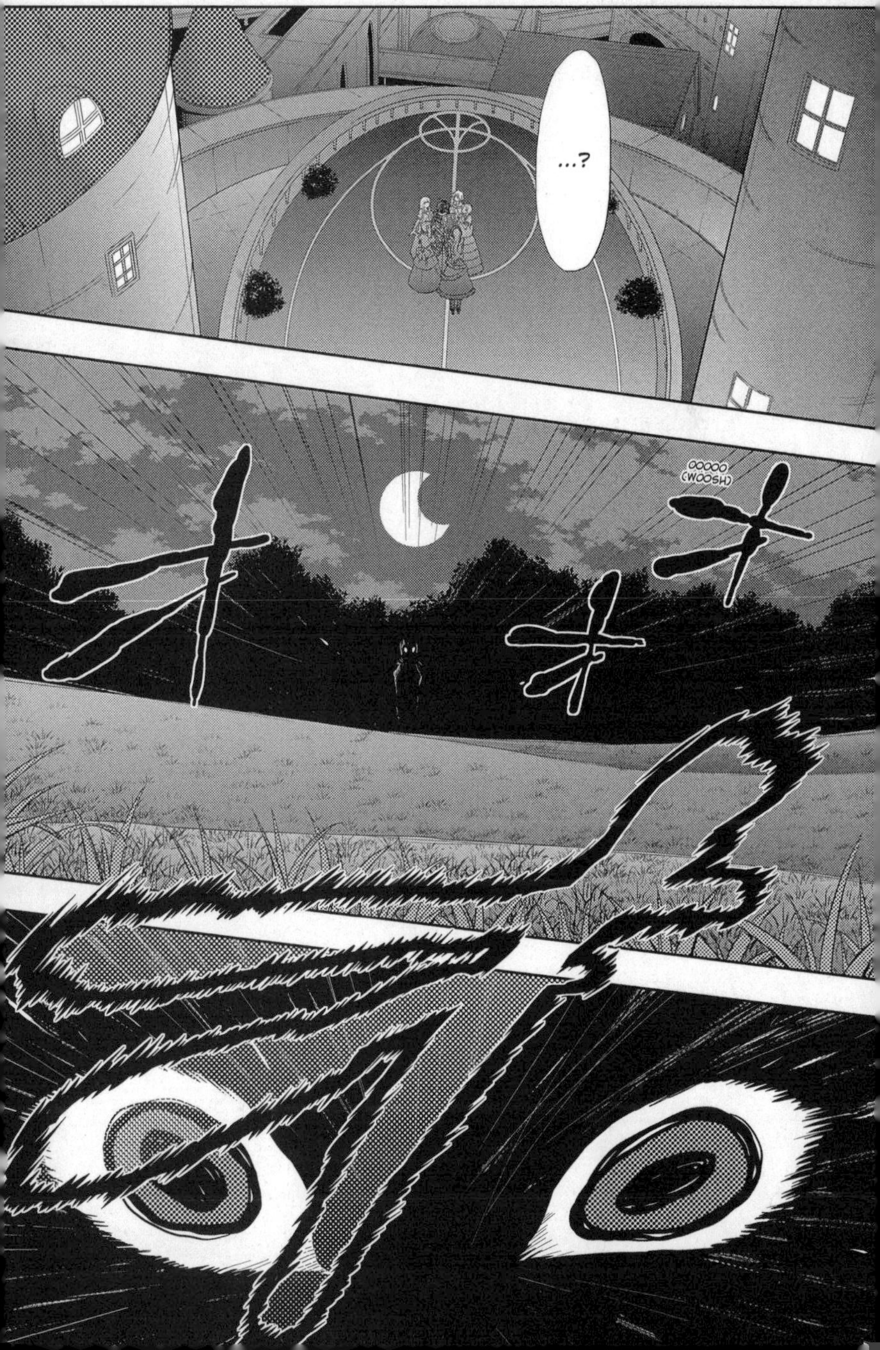
...?
OOOOO
(WOOSH)

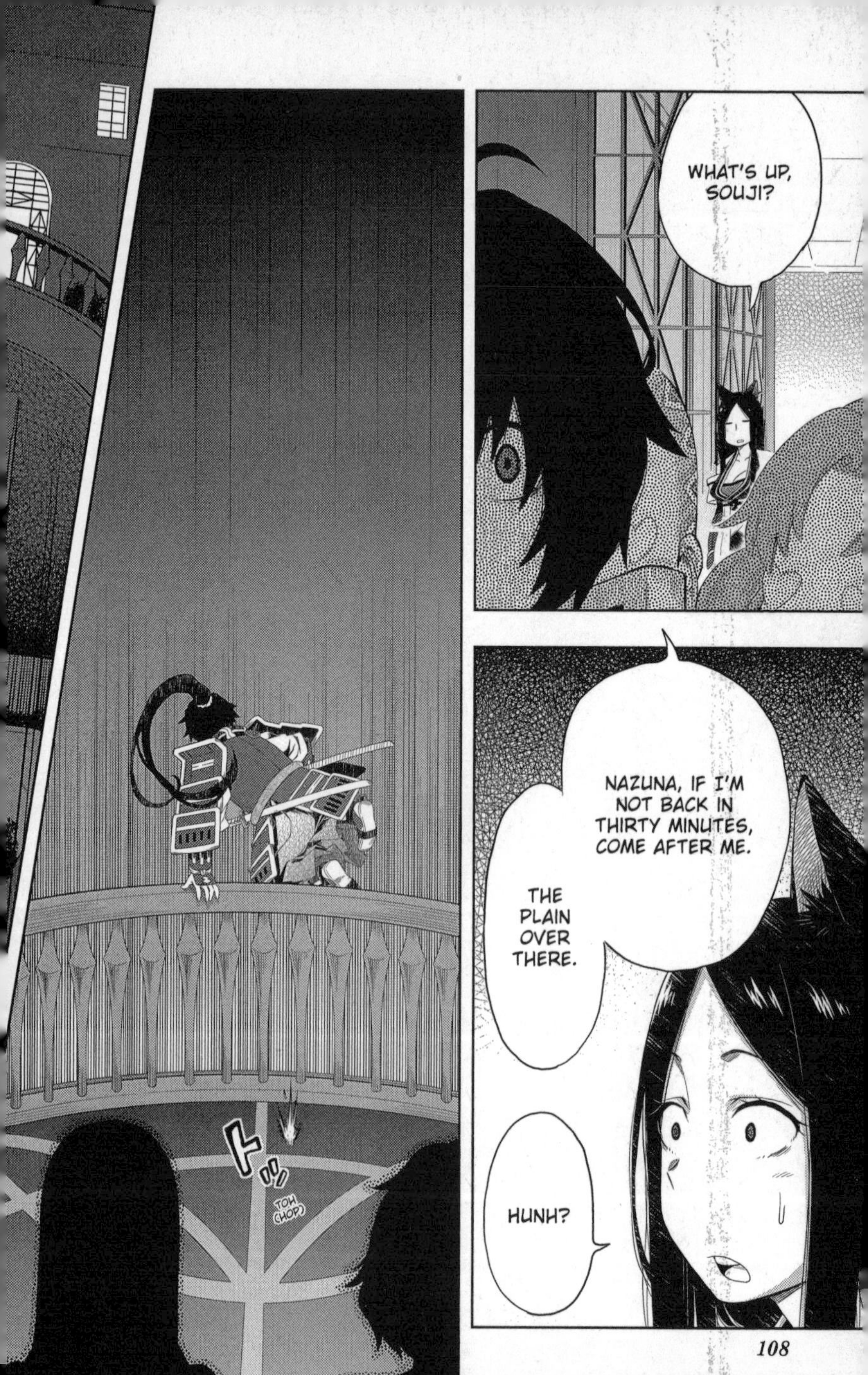
WHAT'S UP, SOUJI?
NAZUNA, IF I'M NOT BACK IN THIRTY MINUTES, COME AFTER ME.
THE PLAIN OVER THERE.
HUNH?
TOH (HOP)

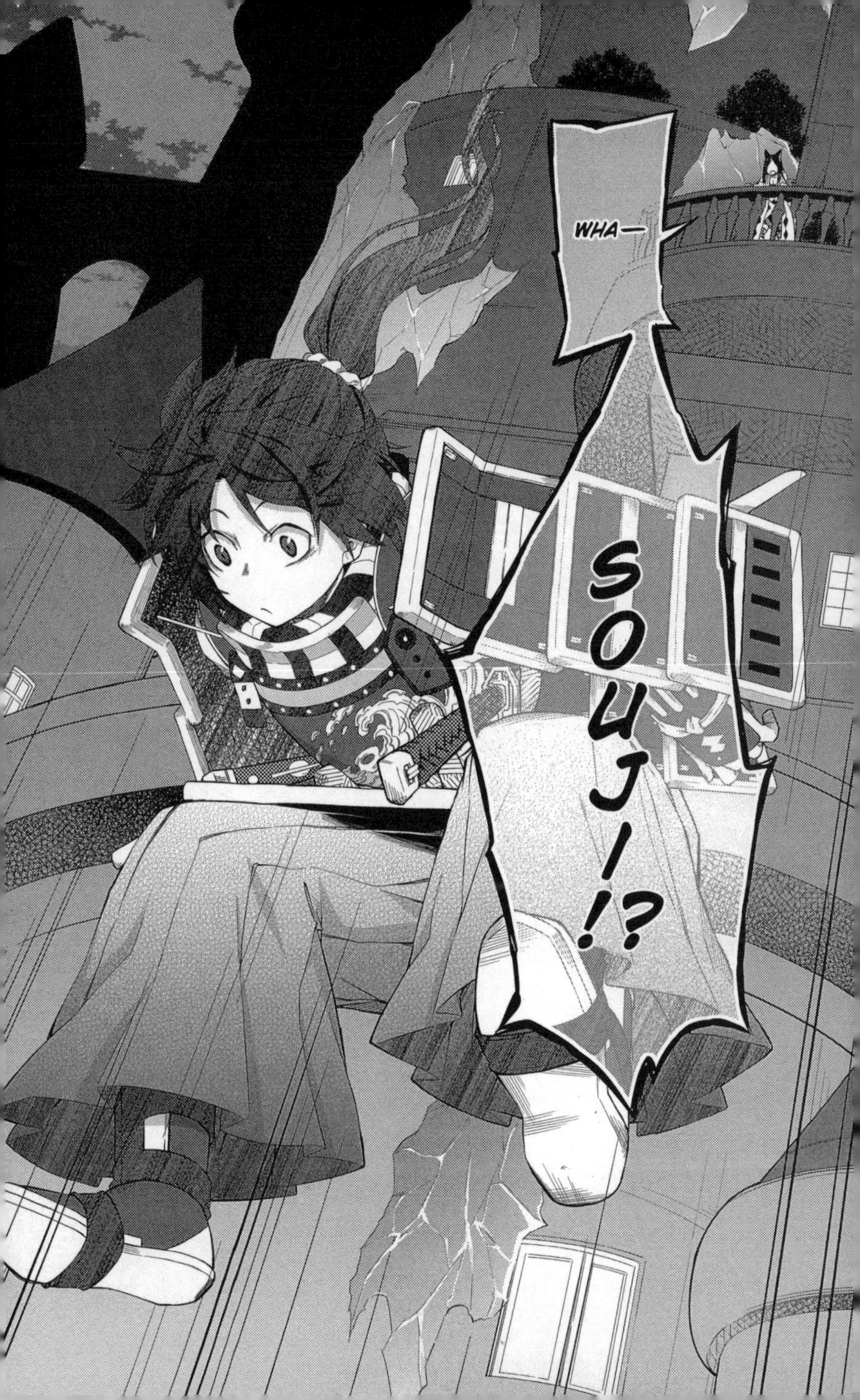
WHA—
SOUJI!?

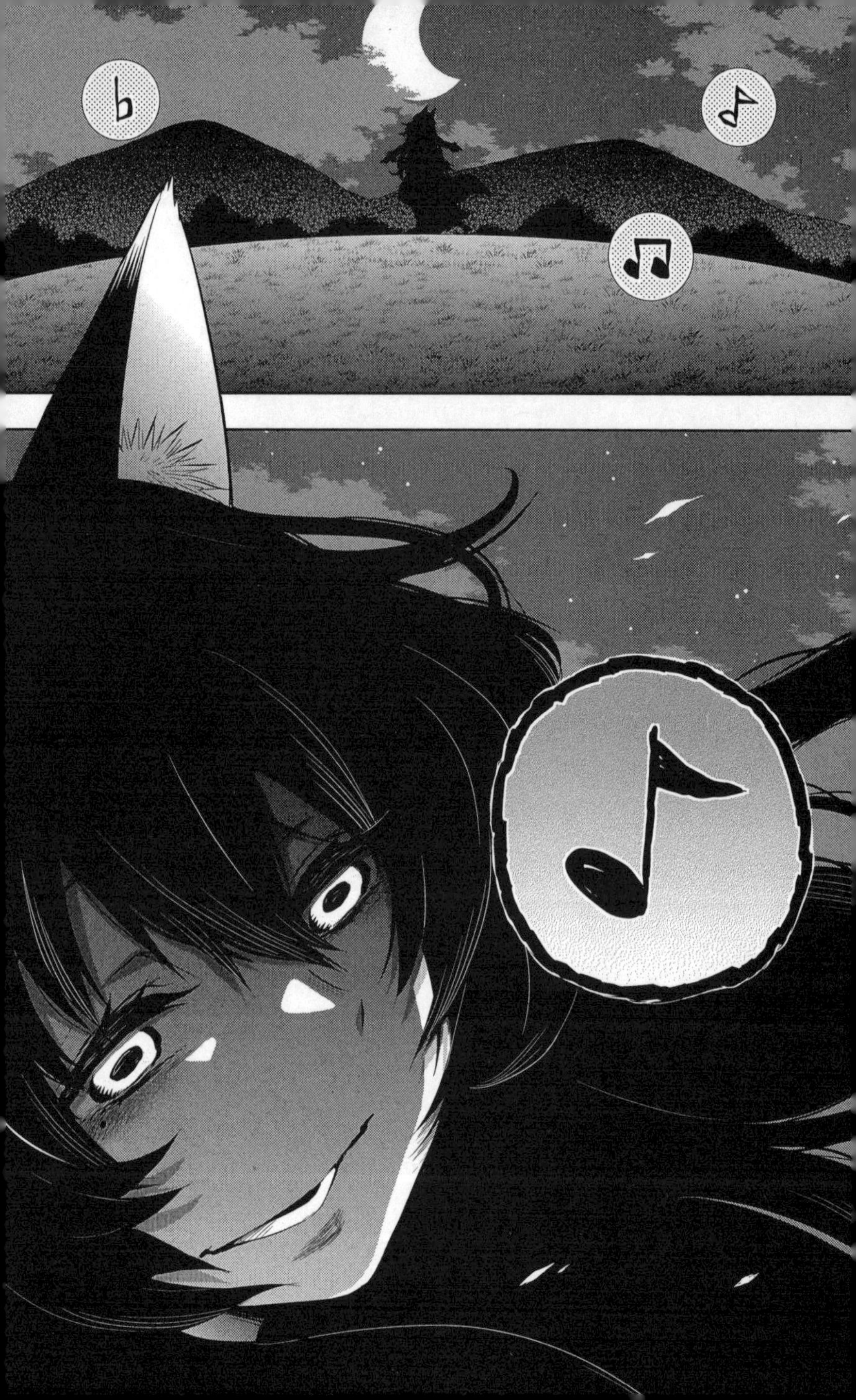

LOG HORIZON
THE WEST WIND BRIGADE

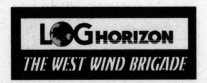

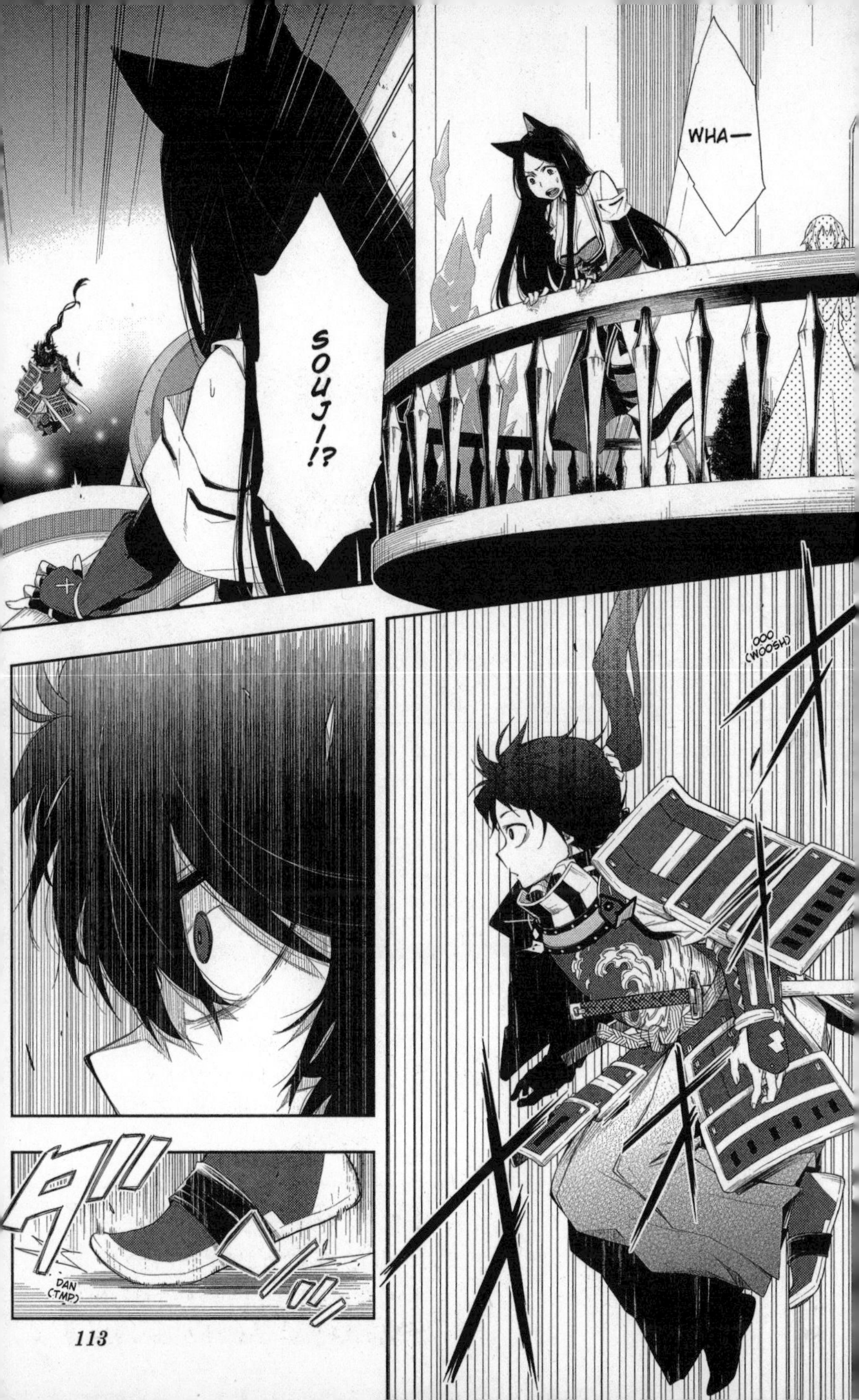
WHA—
SOUJI!?
OOO
(WOOSH)
ダッ
DAN
(TMP)

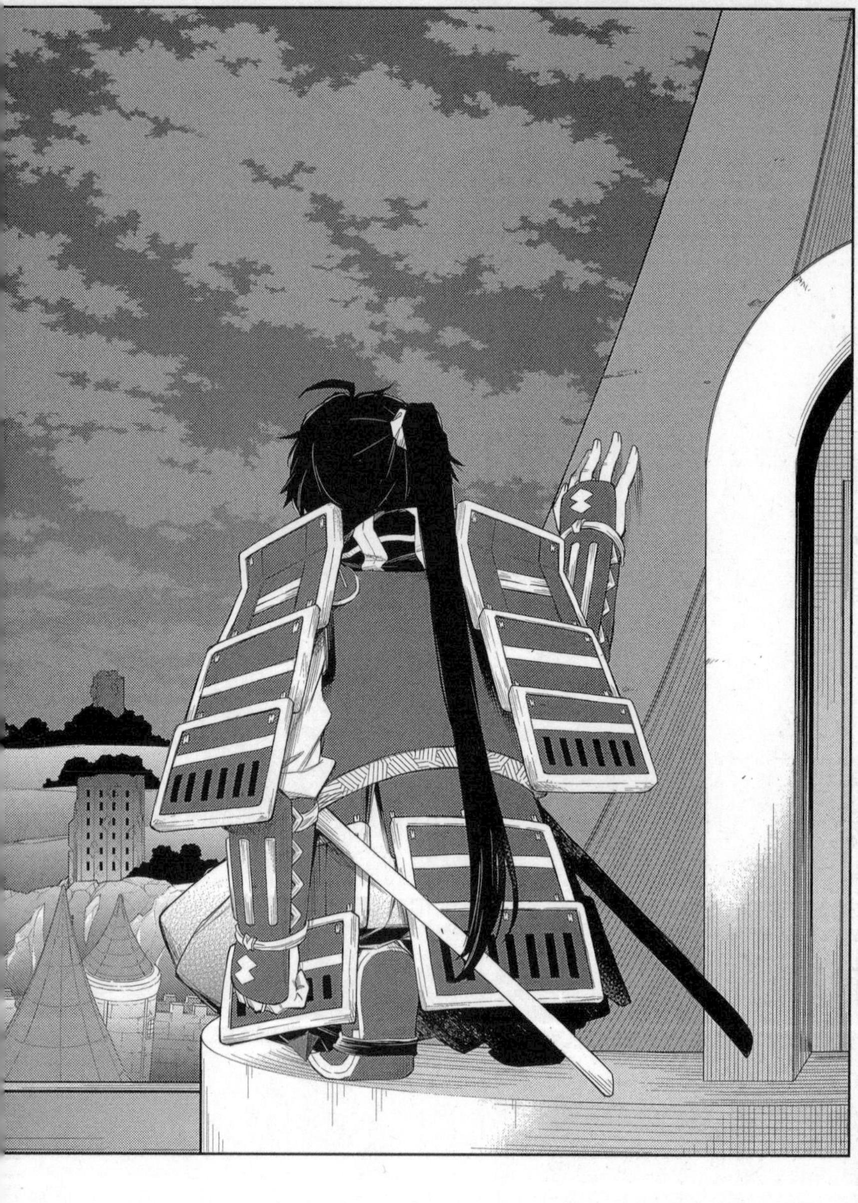

[CHAPTER : 41 **From Deep in the Mud**]

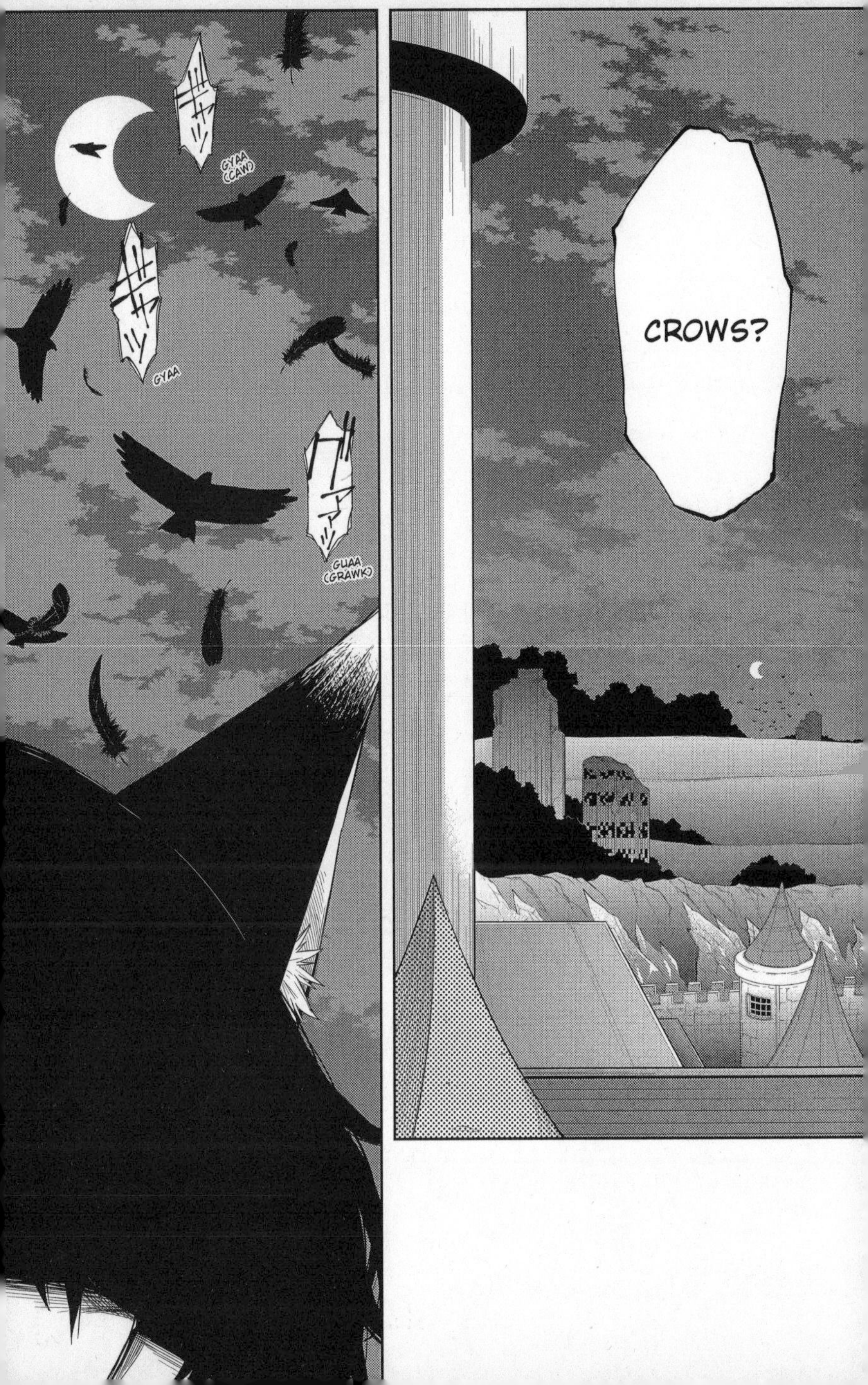
CROWS?
GYAA (CAW)
GYAA
GUAA (GRAWK)

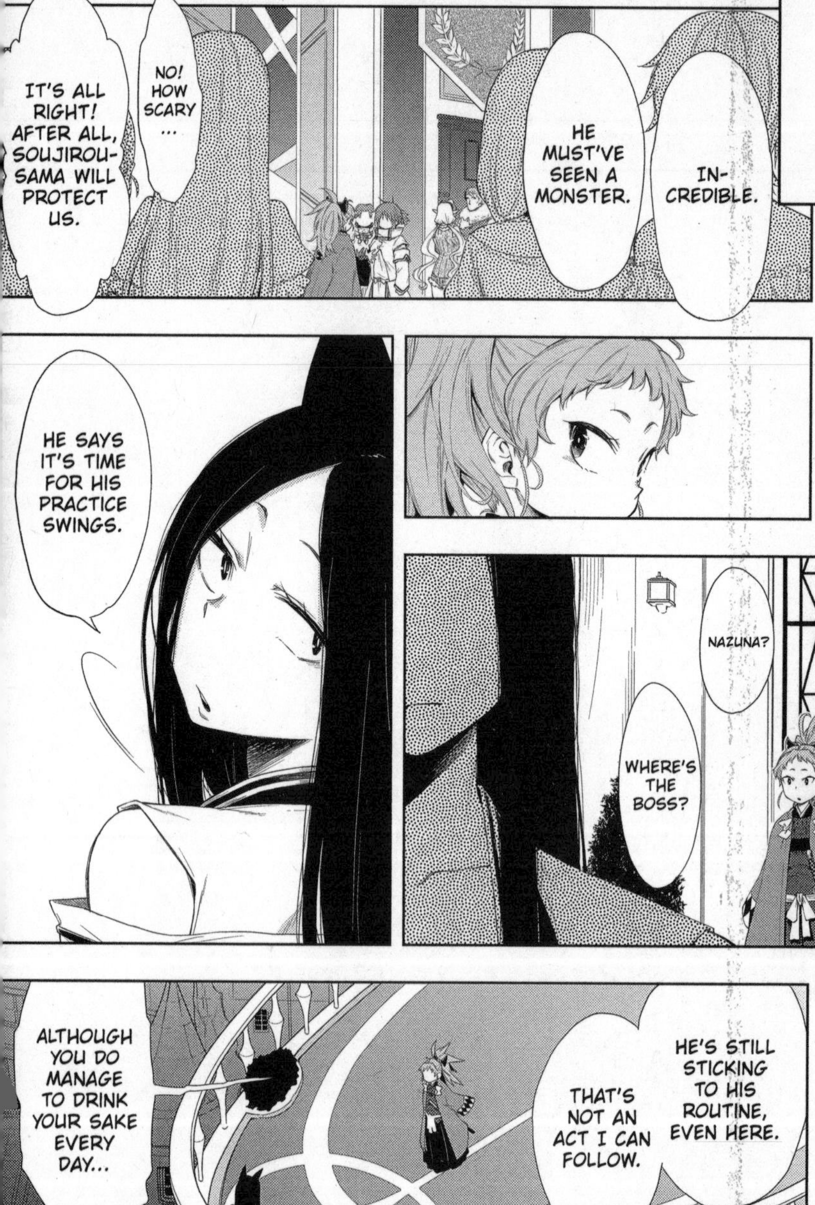
IN-CREDIBLE.
HE MUST'VE SEEN A MONSTER.
NO! HOW SCARY ...
IT'S ALL RIGHT! AFTER ALL, SOUJIROU-SAMA WILL PROTECT US.
NAZUNA?
WHERE'S THE BOSS?
HE SAYS IT'S TIME FOR HIS PRACTICE SWINGS.
HE'S STILL STICKING TO HIS ROUTINE, EVEN HERE.
THAT'S NOT AN ACT I CAN FOLLOW.
ALTHOUGH YOU DO MANAGE TO DRINK YOUR SAKE EVERY DAY...

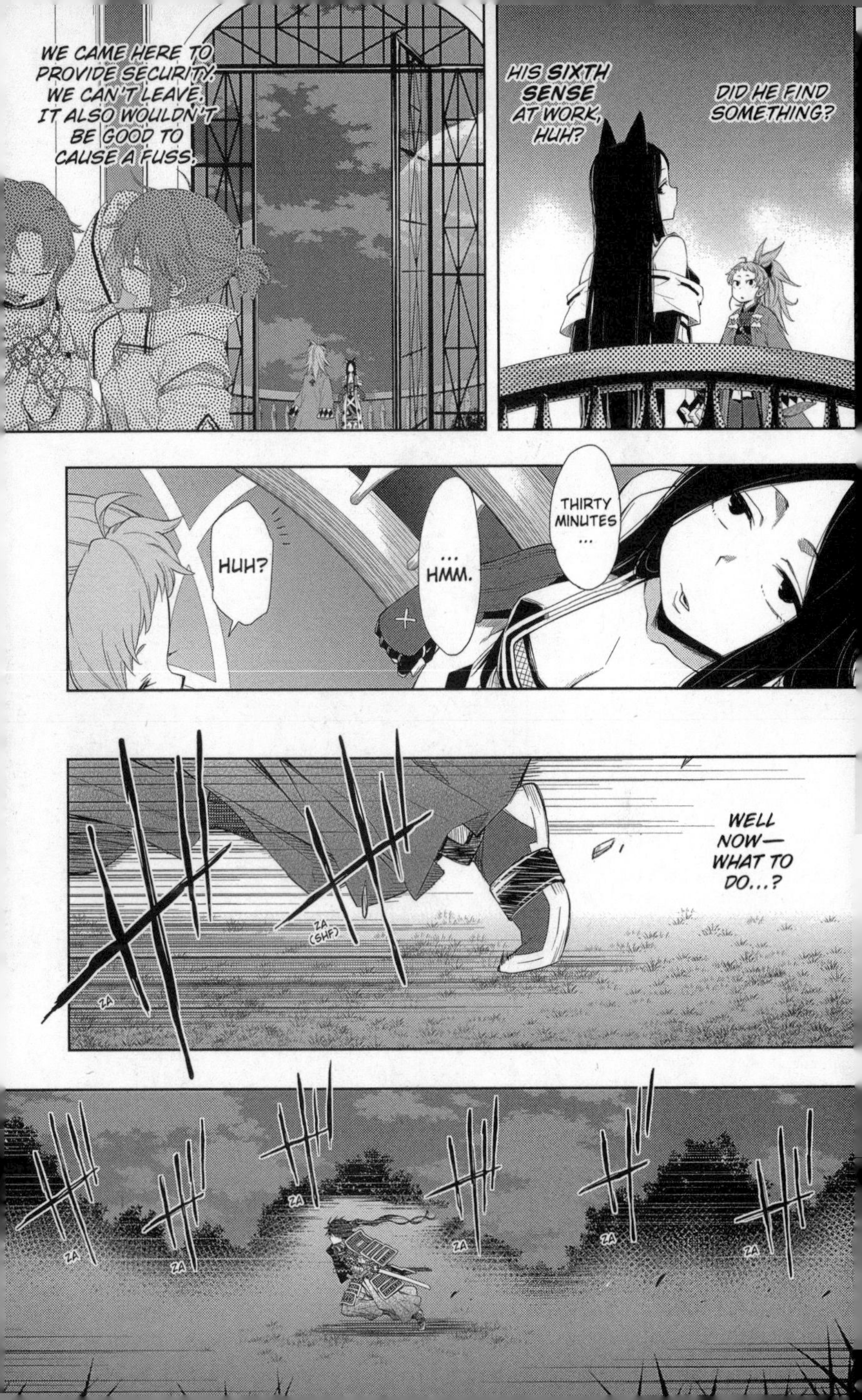
DID HE FIND SOMETHING?
HIS SIXTH SENSE AT WORK, HUH?
WE CAME HERE TO PROVIDE SECURITY. WE CAN'T LEAVE. IT ALSO WOULDN'T BE GOOD TO CAUSE A FUSS.
THIRTY MINUTES...
...HMM.
HUH?
WELL NOW— WHAT TO DO...?
ZA (SHF)
ZA
ZA
ZA
ZA
ZA
ZA
ZA

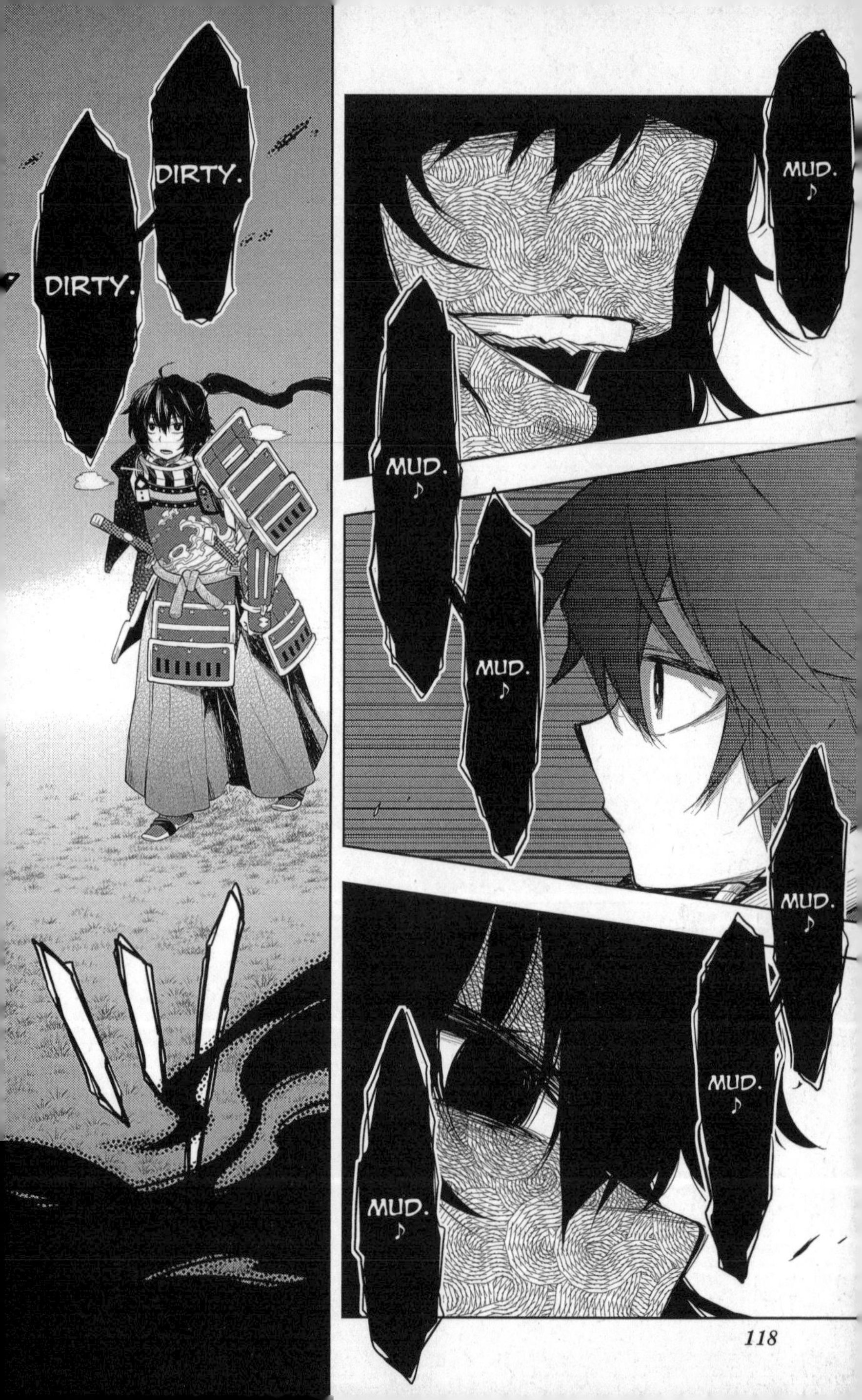
MUD. ♪
MUD. ♪
MUD. ♪
MUD. ♪
MUD. ♪
MUD. ♪
DIRTY.
DIRTY.

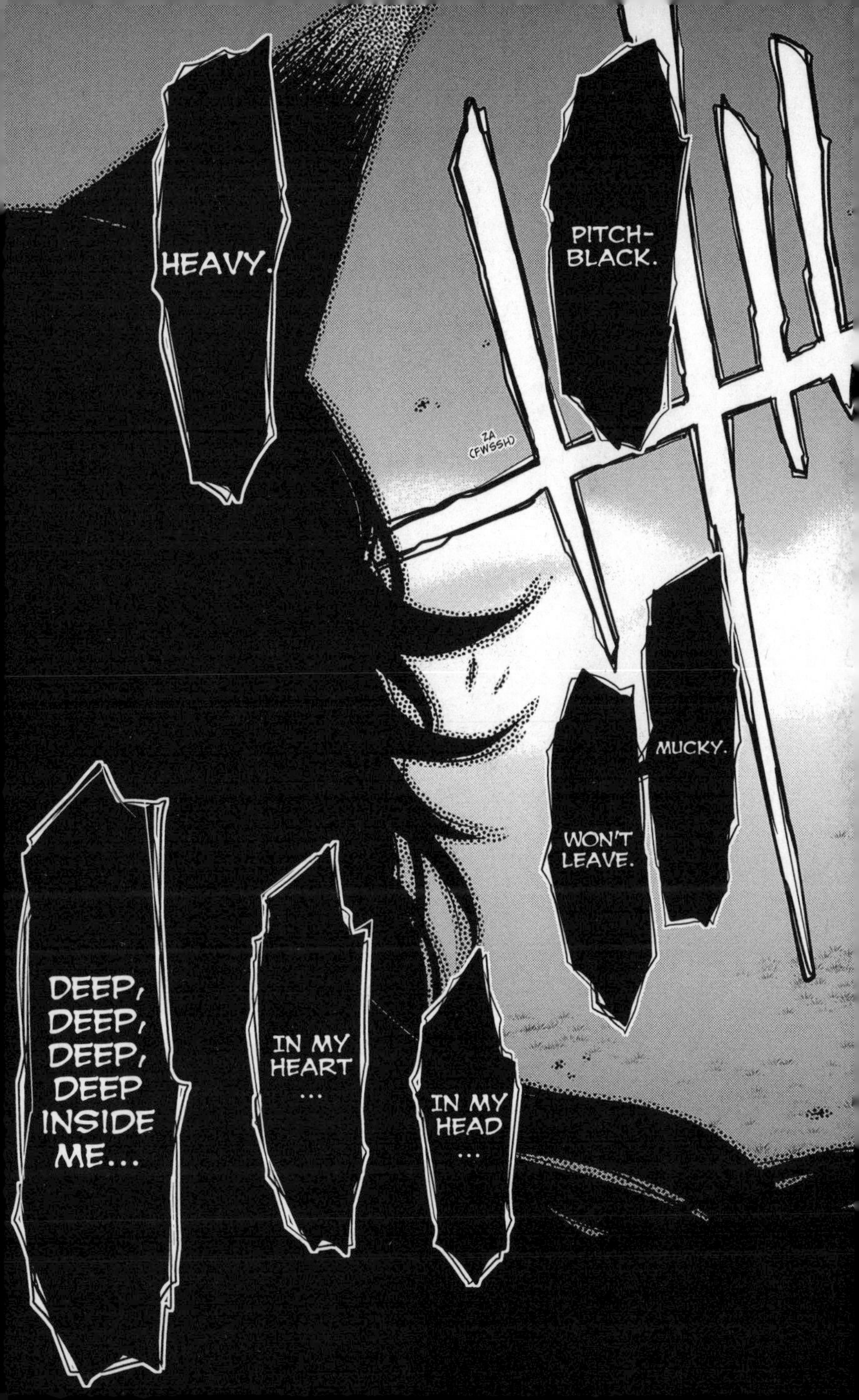
PITCH-BLACK.
HEAVY.
ZA (FWSSH)
MUCKY.
WON'T LEAVE.
IN MY HEAD...
IN MY HEART...
DEEP, DEEP, DEEP, DEEP INSIDE ME...

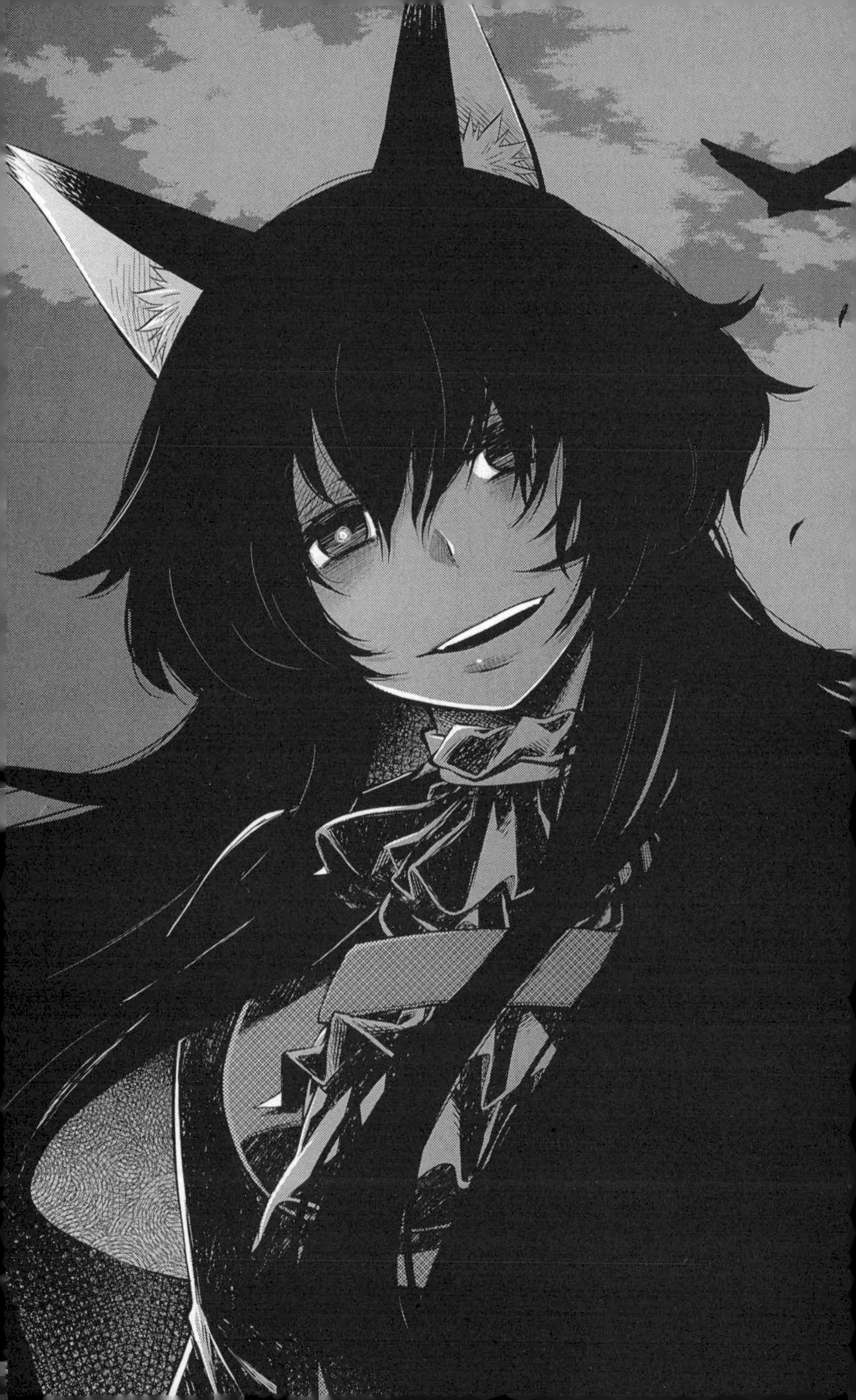

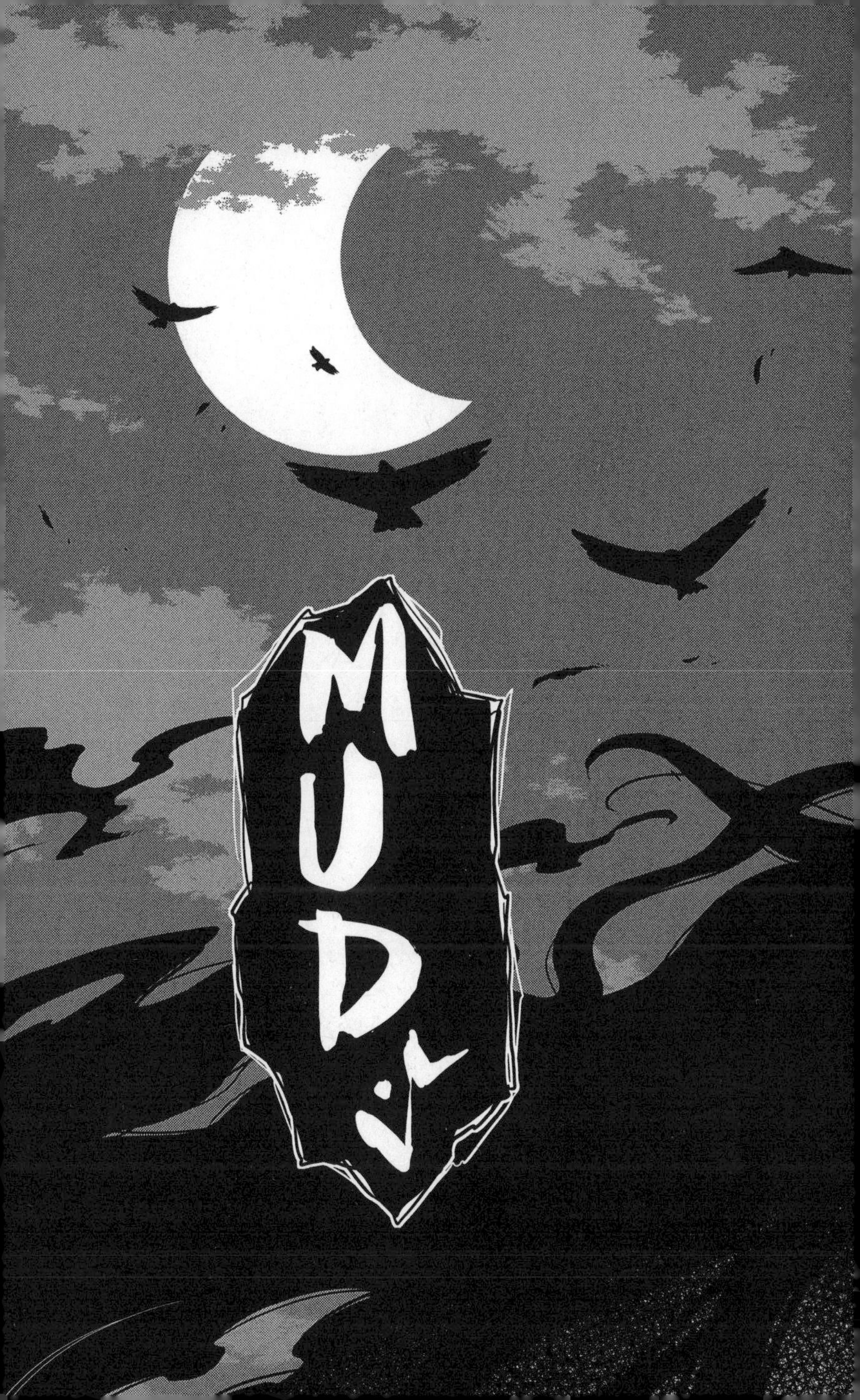
MUD...

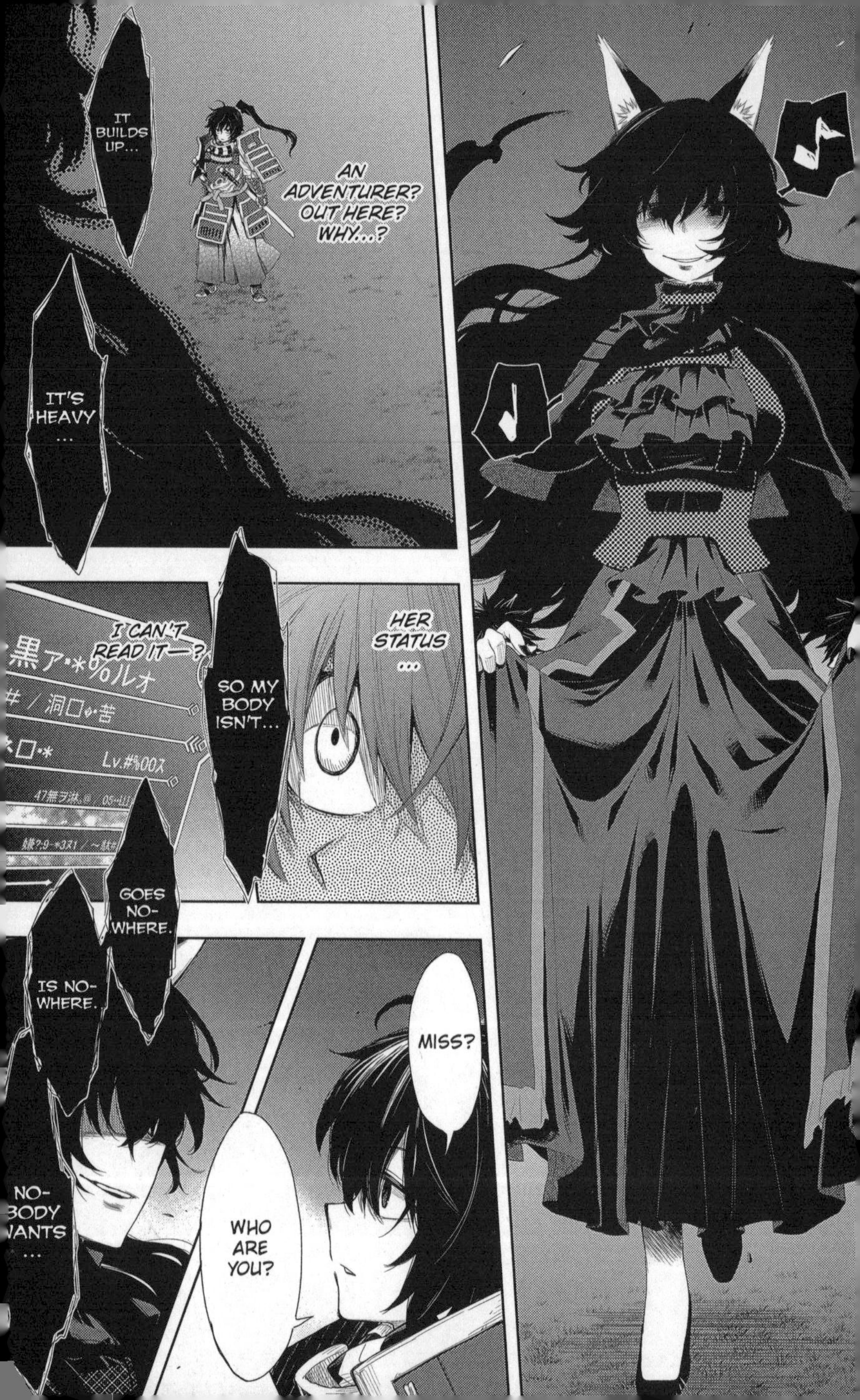
IT BUILDS UP...
AN ADVENTURER? OUT HERE? WHY...?
IT'S HEAVY...
HER STATUS...
SO MY BODY ISN'T...
I CAN'T READ IT—?
MISS?
WHO ARE YOU?
GOES NO-WHERE.
IS NO-WHERE.
NO-BODY WANTS...

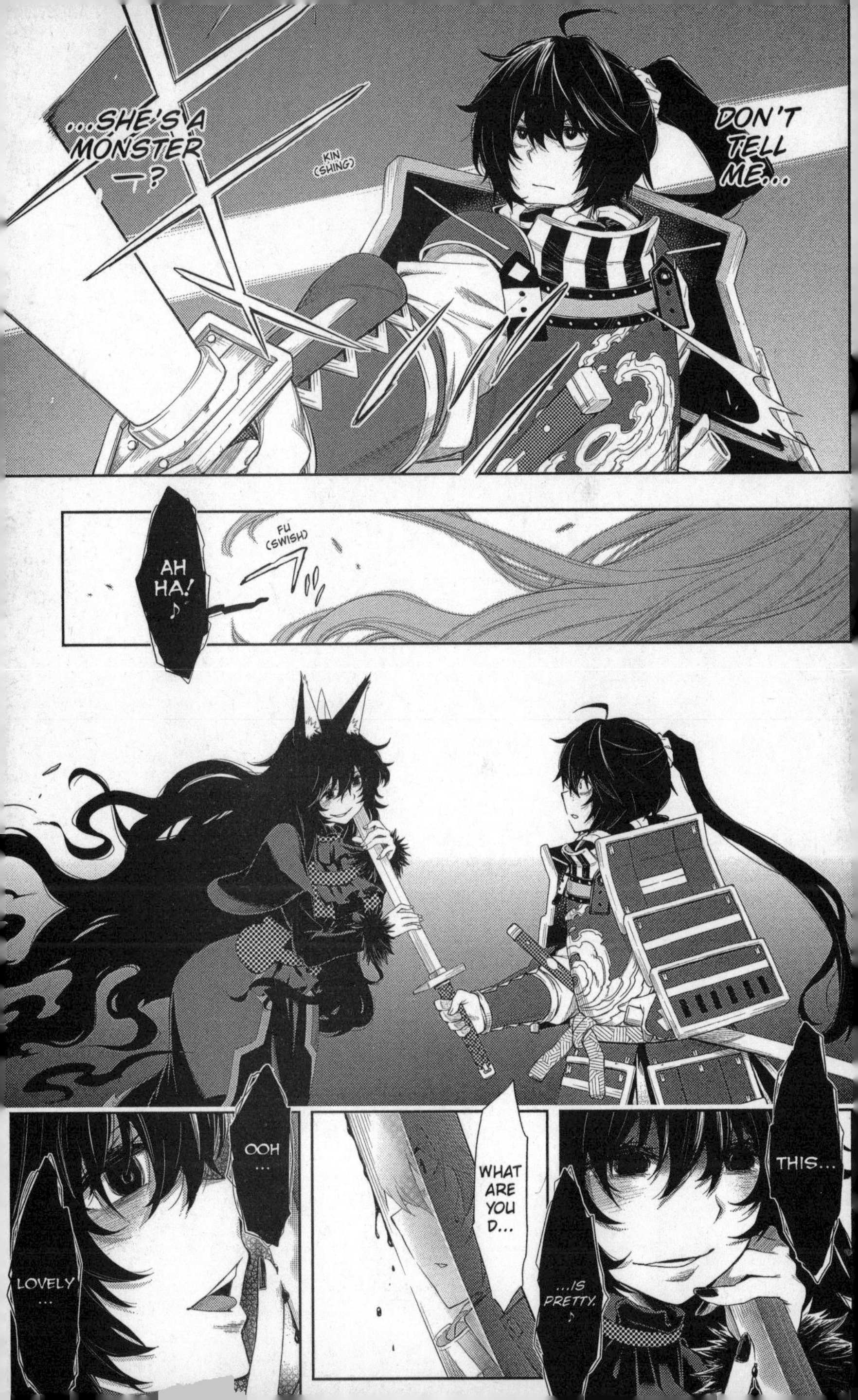
DON'T TELL ME...
KIN (SHING)
...SHE'S A MONSTER—?
FU (SWISH)
AH HA! ♪
THIS...
...IS PRETTY. ♪
WHAT ARE YOU D...
OOH...
LOVELY...

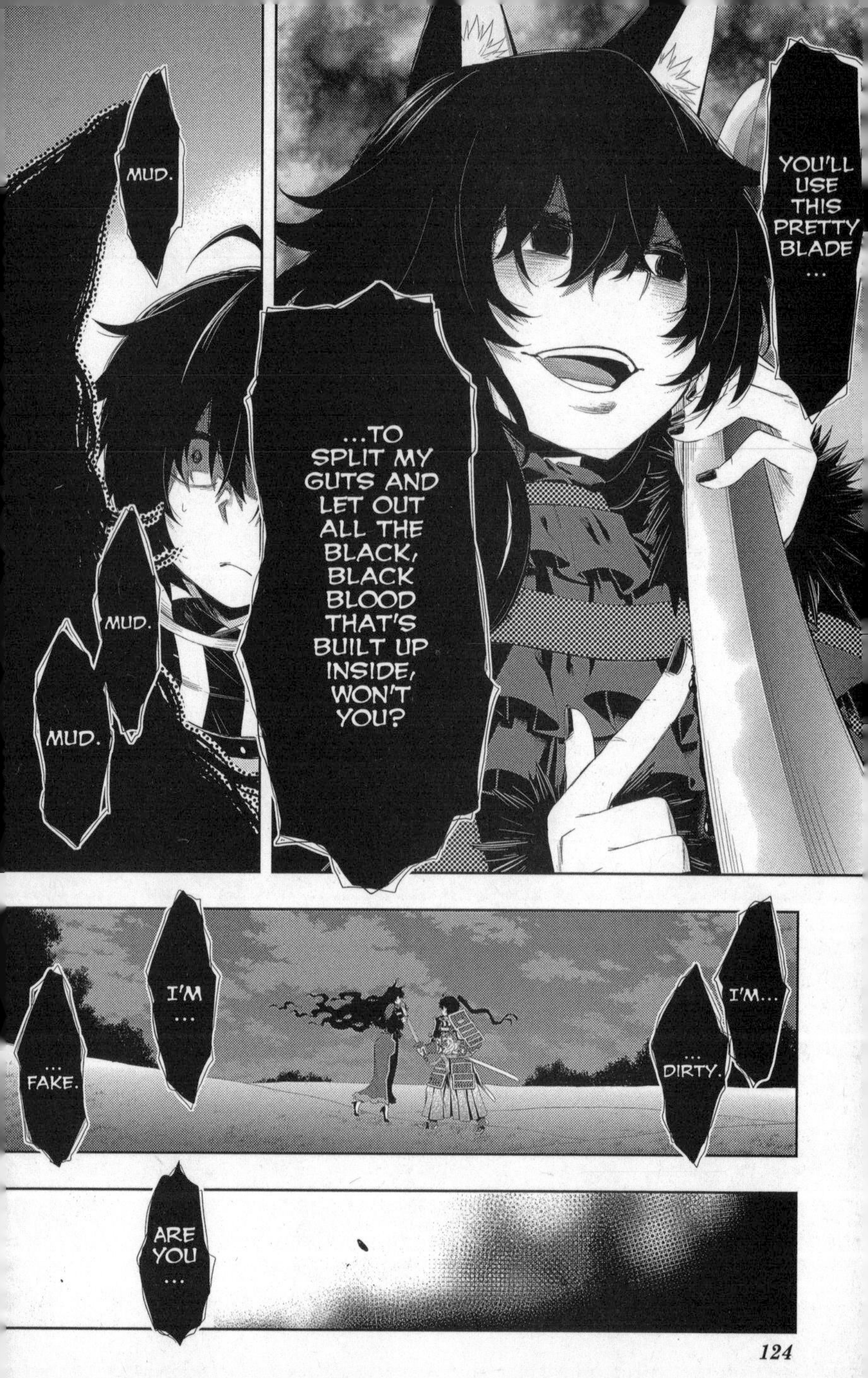
YOU'LL USE THIS PRETTY BLADE...
...TO SPLIT MY GUTS AND LET OUT ALL THE BLACK, BLACK BLOOD THAT'S BUILT UP INSIDE, WON'T YOU?
MUD.
MUD.
MUD.
I'M...
...DIRTY.
I'M...
...FAKE.
ARE YOU...

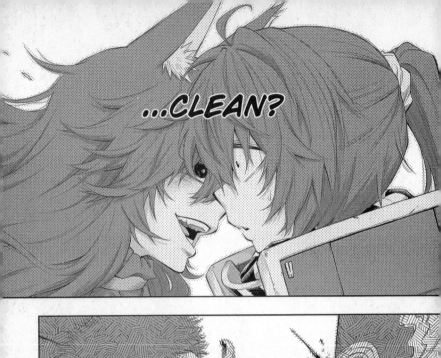

...CLEAN?
DOGA! (WHUD)
GEE (GWEH)
TO
TO (TUP)
GWEH HEH. ♪
THAT KICK MESSED ME UP INSIDE.
...NO...
MY INSIDES...
...WERE ALREADY MESSY.

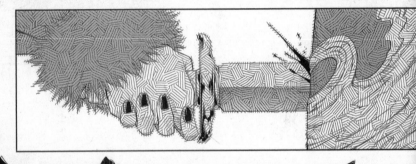

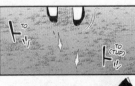

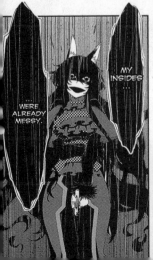

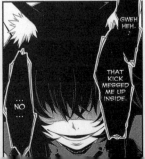

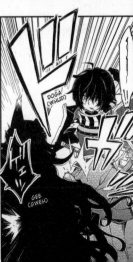

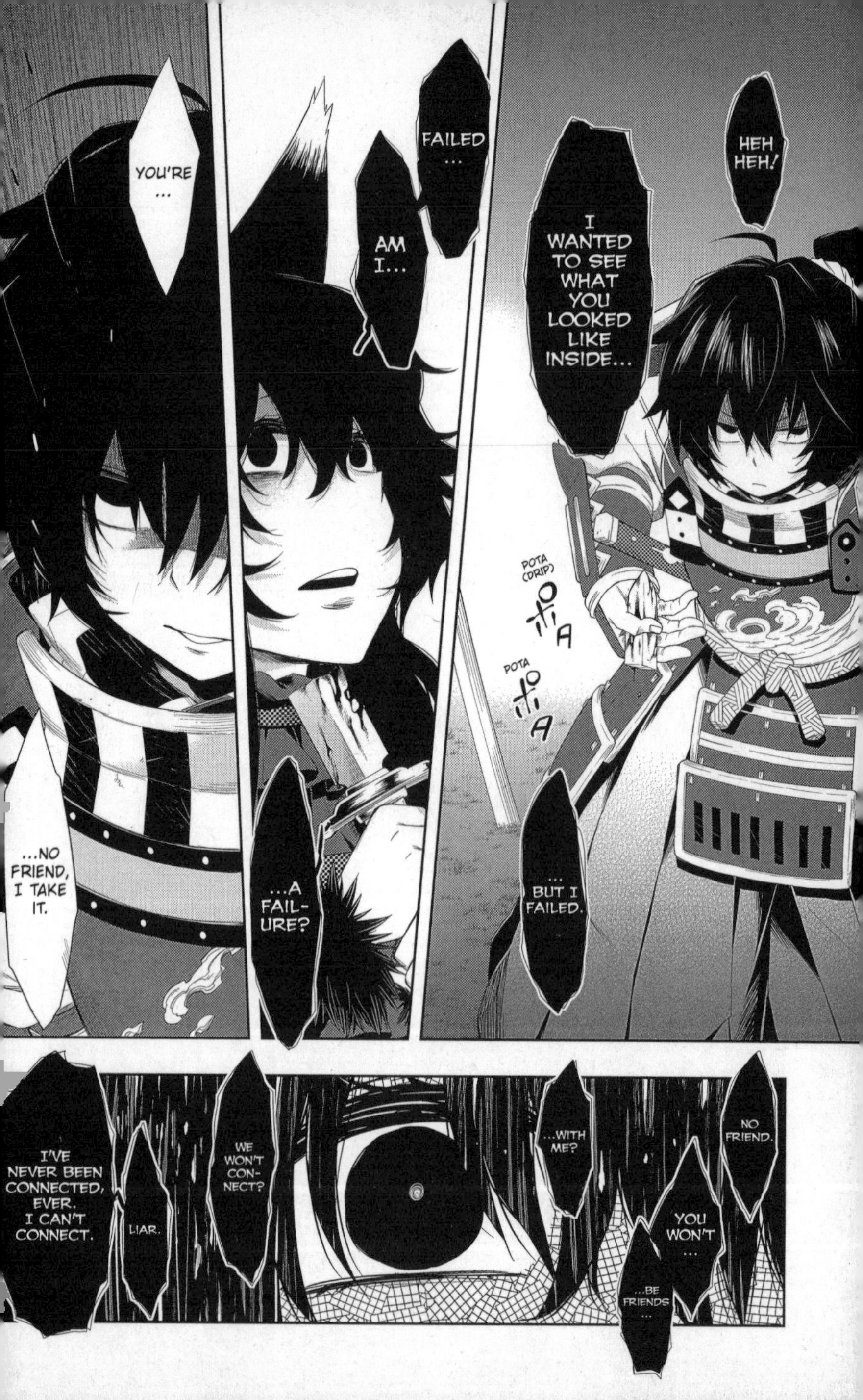
HEH HEH!
I WANTED TO SEE WHAT YOU LOOKED LIKE INSIDE...
POTA (DRIP)
POTA
...BUT I FAILED.
FAILED...
AM I...
...A FAILURE?
YOU'RE...
...NO FRIEND, I TAKE IT.
NO FRIEND.
...WITH ME?
YOU WON'T...
...BE FRIENDS...
WE WON'T CONNECT?
LIAR.
I'VE NEVER BEEN CONNECTED, EVER. I CAN'T CONNECT.

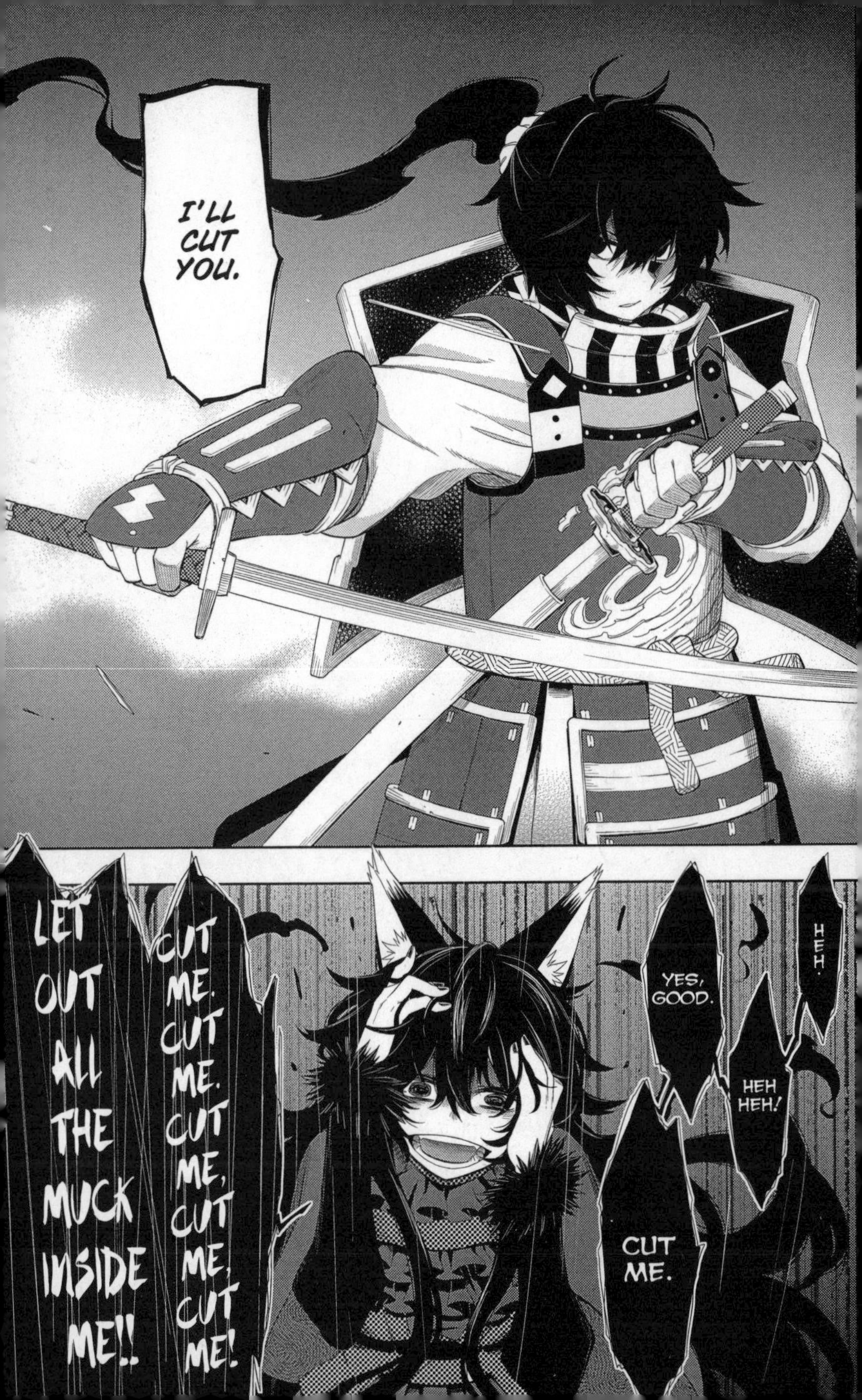
I'LL CUT YOU.
HEH.
YES, GOOD.
HEH HEH!
CUT ME.
CUT ME. CUT ME. CUT ME, CUT ME, CUT ME, CUT ME!
LET OUT ALL THE MUCK INSIDE ME!!

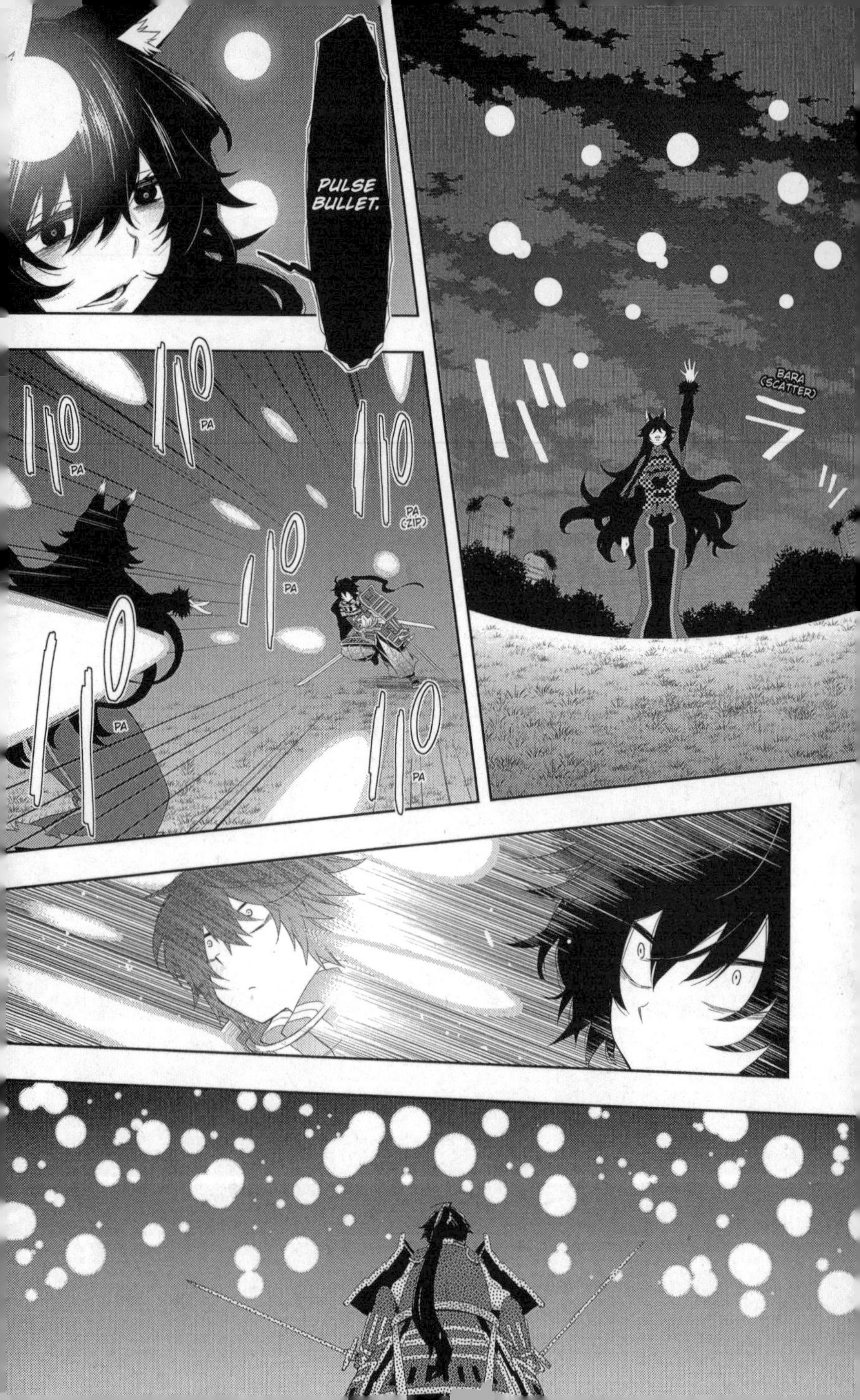
BARA (SCATTER)
PULSE BULLET.
PA (ZIP)
PA
PA
PA
PA
PA

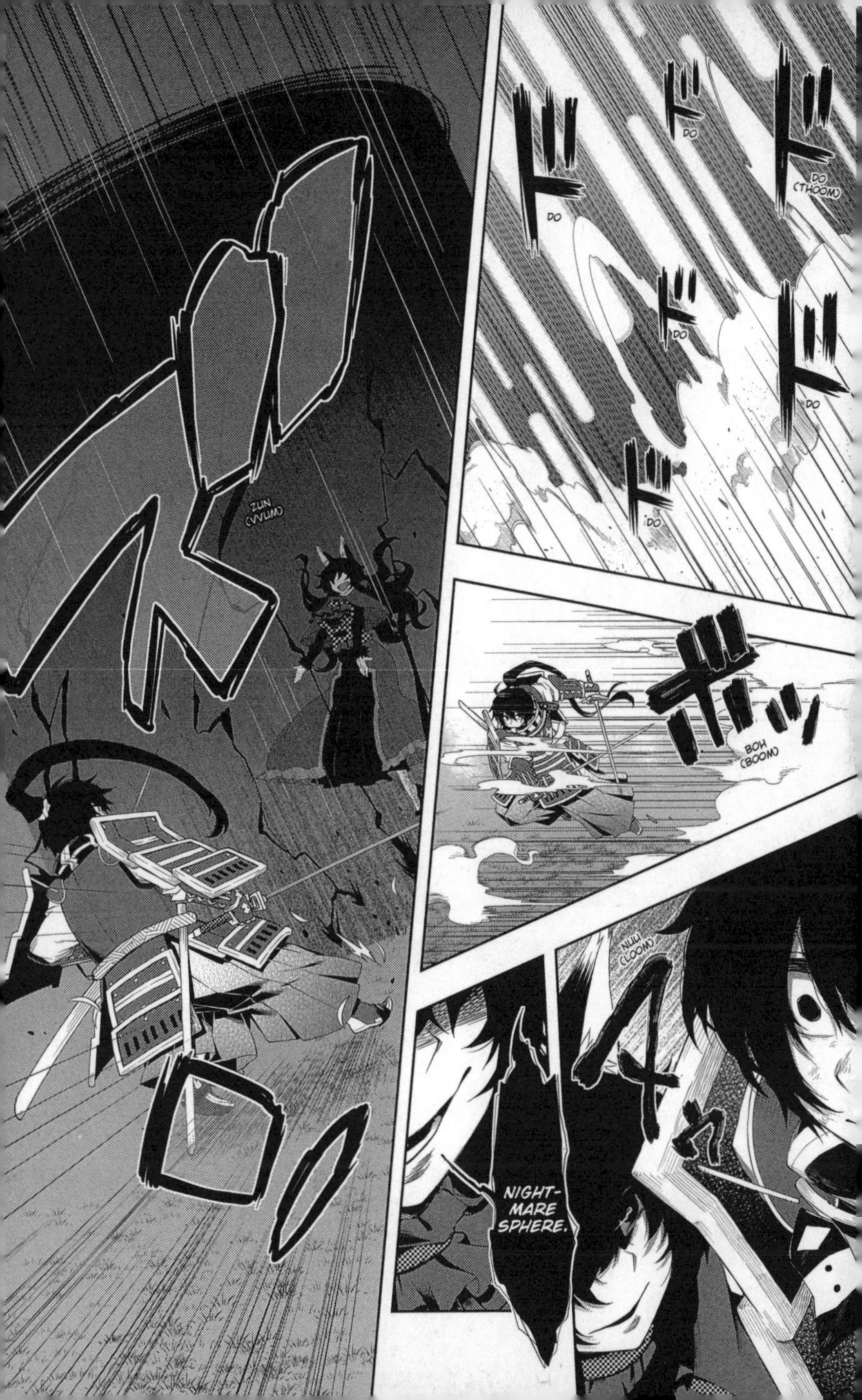
DO
DO (THOOM)
DO
DO
DO
DO
BOH (BOOM)
NUU (LOOM)
NIGHT-MARE SPHERE.
ZUN (VVUM)

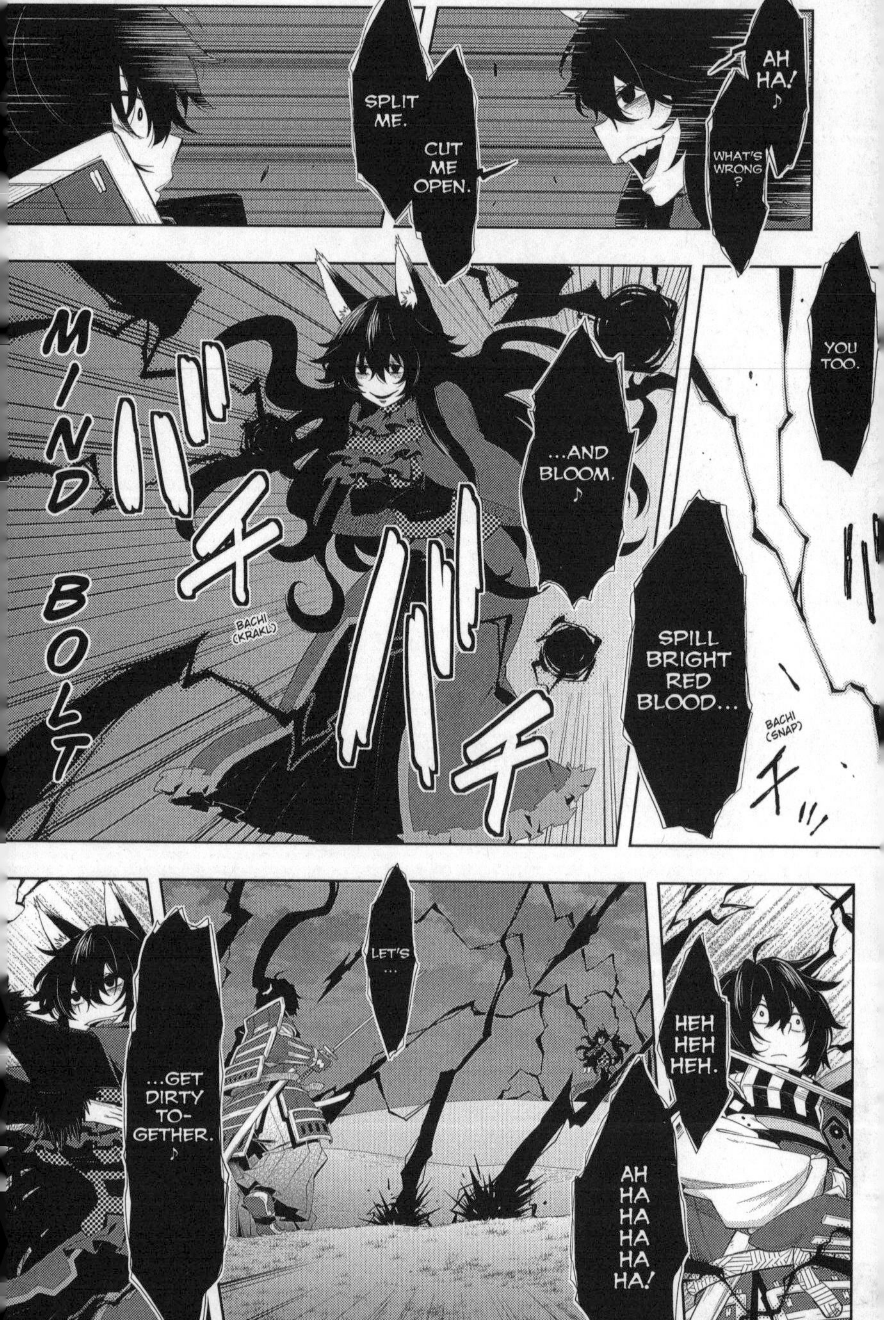
AH HA! ♪
WHAT'S WRONG?
SPLIT ME.
CUT ME OPEN.
YOU TOO.
SPILL BRIGHT RED BLOOD...
BACHI (SNAP)
...AND BLOOM. ♪
BACHI (KRAKL)
MIND BOLT
HEH HEH HEH.
AH HA HA HA HA HA!
LET'S...
...GET DIRTY TO-GETHER. ♪

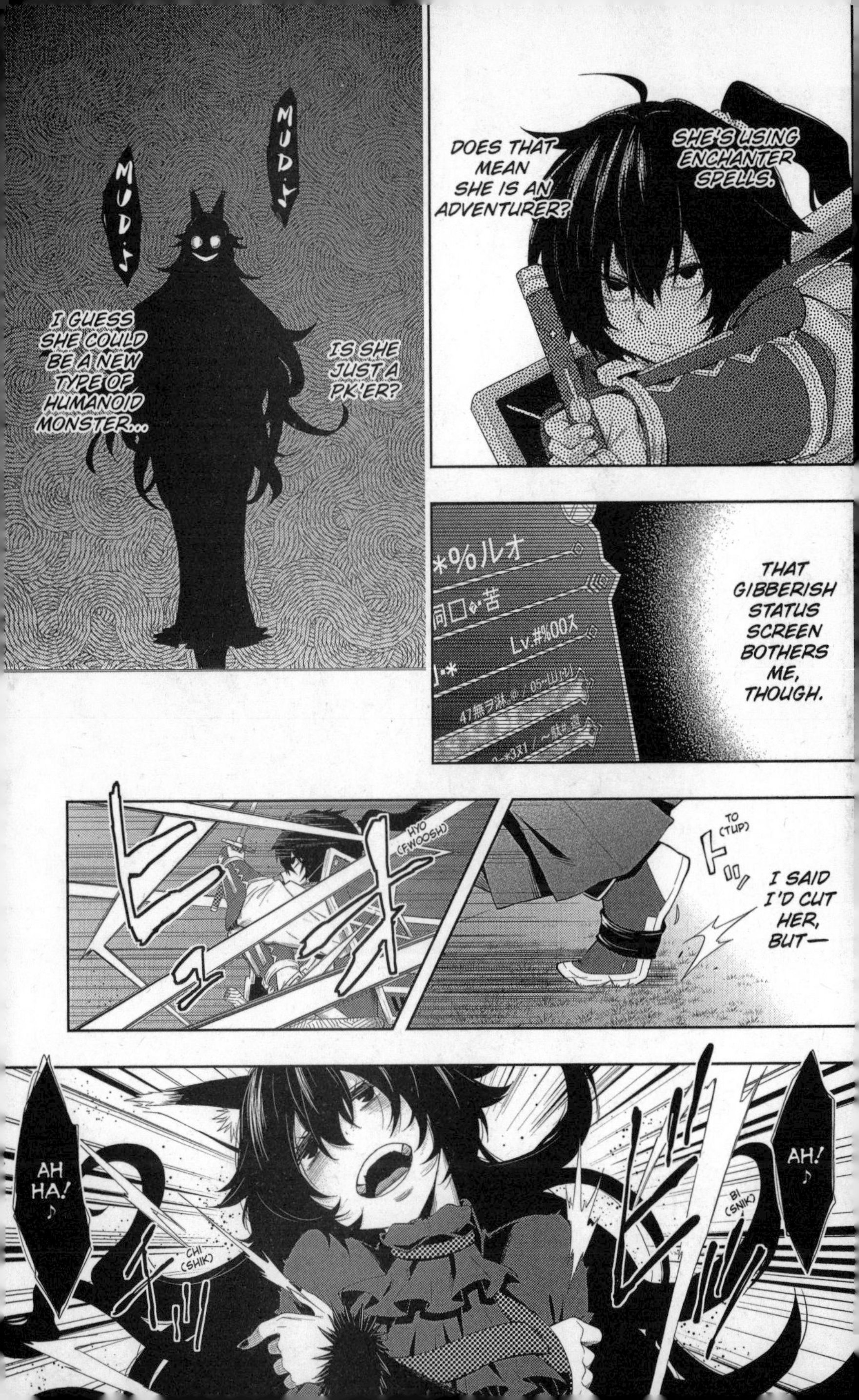
SHE'S USING ENCHANTER SPELLS.
DOES THAT MEAN SHE IS AN ADVENTURER?
THAT GIBBERISH STATUS SCREEN BOTHERS ME, THOUGH.
MUD'S
MUD'S
IS SHE JUST A PK'ER?
I GUESS SHE COULD BE A NEW TYPE OF HUMANOID MONSTER...
TO (TUP)
I SAID I'D CUT HER, BUT—
HYO (FWOOSH)
AH! ♪
BI (SNIK)
CHI (SHIK)
AH HA! ♪

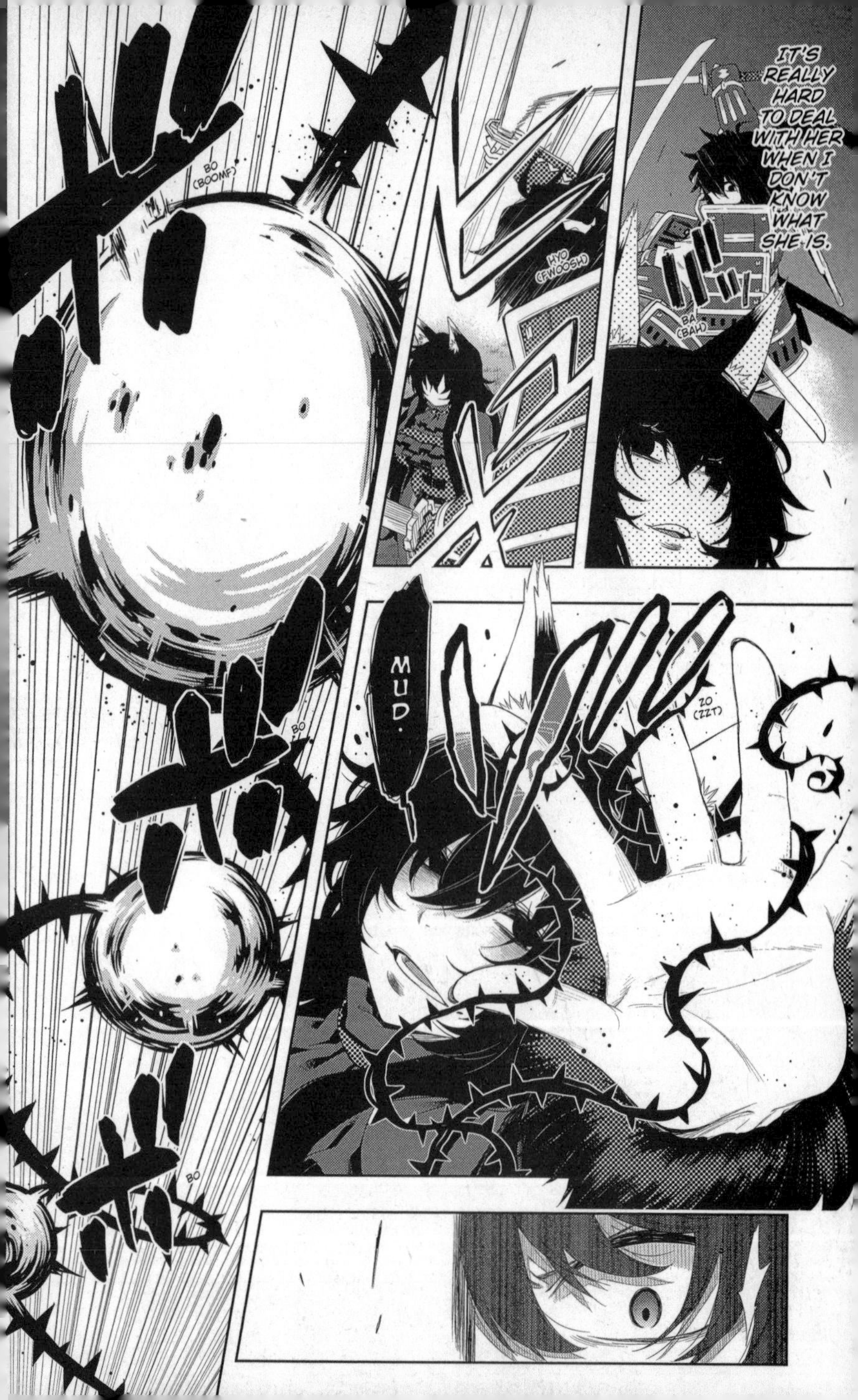
IT'S REALLY HARD TO DEAL WITH HER WHEN I DON'T KNOW WHAT SHE IS.
BA (BAH)
HYO (FWOOSH)
BO (BOOMF)
ZO (ZZT)
MUD.
BO
BO

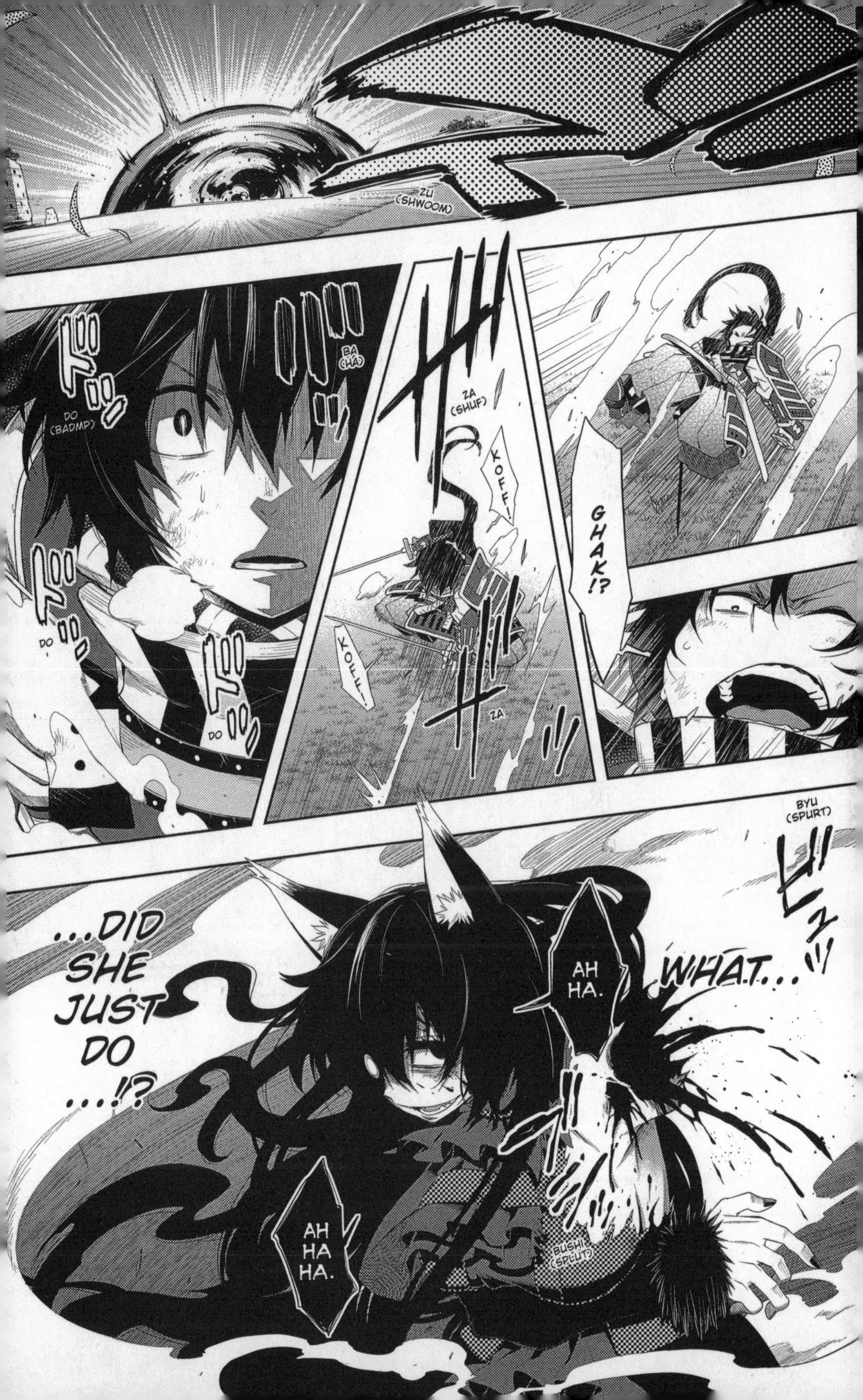
ZU
(SHWOOM)
GHAK!?
ZA
(SHUF)
KOFF!
KOFF!
ZA
BA
(HA)
DO
(BADMP)
DO
DO
BYU
(SPURT)
WHAT...
AH HA.
...DID SHE JUST DO ...!?
BUSHI
(SPLUT)
AH HA HA.

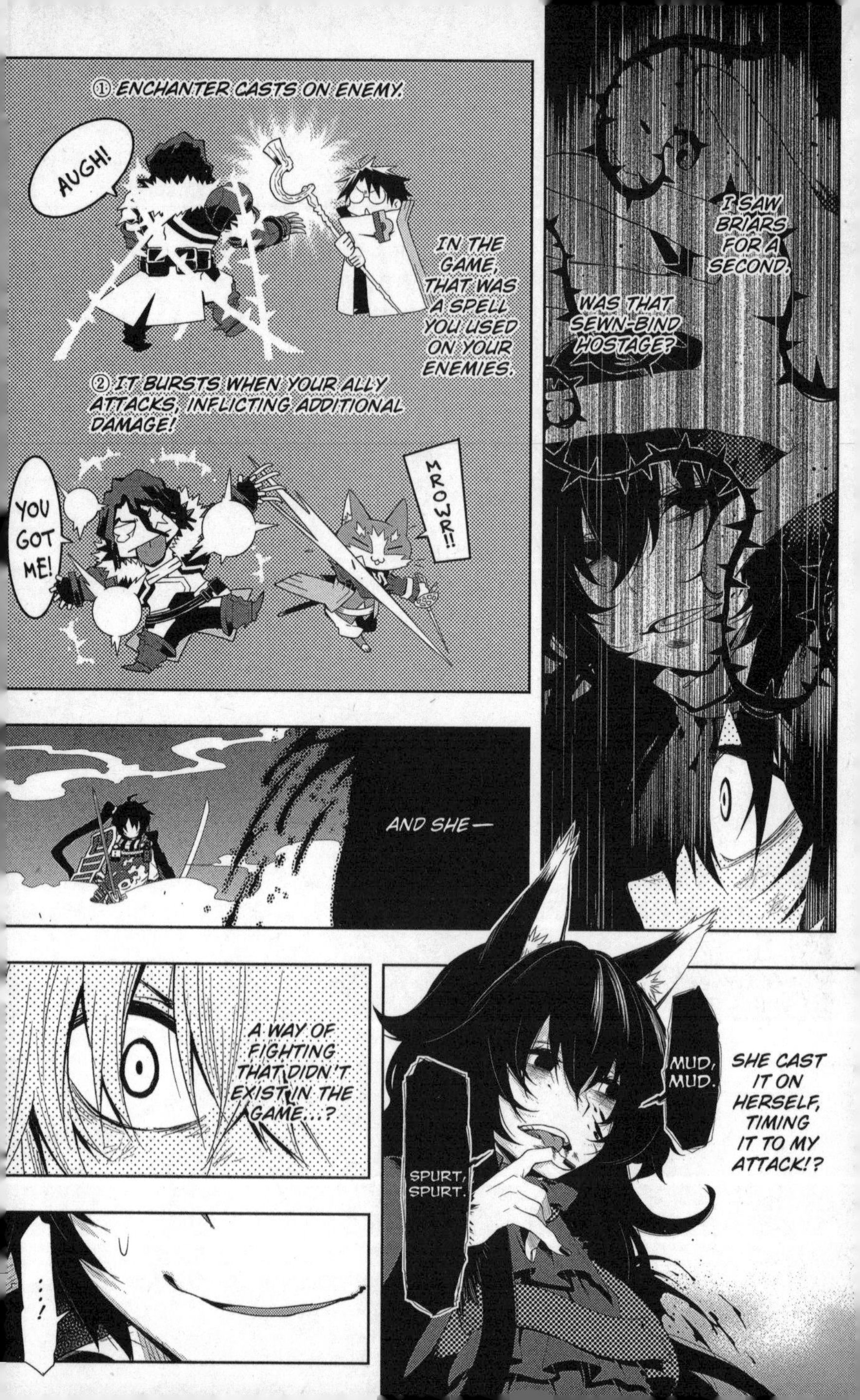
I SAW BRIARS FOR A SECOND.
WAS THAT SEWN-BIND HOSTAGE?
① ENCHANTER CASTS ON ENEMY.
IN THE GAME, THAT WAS A SPELL YOU USED ON YOUR ENEMIES.
AUGH!
② IT BURSTS WHEN YOUR ALLY ATTACKS, INFLICTING ADDITIONAL DAMAGE!
MROWR!!
YOU GOT ME!
AND SHE—
SHE CAST IT ON HERSELF, TIMING IT TO MY ATTACK!?
MUD, MUD.
SPURT, SPURT.
A WAY OF FIGHTING THAT DIDN'T EXIST IN THE GAME...?
...!

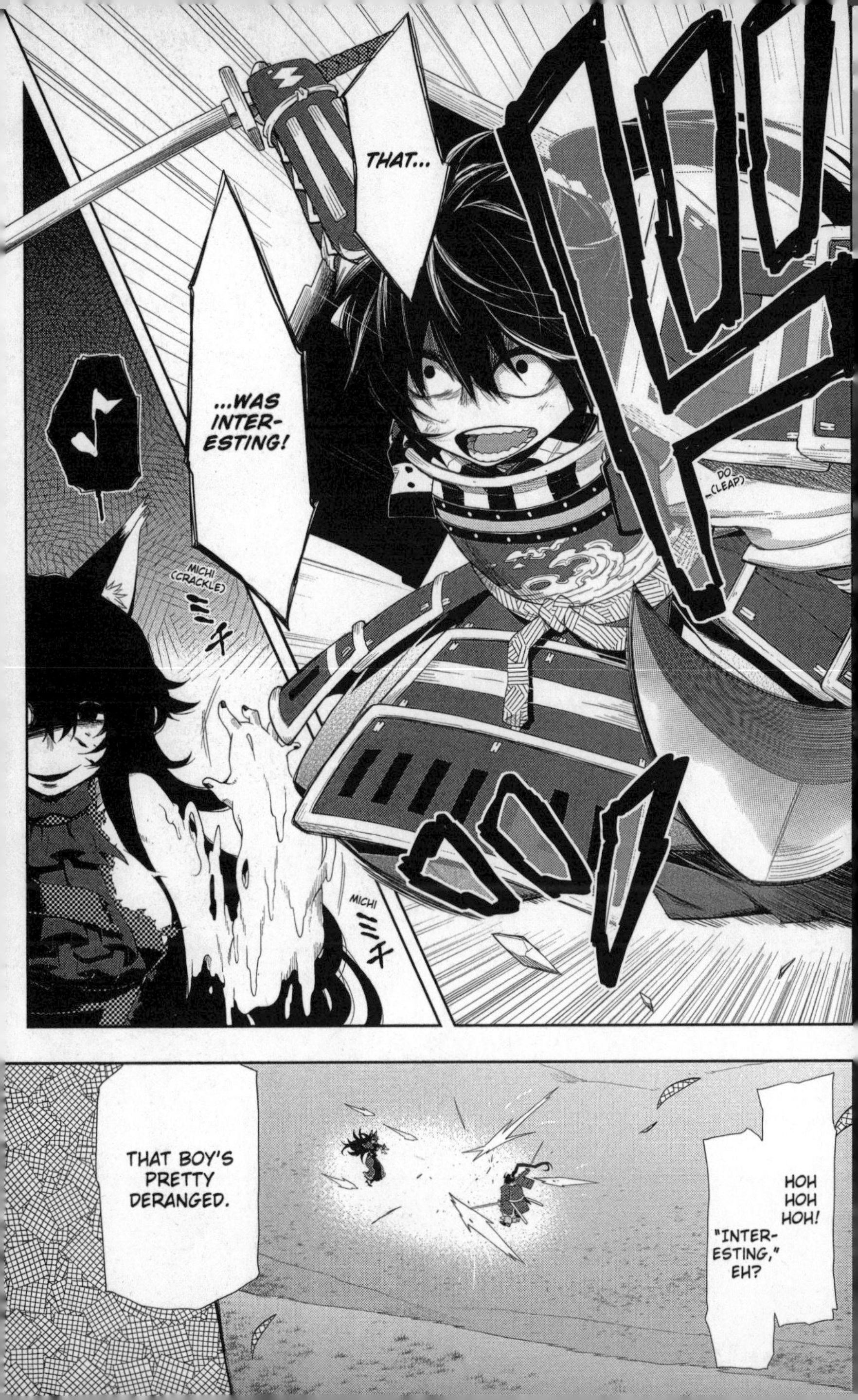
THAT...
...WAS INTER-ESTING!
DO (LEAP)
MICHI (CRACKLE)
MICHI
HOH HOH HOH! "INTER-ESTING," EH?
THAT BOY'S PRETTY DERANGED.

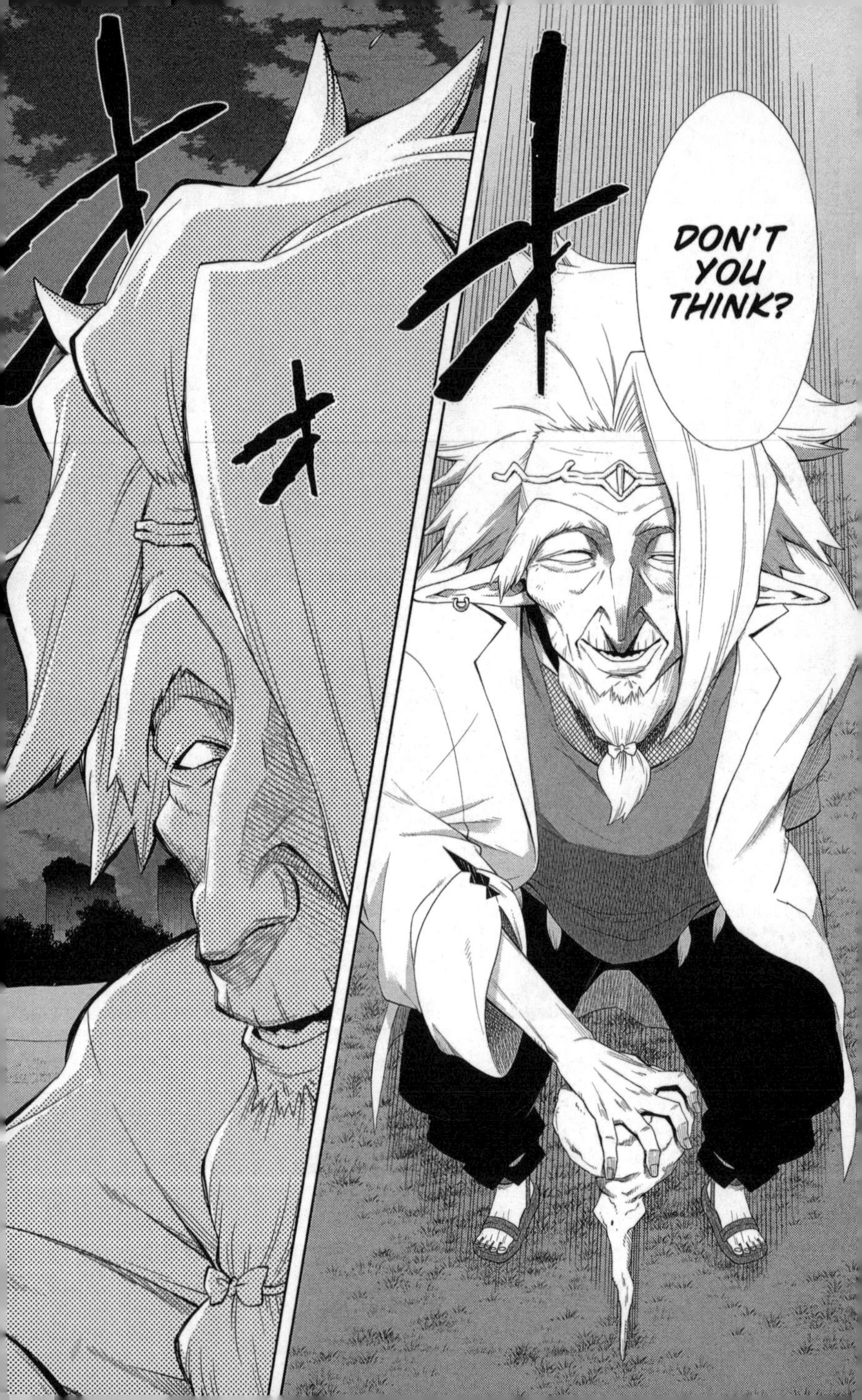
DON'T YOU THINK?

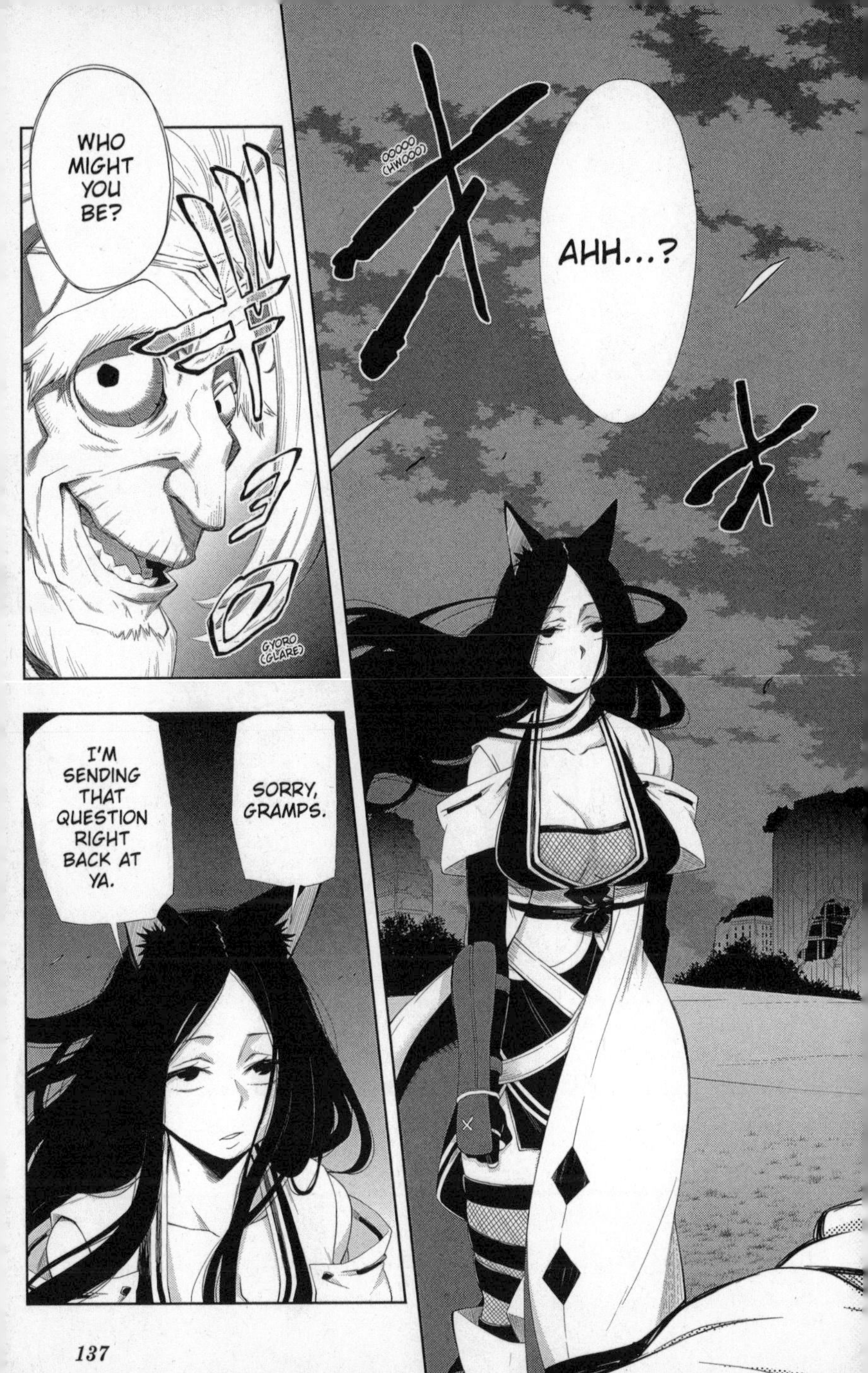
AHH...?
OOOOO (HWOOO)
WHO MIGHT YOU BE?
GYORO (GLARE)
SORRY, GRAMPS.
I'M SENDING THAT QUESTION RIGHT BACK AT YA.

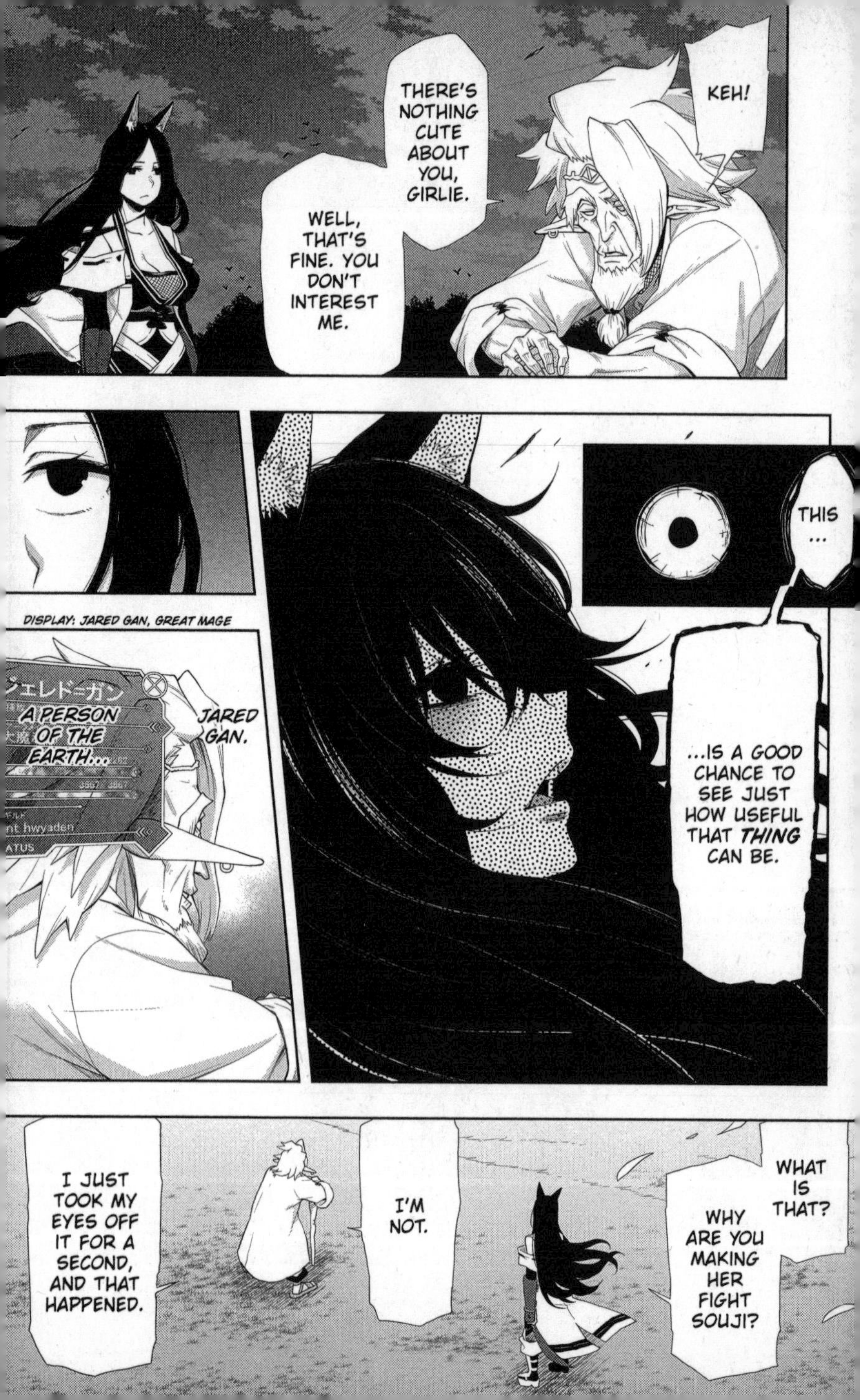
KEH!
THERE'S NOTHING CUTE ABOUT YOU, GIRLIE.
WELL, THAT'S FINE. YOU DON'T INTEREST ME.
THIS ...
...IS A GOOD CHANCE TO SEE JUST HOW USEFUL THAT *THING* CAN BE.
DISPLAY: JARED GAN, GREAT MAGE
ジェレド=ガン
A PERSON OF THE EARTH...
JARED GAN.
WHAT IS THAT?
WHY ARE YOU MAKING HER FIGHT SOUJI?
I'M NOT.
I JUST TOOK MY EYES OFF IT FOR A SECOND, AND THAT HAPPENED.

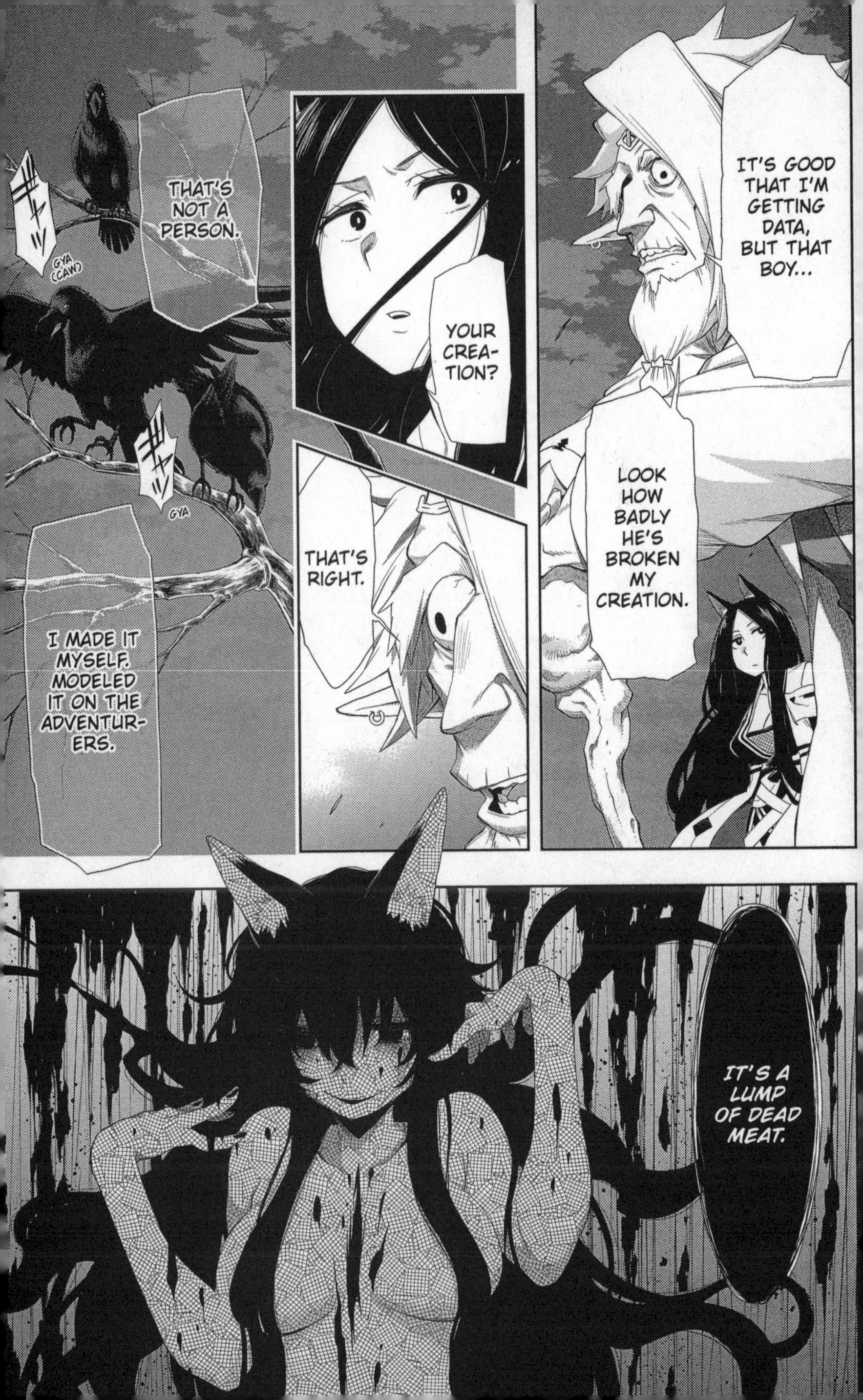
IT'S GOOD THAT I'M GETTING DATA, BUT THAT BOY...
LOOK HOW BADLY HE'S BROKEN MY CREATION.
YOUR CREATION?
THAT'S RIGHT.
THAT'S NOT A PERSON.
GYA (CAW)
GYA
I MADE IT MYSELF. MODELED IT ON THE ADVENTURERS.
IT'S A LUMP OF DEAD MEAT.

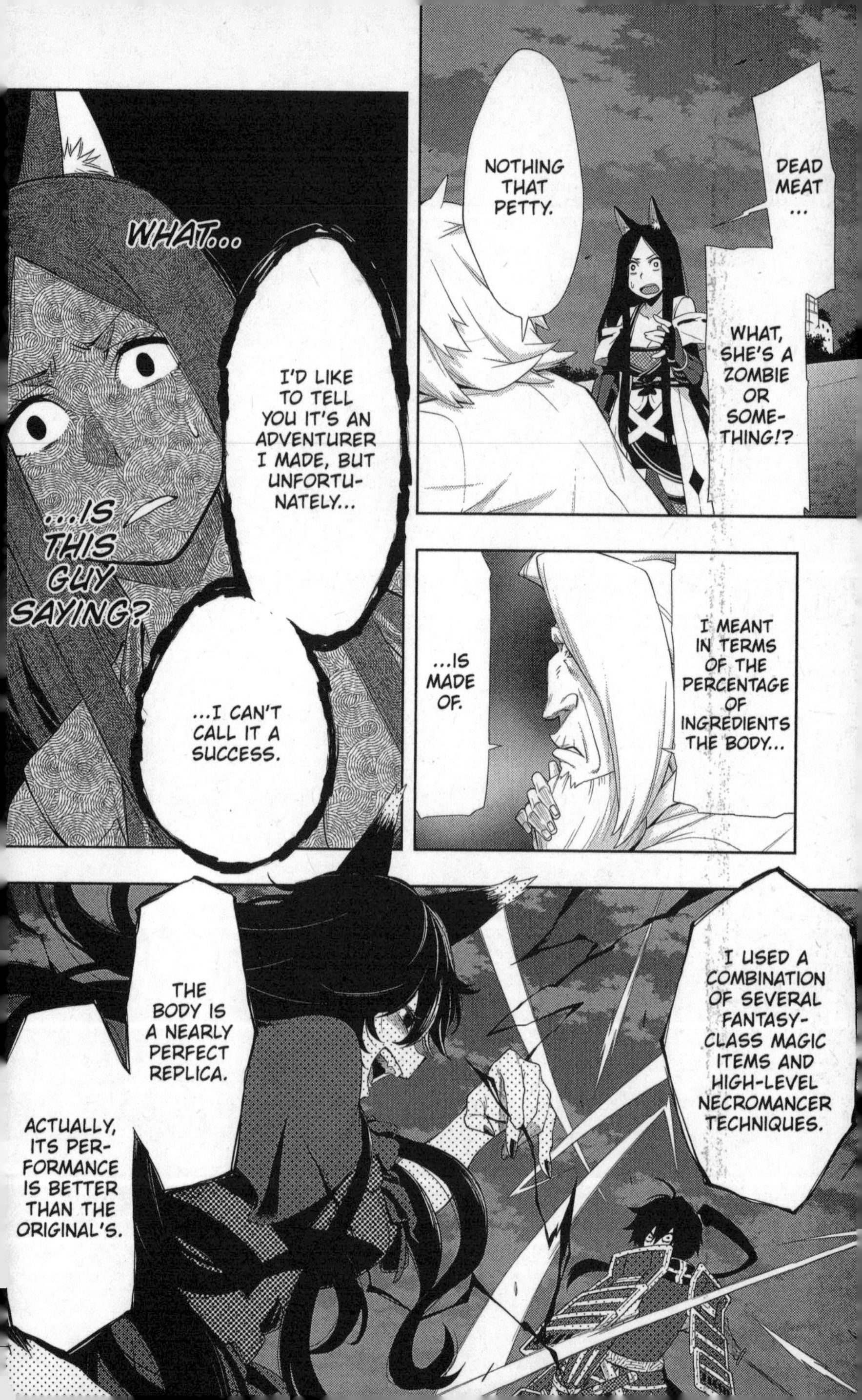
DEAD MEAT...
WHAT, SHE'S A ZOMBIE OR SOMETHING!?
NOTHING THAT PETTY.
I MEANT IN TERMS OF THE PERCENTAGE OF INGREDIENTS THE BODY...
...IS MADE OF.
I'D LIKE TO TELL YOU IT'S AN ADVENTURER I MADE, BUT UNFORTUNATELY...
...I CAN'T CALL IT A SUCCESS.
WHAT...
...IS THIS GUY SAYING?
I USED A COMBINATION OF SEVERAL FANTASY-CLASS MAGIC ITEMS AND HIGH-LEVEL NECROMANCER TECHNIQUES.
THE BODY IS A NEARLY PERFECT REPLICA.
ACTUALLY, ITS PERFORMANCE IS BETTER THAN THE ORIGINAL'S.

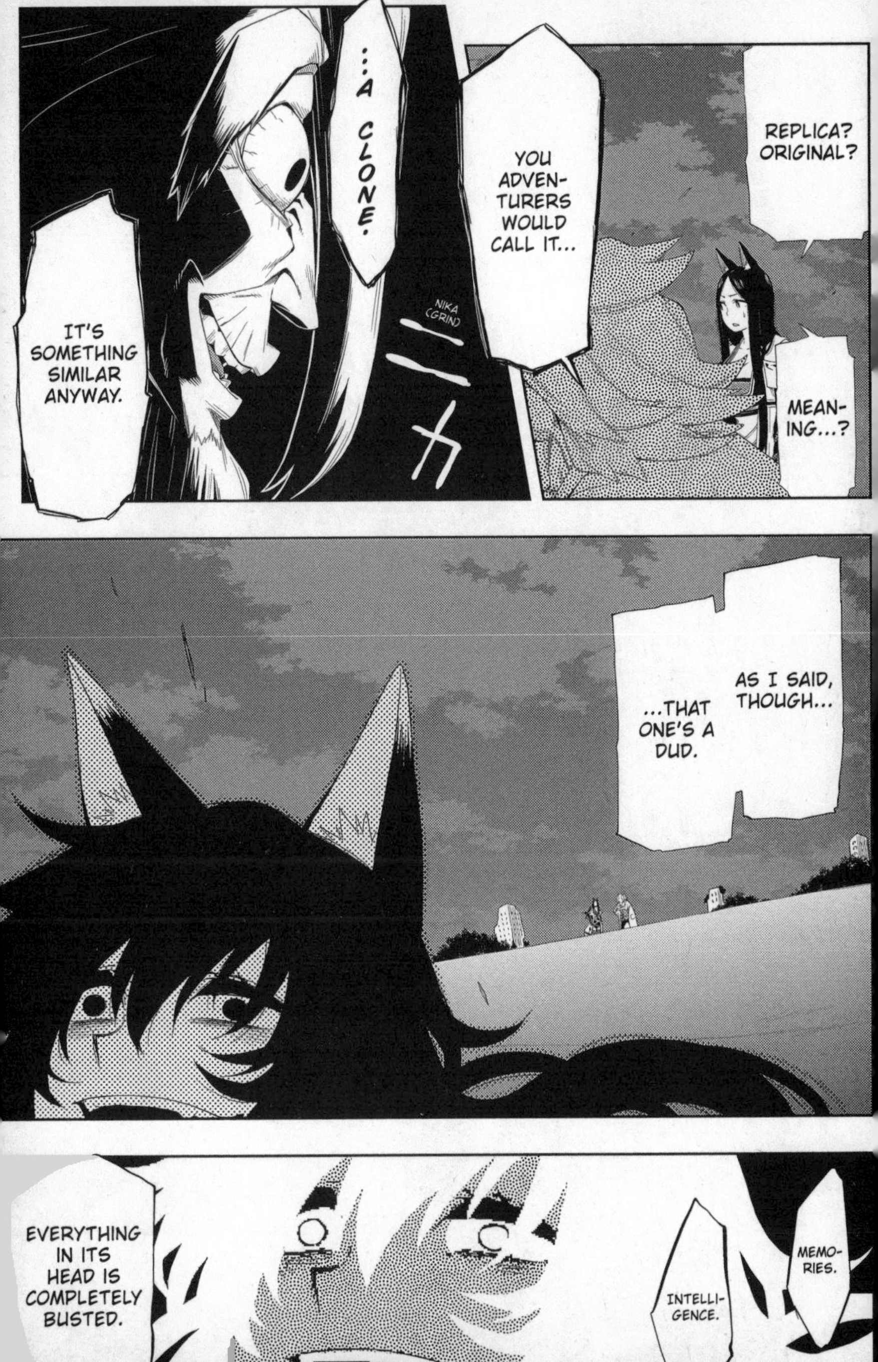
REPLICA? ORIGINAL?
MEAN-ING...?
YOU ADVEN-TURERS WOULD CALL IT...
...A CLONE.
NIKA (GRIN)
IT'S SOMETHING SIMILAR ANYWAY.
AS I SAID, THOUGH...
...THAT ONE'S A DUD.
MEMO-RIES.
INTELLI-GENCE.
EVERYTHING IN ITS HEAD IS COMPLETELY BUSTED.

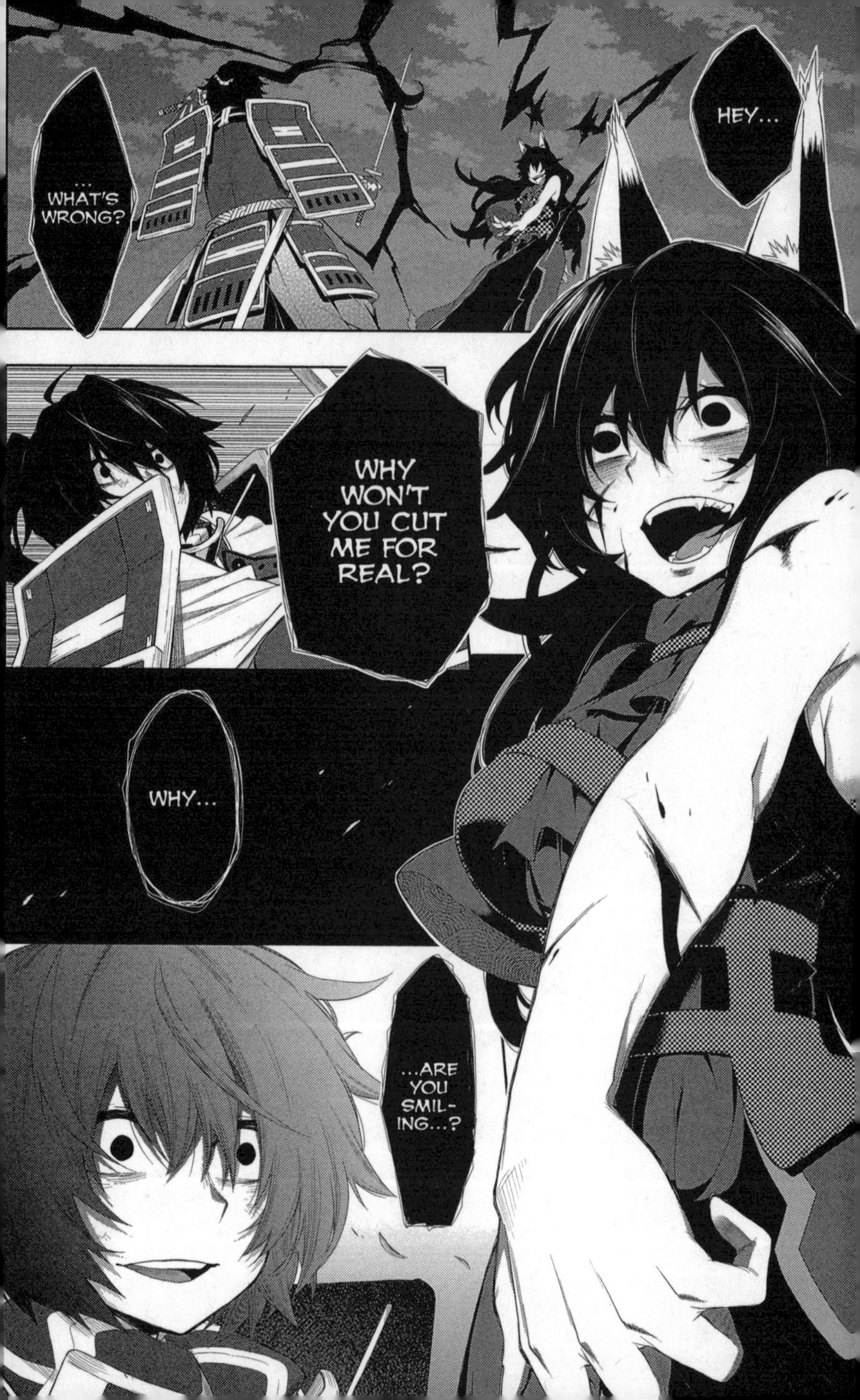
HEY...
...WHAT'S WRONG?
WHY WON'T YOU CUT ME FOR REAL?
WHY...
...ARE YOU SMIL-ING...?

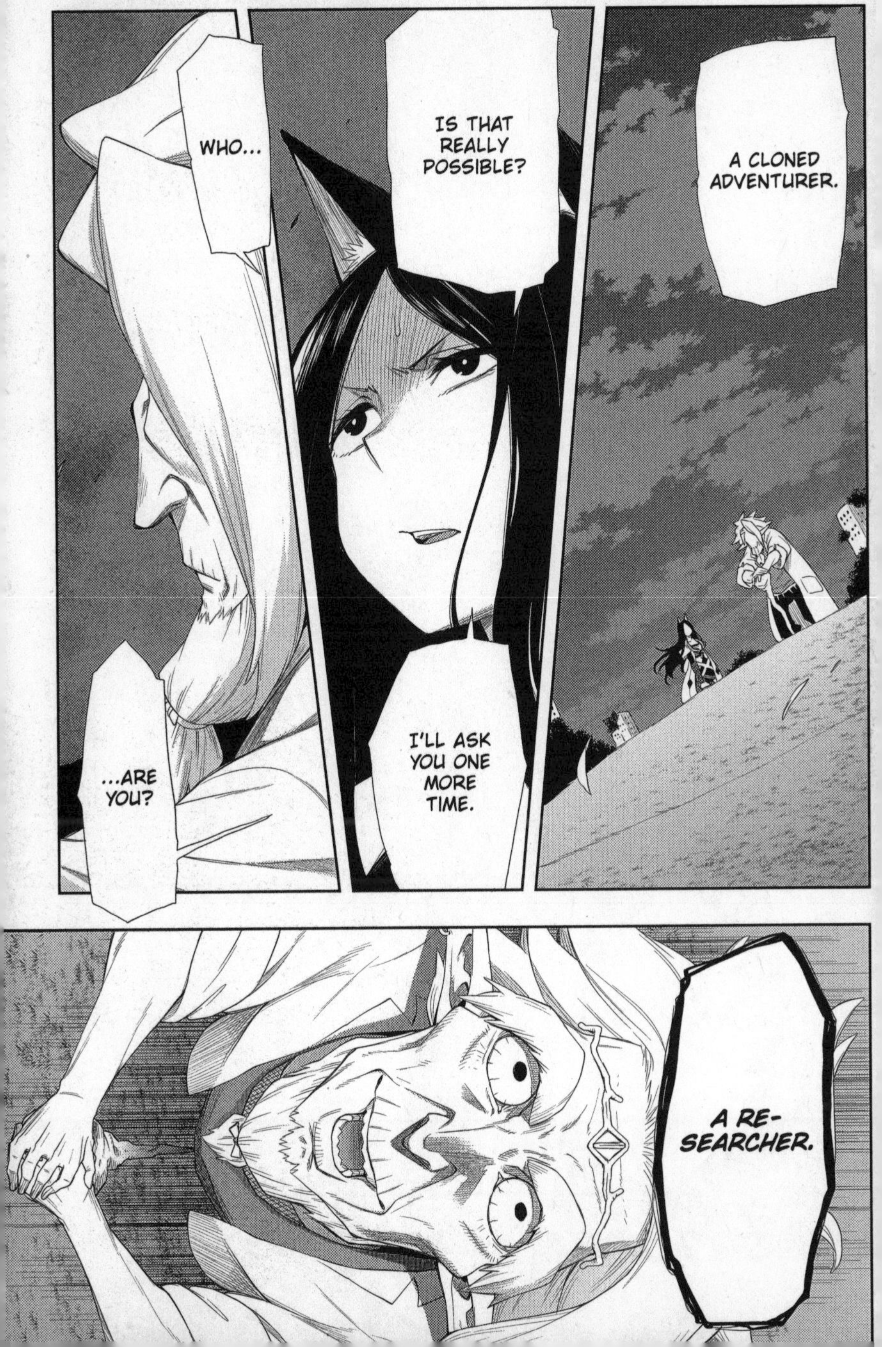

A CLONED ADVENTURER.
IS THAT REALLY POSSIBLE?
I'LL ASK YOU ONE MORE TIME.
WHO...
...ARE YOU?
A RE-SEARCHER.

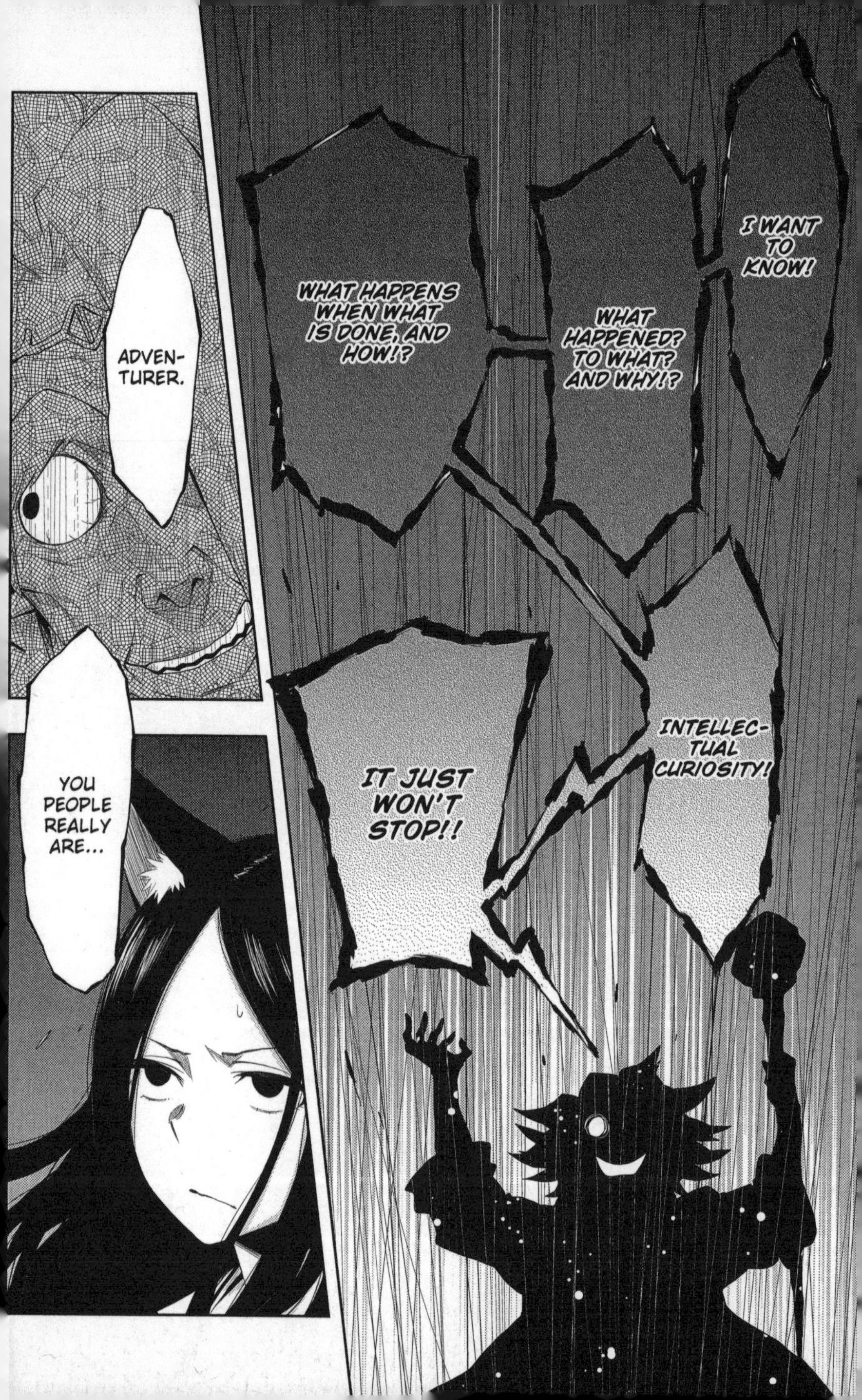
I WANT TO KNOW!
WHAT HAPPENED? TO WHAT? AND WHY!?
WHAT HAPPENS WHEN WHAT IS DONE, AND HOW!?
INTELLEC-TUAL CURIOSITY!
IT JUST WON'T STOP!!
ADVEN-TURER.
YOU PEOPLE REALLY ARE...

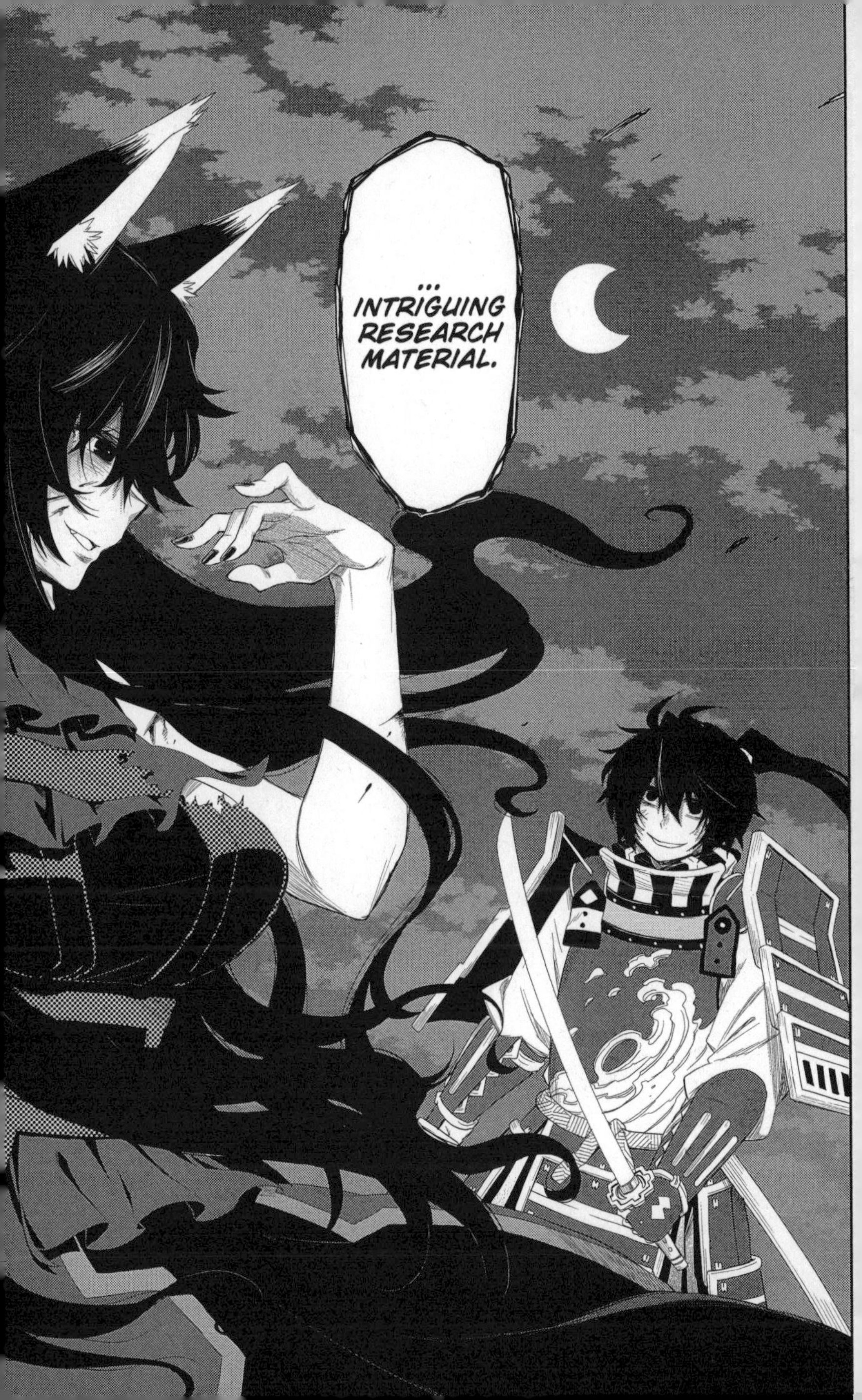
...INTRIGUING RESEARCH MATERIAL.

LOG HORIZON

THE WEST WIND BRIGADE

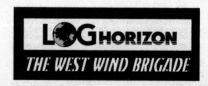

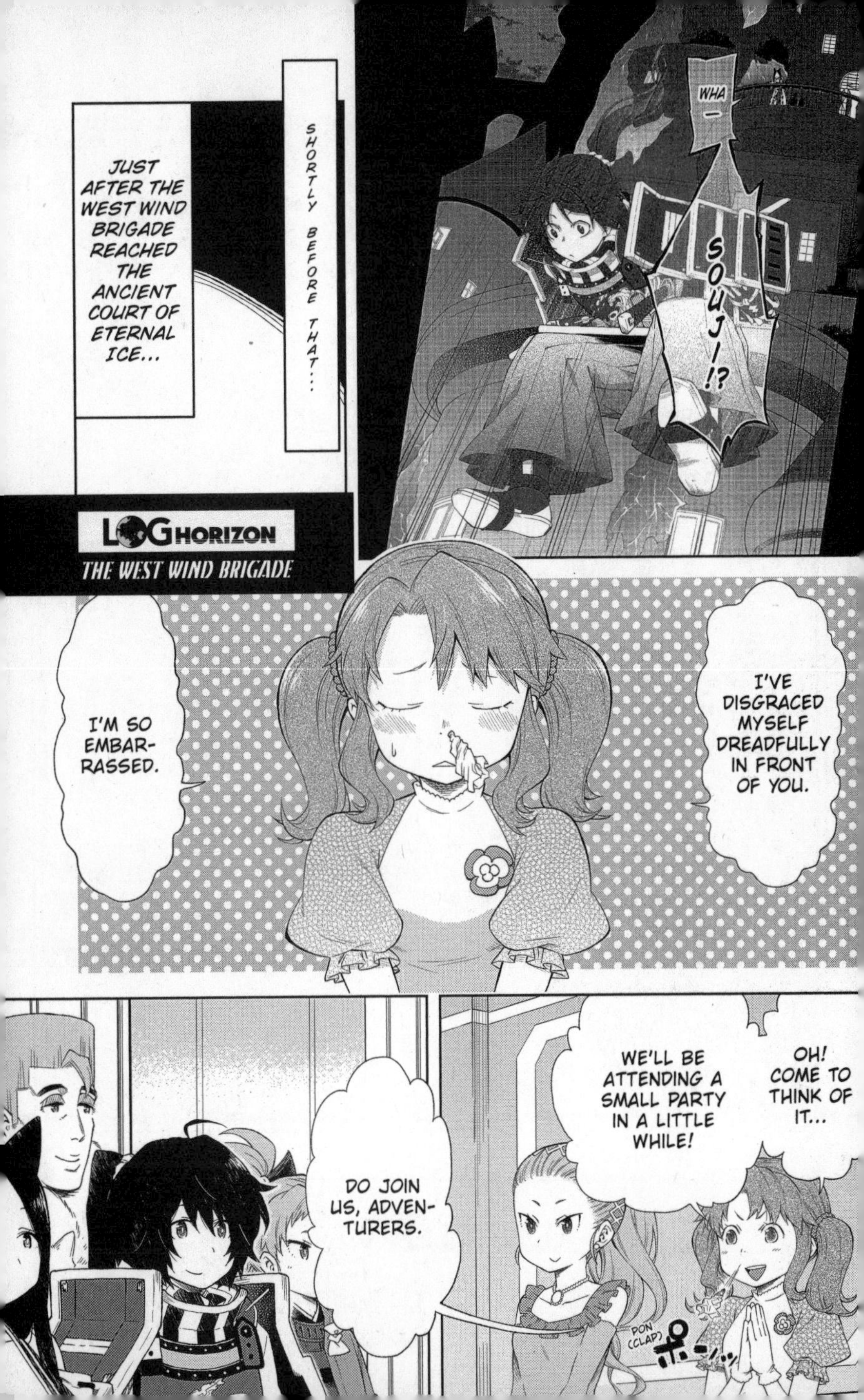
WHA—
SOUJI!?
SHORTLY BEFORE THAT...
JUST AFTER THE WEST WIND BRIGADE REACHED THE ANCIENT COURT OF ETERNAL ICE...
LOG HORIZON
THE WEST WIND BRIGADE
I'VE DISGRACED MYSELF DREADFULLY IN FRONT OF YOU.
I'M SO EMBARRASSED.
OH! COME TO THINK OF IT...
WE'LL BE ATTENDING A SMALL PARTY IN A LITTLE WHILE!
PON (CLAP)
DO JOIN US, ADVENTURERS.

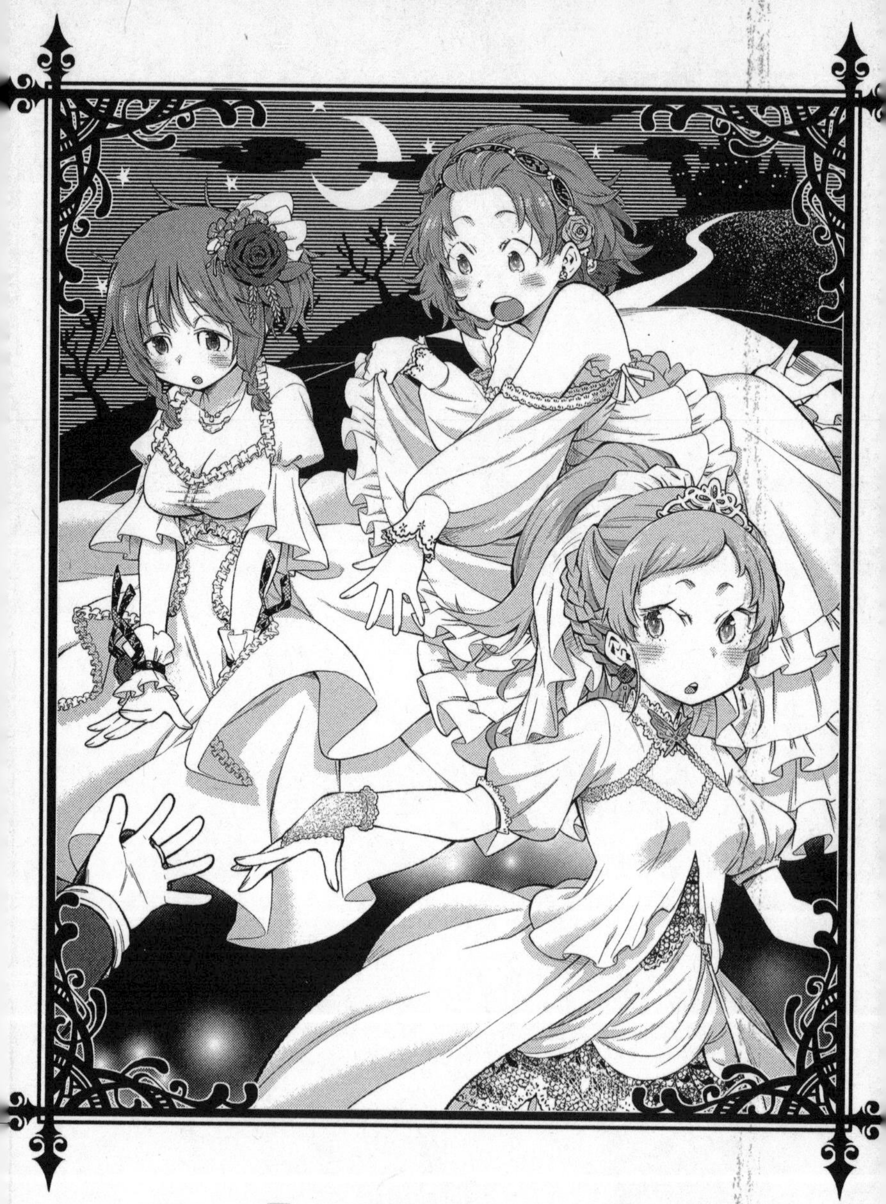

CHAPTER : 40.5 Wait Time

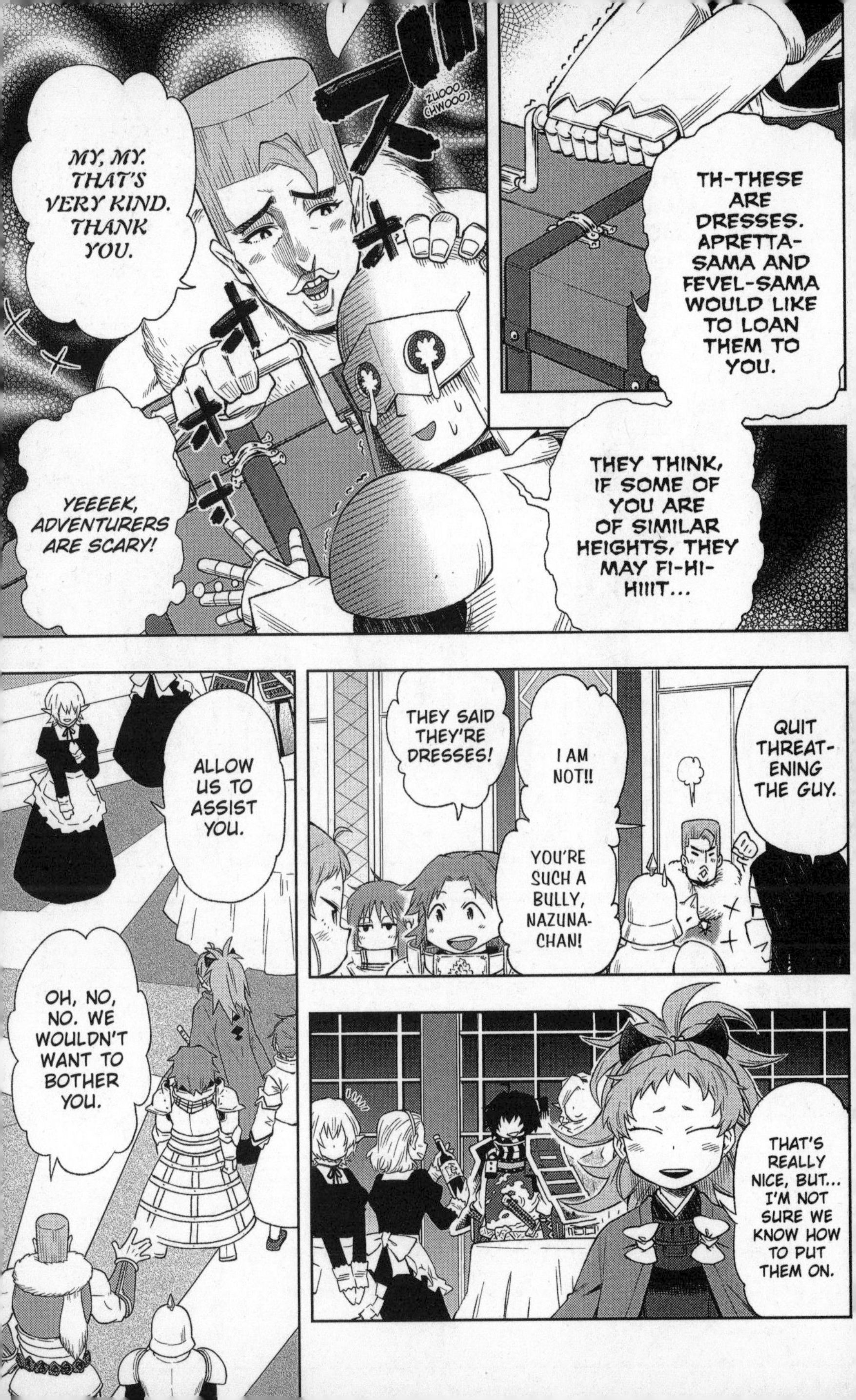
TH-THESE ARE DRESSES. APRETTA-SAMA AND FEVEL-SAMA WOULD LIKE TO LOAN THEM TO YOU.
THEY THINK, IF SOME OF YOU ARE OF SIMILAR HEIGHTS, THEY MAY FI-HI-HIIIT...
ZUOOO (CHWOOO)
MY, MY. THAT'S VERY KIND. THANK YOU.
YEEEEK, ADVENTURERS ARE SCARY!
QUIT THREATEN-ING THE GUY.
I AM NOT!!
THEY SAID THEY'RE DRESSES!
YOU'RE SUCH A BULLY, NAZUNA-CHAN!
THAT'S REALLY NICE, BUT... I'M NOT SURE WE KNOW HOW TO PUT THEM ON.
ALLOW US TO ASSIST YOU.
OH, NO, NO. WE WOULDN'T WANT TO BOTHER YOU.

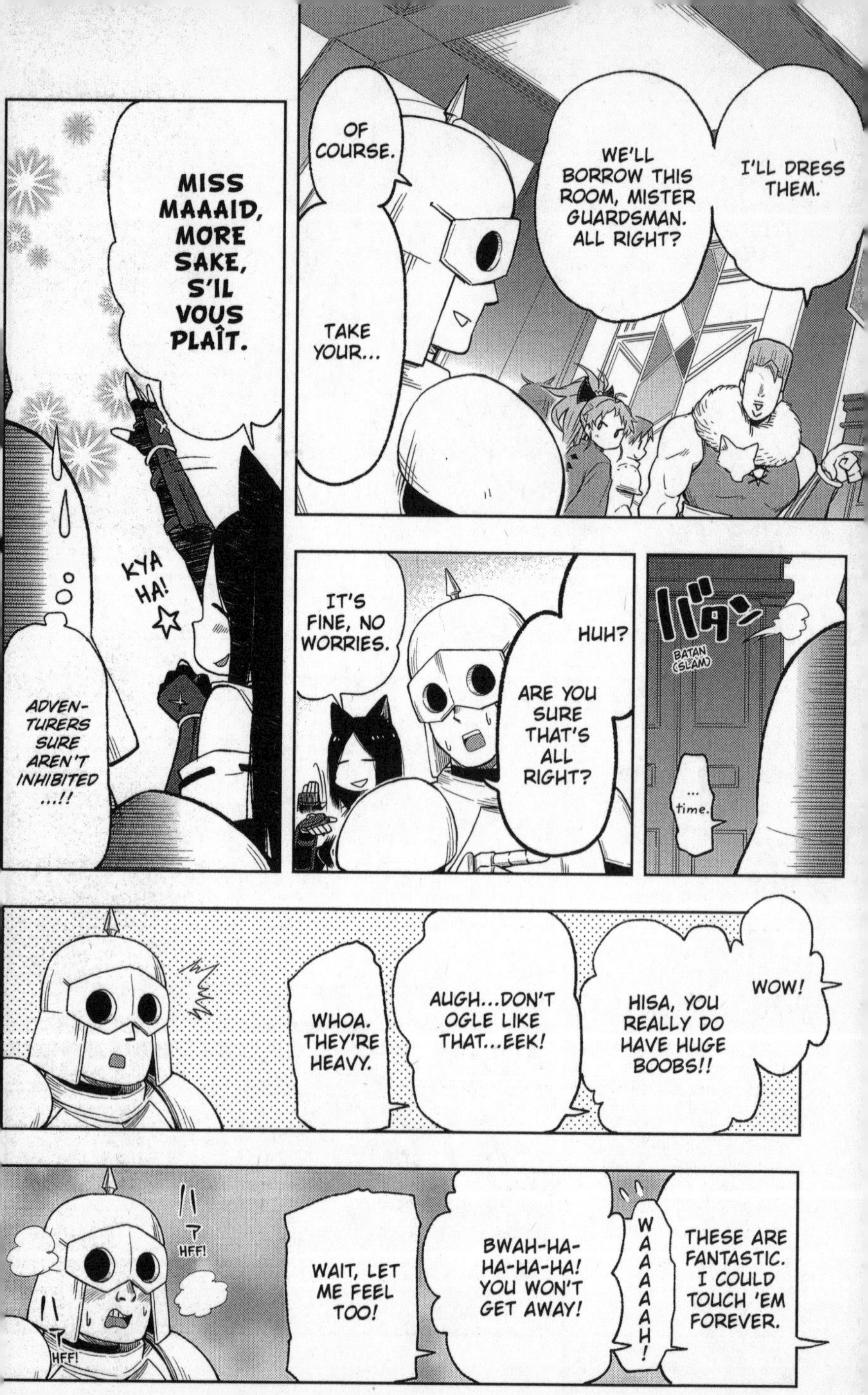

I'LL DRESS THEM.
WE'LL BORROW THIS ROOM, MISTER GUARDSMAN. ALL RIGHT?
OF COURSE.
TAKE YOUR...
バタン
BATAN (SLAM)
...time.
HUH?
ARE YOU SURE THAT'S ALL RIGHT?
IT'S FINE, NO WORRIES.
MISS MAAAID, MORE SAKE, S'IL VOUS PLAÎT.
KYA HA!
ADVEN-TURERS SURE AREN'T INHIBITED...!!
WOW!
HISA, YOU REALLY DO HAVE HUGE BOOBS!!
AUGH...DON'T OGLE LIKE THAT...EEK!
WHOA. THEY'RE HEAVY.
THESE ARE FANTASTIC. I COULD TOUCH 'EM FOREVER.
WAAAAAAH!
BWAH-HA-HA-HA-HA! YOU WON'T GET AWAY!
WAIT, LET ME FEEL TOO!
ハァ
HFF!
ハァ
HFF!

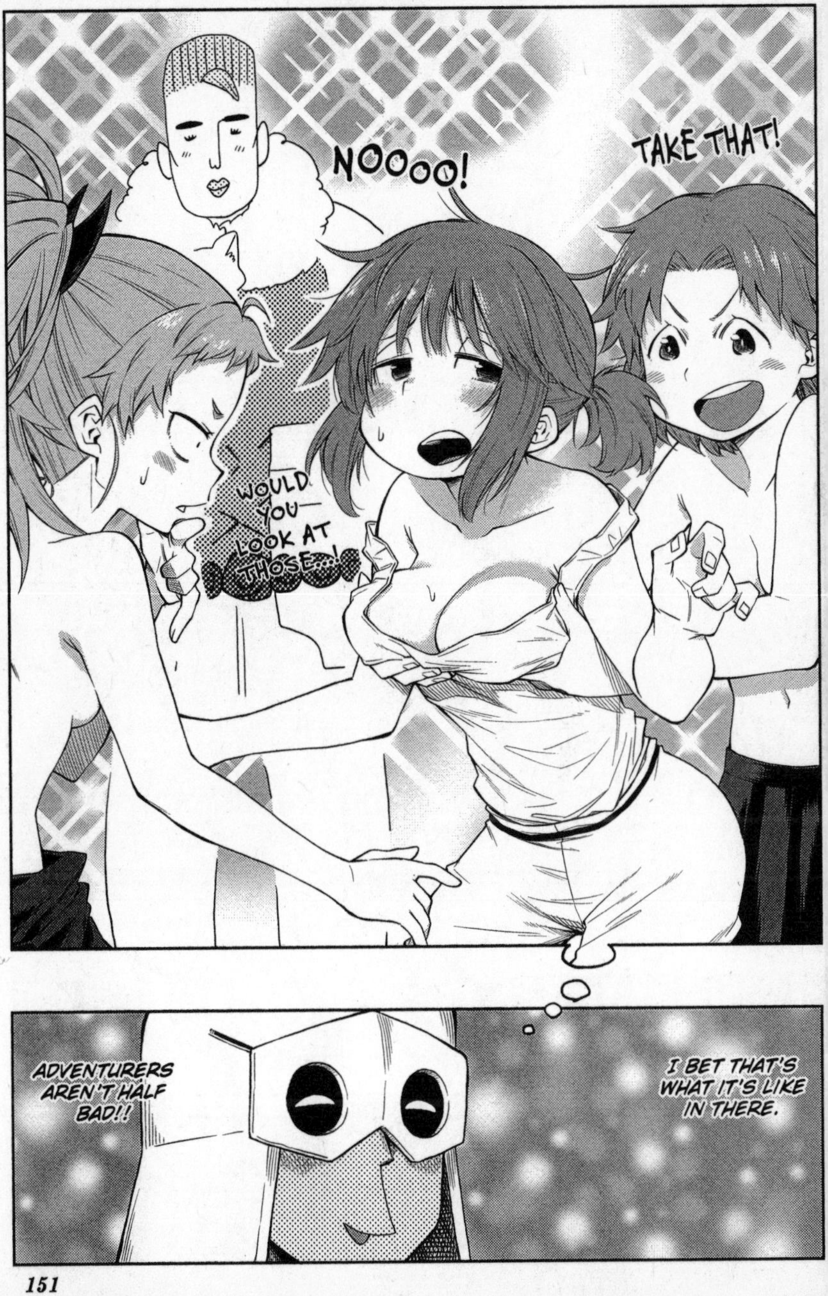
TAKE THAT!
NOOOO!
WOULD YOU LOOK AT THOSE...!
I BET THAT'S WHAT IT'S LIKE IN THERE.
ADVENTURERS AREN'T HALF BAD!!

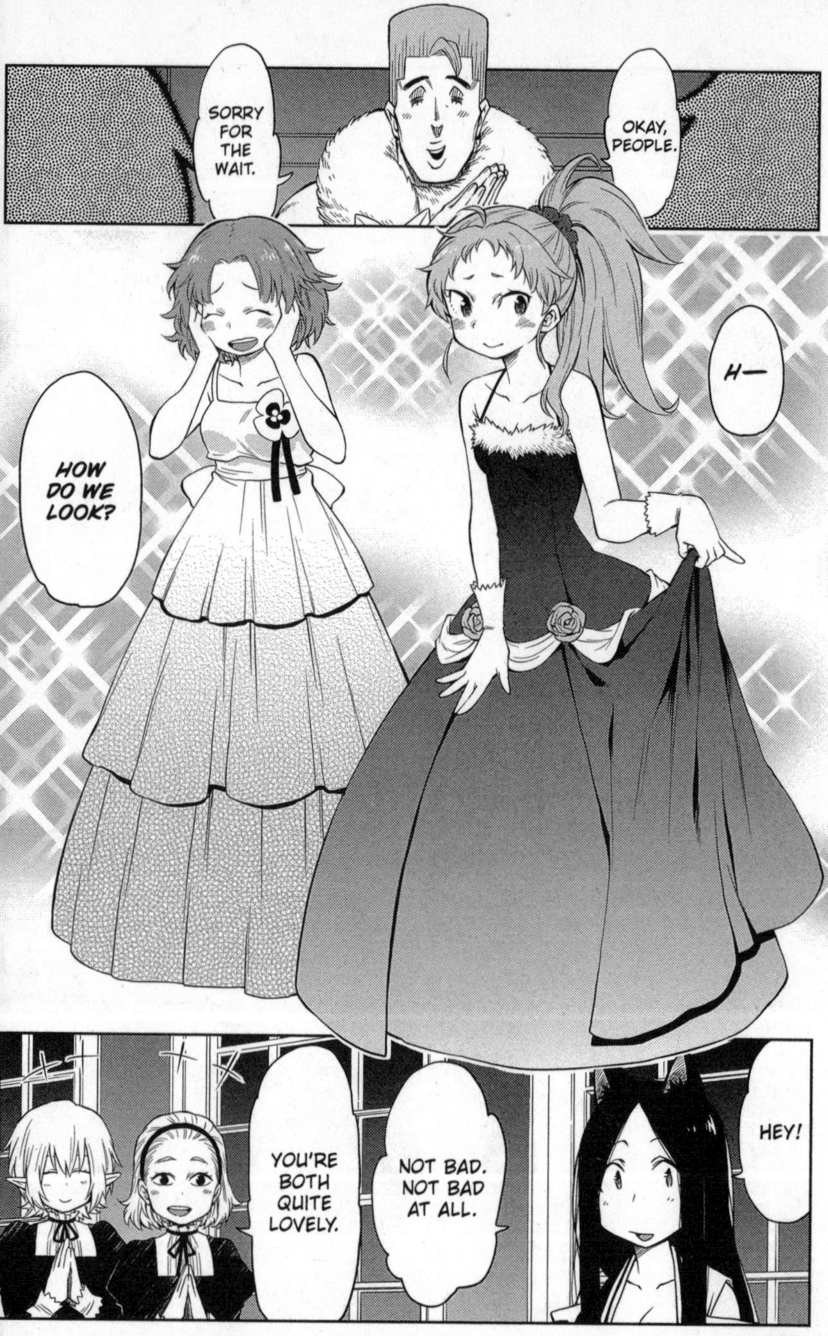
OKAY, PEOPLE.
SORRY FOR THE WAIT.
H—
HOW DO WE LOOK?
HEY!
NOT BAD. NOT BAD AT ALL.
YOU'RE BOTH QUITE LOVELY.

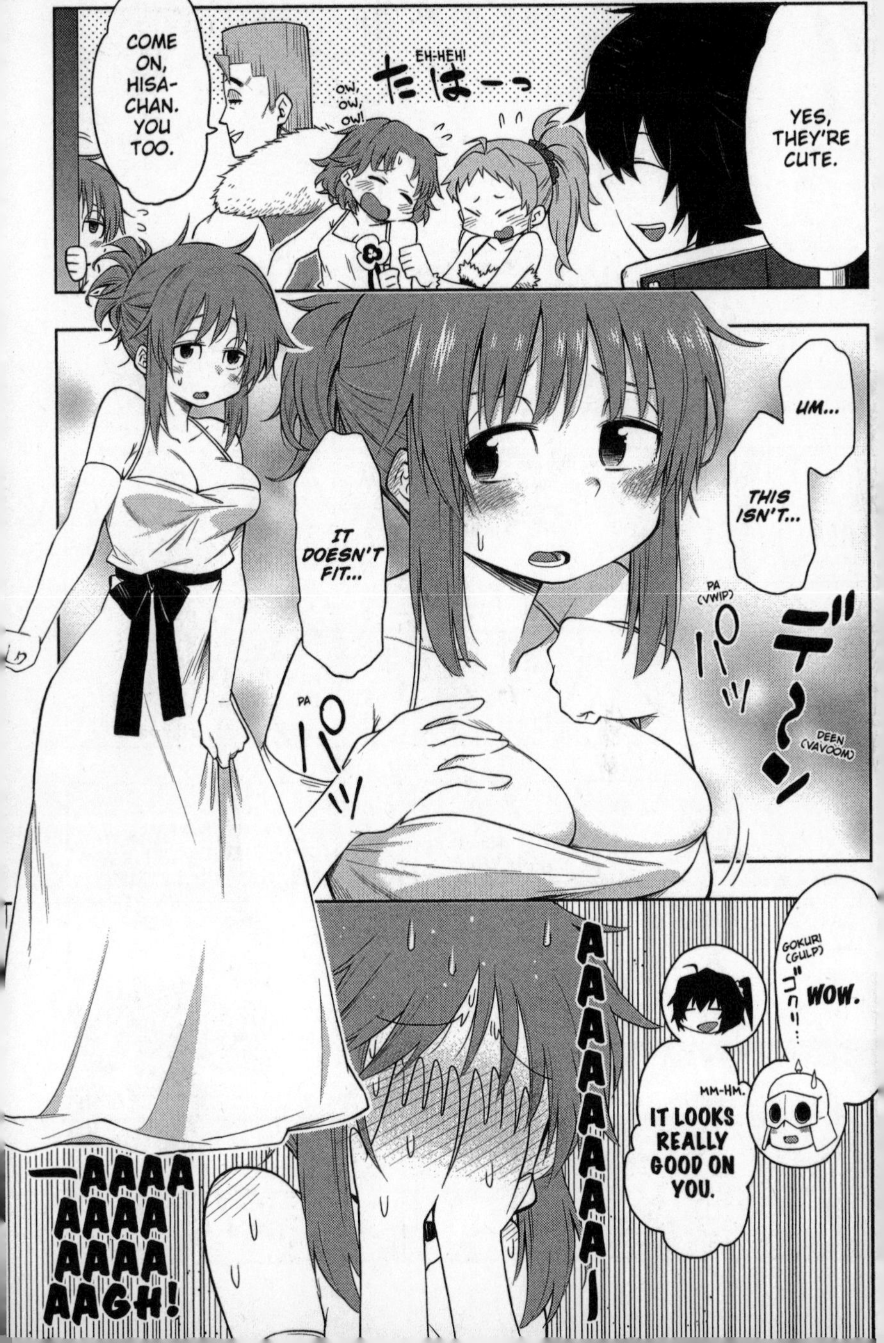
YES, THEY'RE CUTE.
EH-HEH!
たはーっ
OW, OW, OW!
COME ON, HISA-CHAN. YOU TOO.
UM...
THIS ISN'T...
デ〜ン
DEEN (VAVOOM)
パッ
PA (VWIP)
IT DOESN'T FIT...
パッ
PA
WOW.
ゴクリ…
GOKURI (GULP)
MM-HM.
IT LOOKS REALLY GOOD ON YOU.
AAAAAAAAAA!
—AAAA AAAA AAAA AAGH!

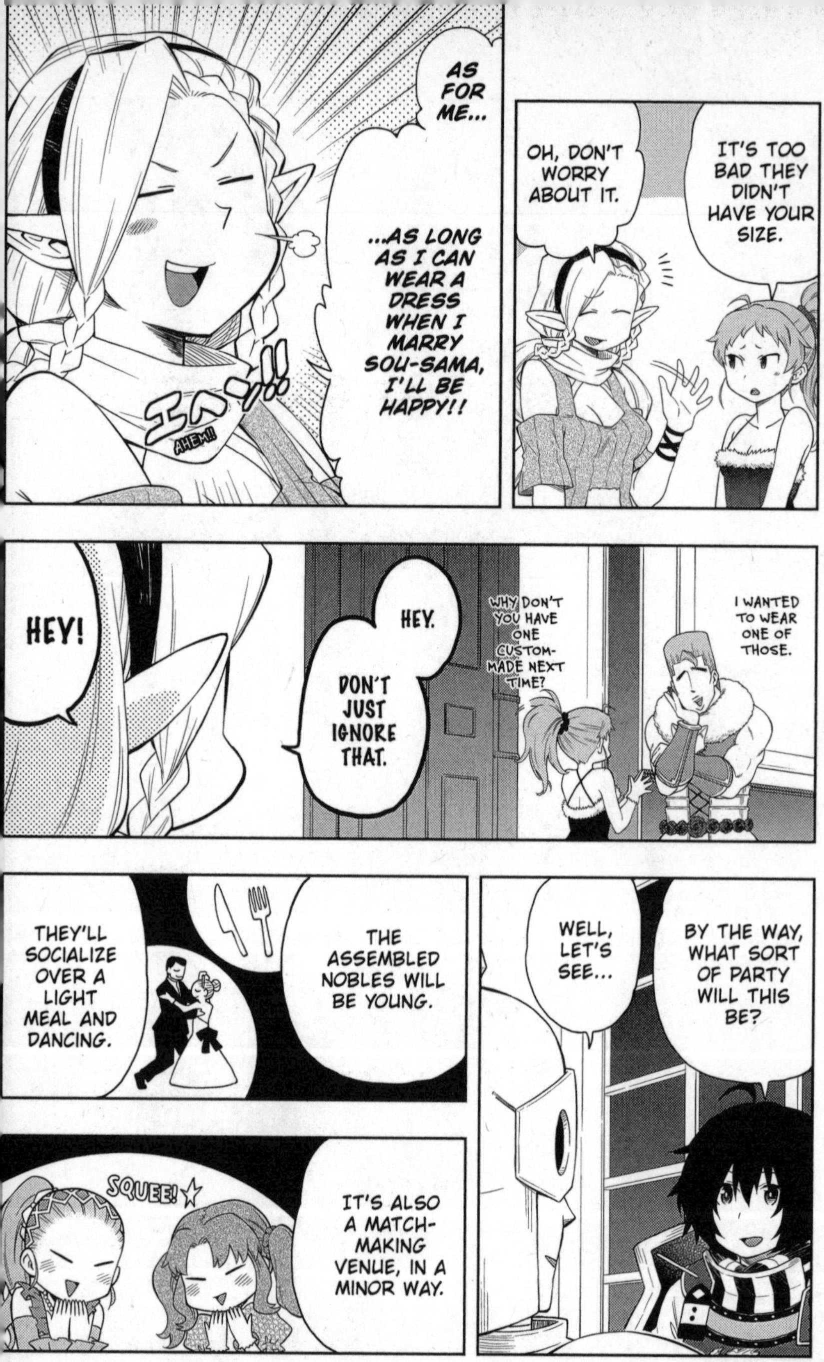
IT'S TOO BAD THEY DIDN'T HAVE YOUR SIZE.
OH, DON'T WORRY ABOUT IT.
AS FOR ME...
...AS LONG AS I CAN WEAR A DRESS WHEN I MARRY SOU-SAMA, I'LL BE HAPPY!!
エヘン!!
AHEM!!
I WANTED TO WEAR ONE OF THOSE.
WHY DON'T YOU HAVE ONE CUSTOM-MADE NEXT TIME?
HEY.
DON'T JUST IGNORE THAT.
HEY!
BY THE WAY, WHAT SORT OF PARTY WILL THIS BE?
WELL, LET'S SEE...
THE ASSEMBLED NOBLES WILL BE YOUNG.
THEY'LL SOCIALIZE OVER A LIGHT MEAL AND DANCING.
IT'S ALSO A MATCH-MAKING VENUE, IN A MINOR WAY.
SQUEE!

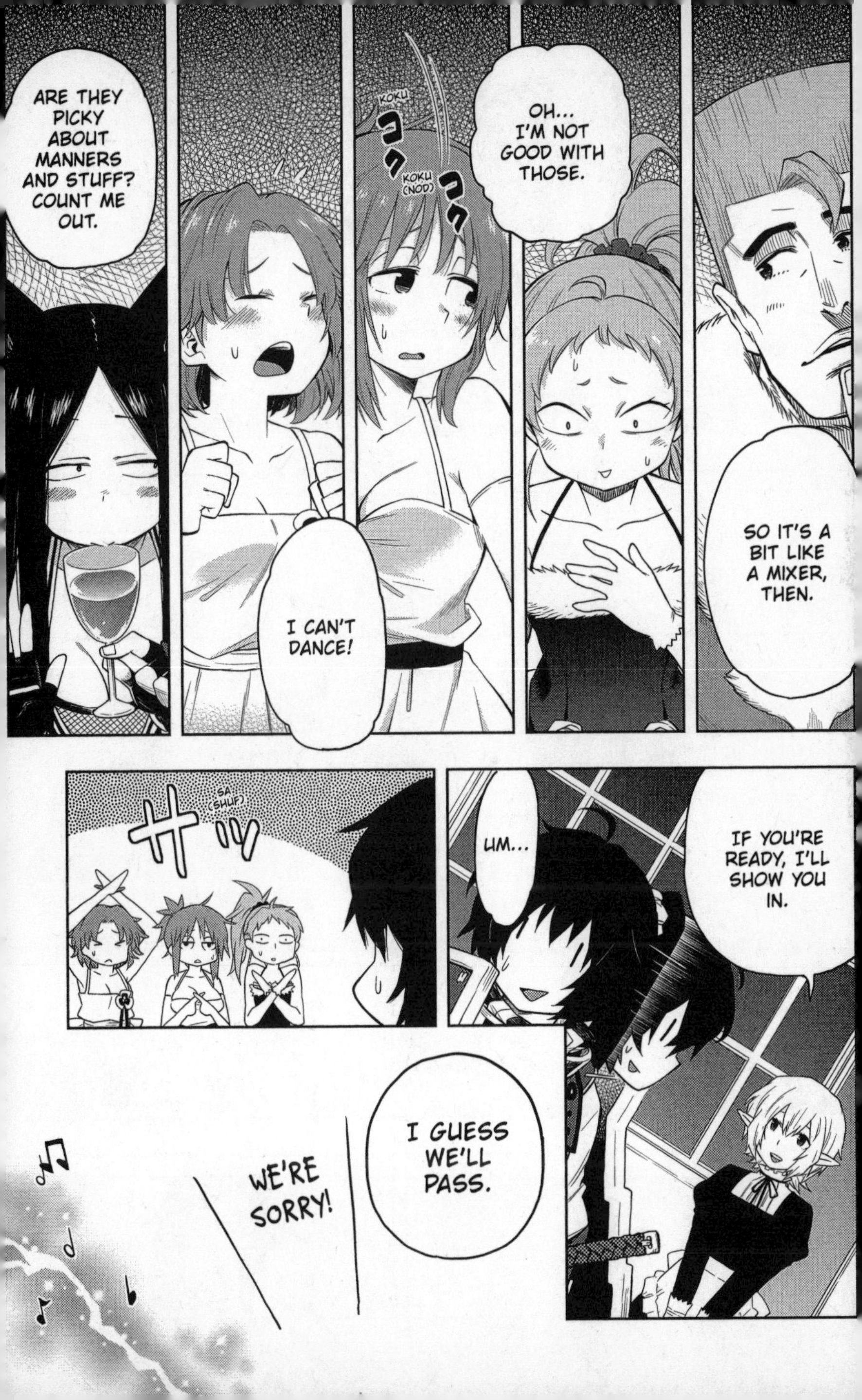
SO IT'S A BIT LIKE A MIXER, THEN.
OH... I'M NOT GOOD WITH THOSE.
KOKU
KOKU (NOD)
I CAN'T DANCE!
ARE THEY PICKY ABOUT MANNERS AND STUFF? COUNT ME OUT.
IF YOU'RE READY, I'LL SHOW YOU IN.
UM...
SA (SHUF)
I GUESS WE'LL PASS.
WE'RE SORRY!

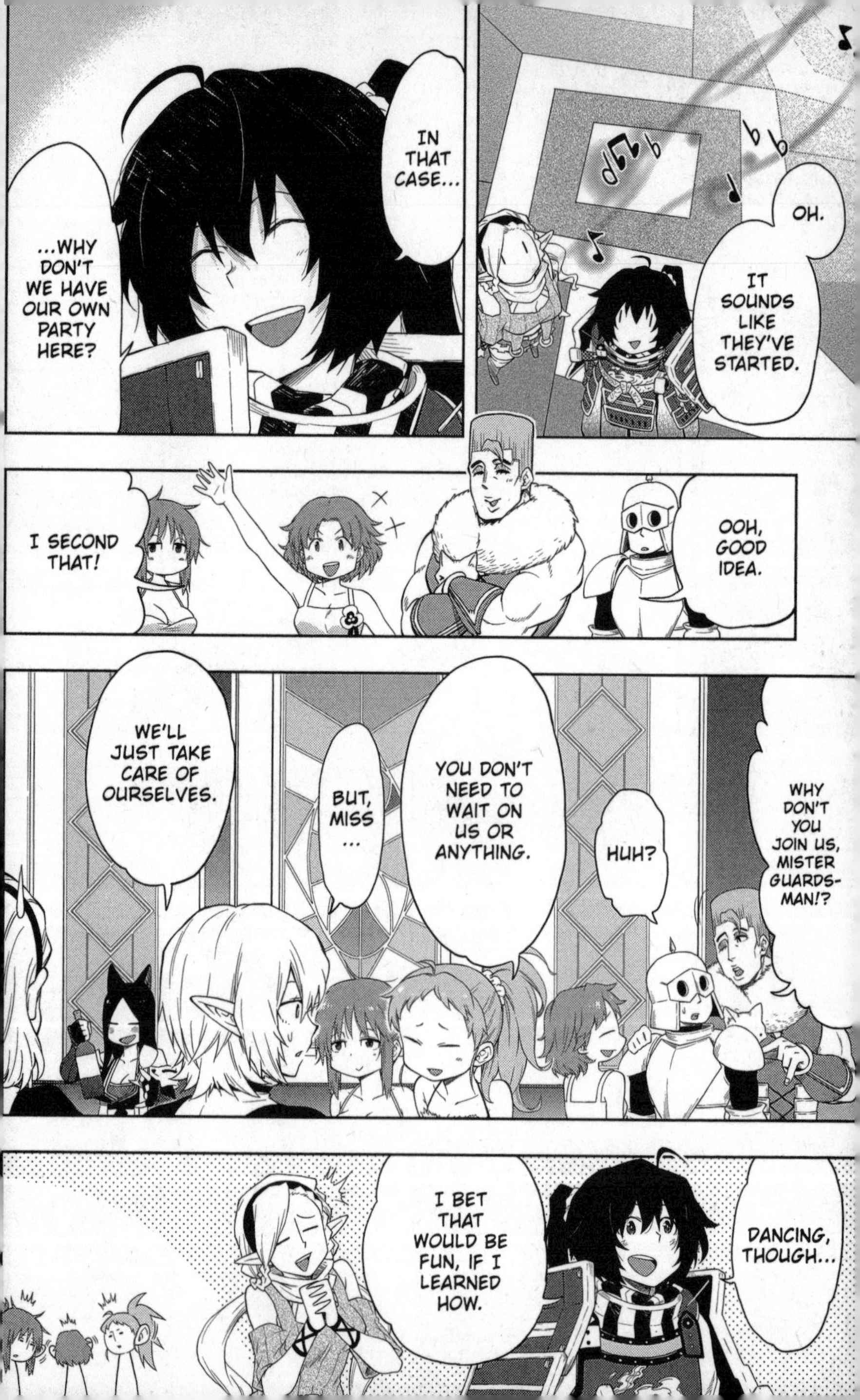
OH.
IT SOUNDS LIKE THEY'VE STARTED.
IN THAT CASE...
...WHY DON'T WE HAVE OUR OWN PARTY HERE?
OOH, GOOD IDEA.
I SECOND THAT!
WHY DON'T YOU JOIN US, MISTER GUARDS-MAN!?
HUH?
YOU DON'T NEED TO WAIT ON US OR ANYTHING.
BUT, MISS...
WE'LL JUST TAKE CARE OF OURSELVES.
DANCING, THOUGH...
I BET THAT WOULD BE FUN, IF I LEARNED HOW.

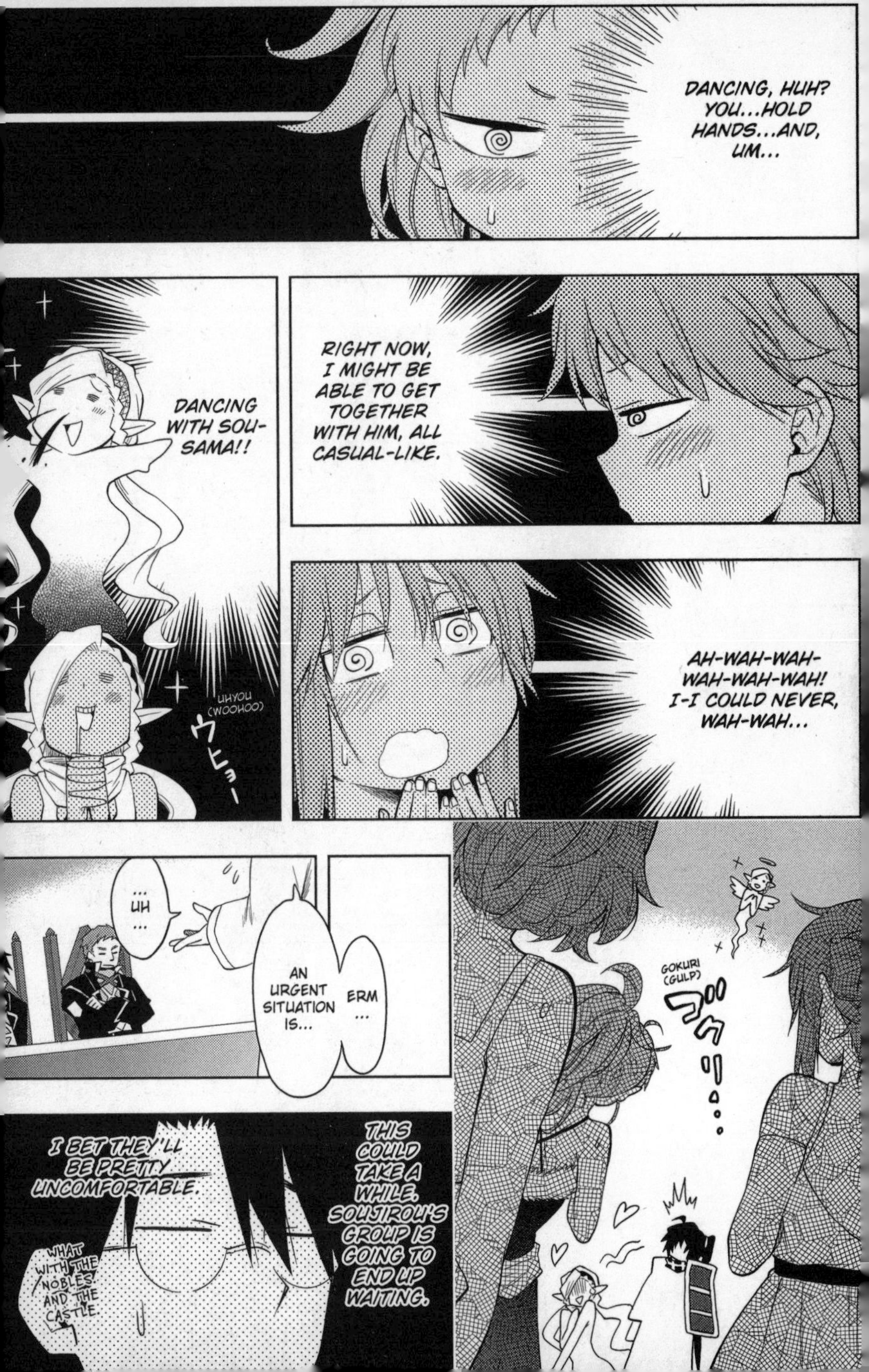
DANCING, HUH? YOU...HOLD HANDS...AND, UM...
RIGHT NOW, I MIGHT BE ABLE TO GET TOGETHER WITH HIM, ALL CASUAL-LIKE.
AH-WAH-WAH-WAH-WAH-WAH! I-I COULD NEVER, WAH-WAH...
DANCING WITH SOU-SAMA!!
UHYOU (WOOHOO)
ウヒョー
GOKURI (GULP)
ゴクリ
ERM...
AN URGENT SITUATION IS...
...UH...
THIS COULD TAKE A WHILE. SOUJIROU'S GROUP IS GOING TO END UP WAITING.
I BET THEY'LL BE PRETTY UNCOMFORTABLE.
WHAT WITH THE NOBLES AND THE CASTLE.

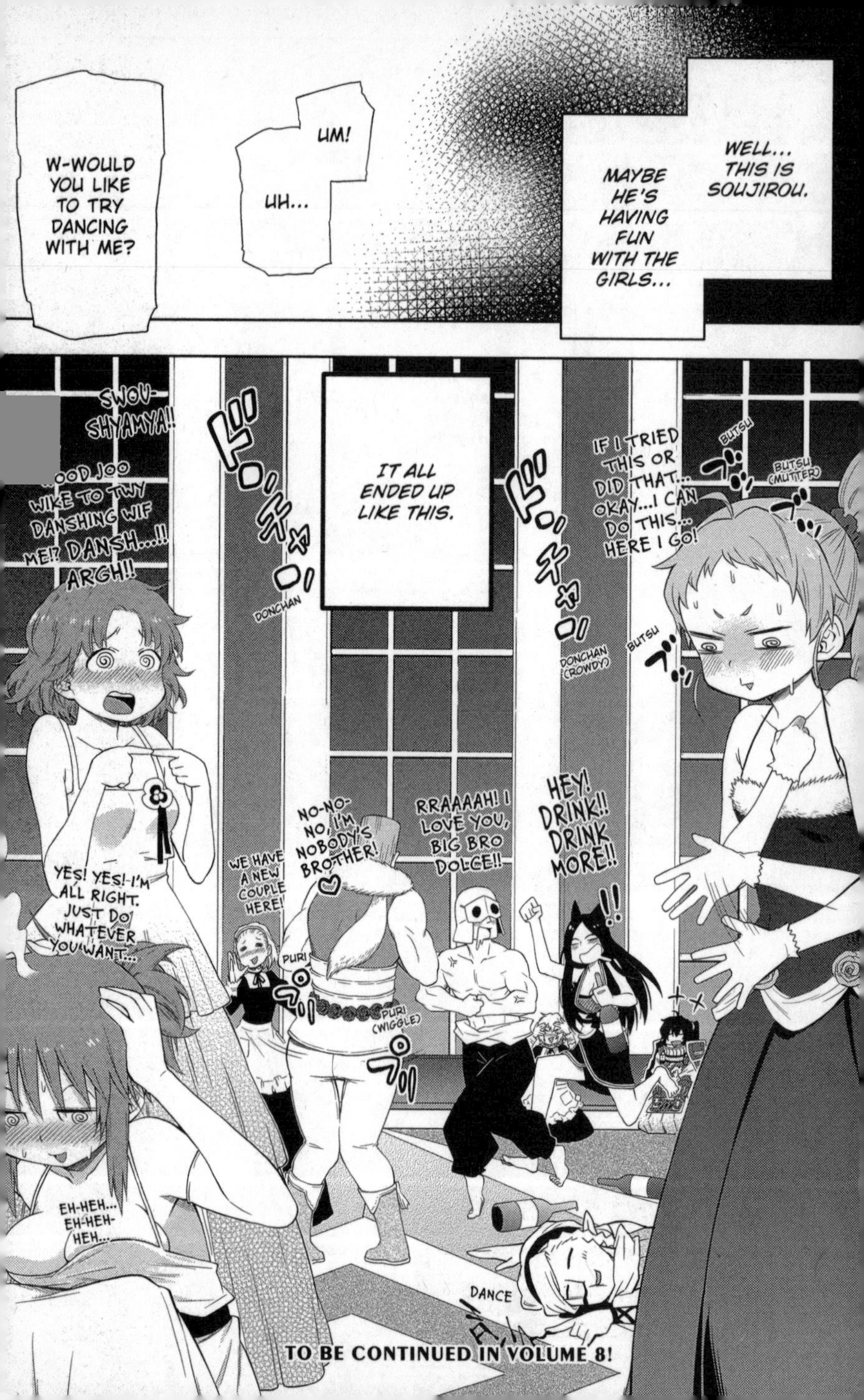
WELL... THIS IS SOUJIROU.
MAYBE HE'S HAVING FUN WITH THE GIRLS...
UM!
UH...
W-WOULD YOU LIKE TO TRY DANCING WITH ME?
IF I TRIED THIS OR DID THAT... OKAY...I CAN DO THIS... HERE I GO!
BUTSU
BUTSU (MUTTER)
BUTSU
DONCHAN (ROWDY)
IT ALL ENDED UP LIKE THIS.
DONCHAN
SWOU-SHYAMYA!!
...OOD JOO WIKE TO TWY DANSHING WIF ME!? DANSH...!! ARGH!!
HEY! DRINK!! DRINK MORE!!
!!
RRAAAAH! I LOVE YOU, BIG BRO DOLCE!!
NO-NO-NO, I'M NOBODY'S BROTHER!
WE HAVE A NEW COUPLE HERE!
PURI
PURI (WIGGLE)
YES! YES! I'M ALL RIGHT. JUST DO WHATEVER YOU WANT...
DANCE
EH-HEH... EH-HEH-HEH...
TO BE CONTINUED IN VOLUME 8!

LOG HORIZON

THE WEST WIND BRIGADE

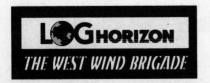

BONUS MANGA

HORROR GHOULRIZON

~ THE ROTTEN MEAT PARADE ~

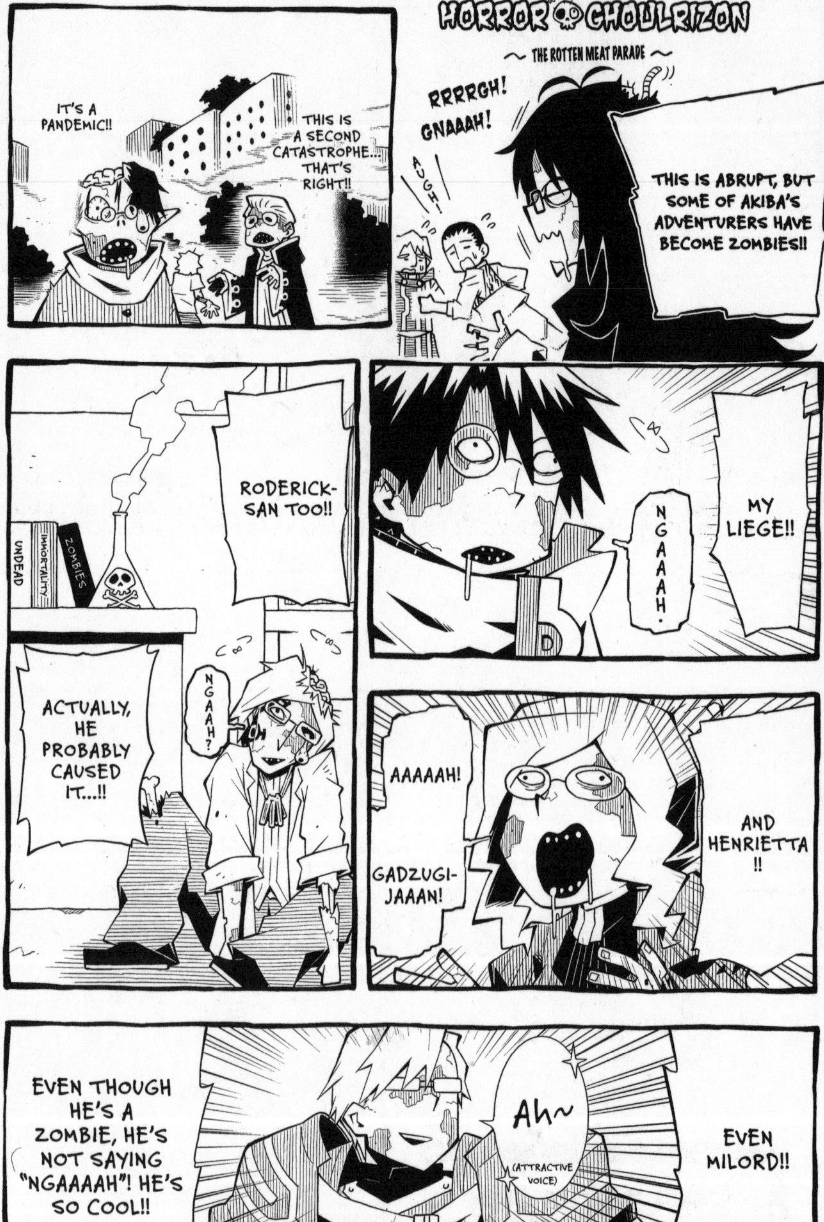
THIS IS ABRUPT, BUT SOME OF AKIBA'S ADVENTURERS HAVE BECOME ZOMBIES!!
RRRRGH!
GNAAAH!
AUGH!
THIS IS A SECOND CATASTROPHE... THAT'S RIGHT!!
IT'S A PANDEMIC!!
MY LIEGE!!
NGAAAAH.
AND HENRIETTA!!
AAAAAH!
GADZUGI-JAAAN!
RODERICK-SAN TOO!!
ZOMBIES
IMMORTALITY
UNDEAD
NGAAAH?
ACTUALLY, HE PROBABLY CAUSED IT...!!
EVEN MILORD!!
Ah~
(ATTRACTIVE VOICE)
EVEN THOUGH HE'S A ZOMBIE, HE'S NOT SAYING "NGAAAAH"! HE'S SO COOL!!

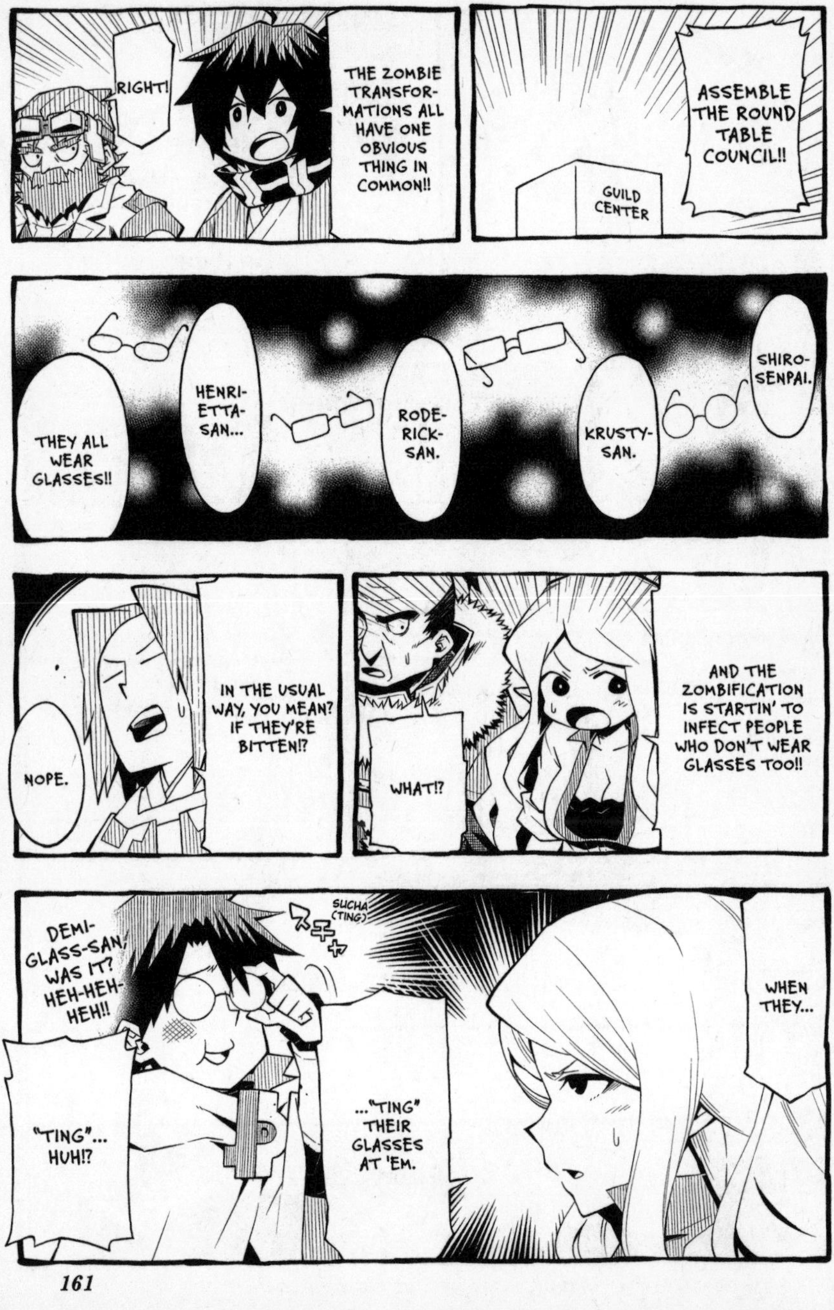
ASSEMBLE THE ROUND TABLE COUNCIL!!
GUILD CENTER
THE ZOMBIE TRANSFOR-MATIONS ALL HAVE ONE OBVIOUS THING IN COMMON!!
RIGHT!
SHIRO-SENPAI.
KRUSTY-SAN.
RODE-RICK-SAN.
HENRI-ETTA-SAN...
THEY ALL WEAR GLASSES!!
AND THE ZOMBIFICATION IS STARTIN' TO INFECT PEOPLE WHO DON'T WEAR GLASSES TOO!!
WHAT!?
IN THE USUAL WAY, YOU MEAN? IF THEY'RE BITTEN!?
NOPE.
WHEN THEY...
..."TING" THEIR GLASSES AT 'EM.
"TING"... HUH!?
SUCHA (TING)
DEMI-GLASS-SAN, WAS IT? HEH-HEH-HEH!!

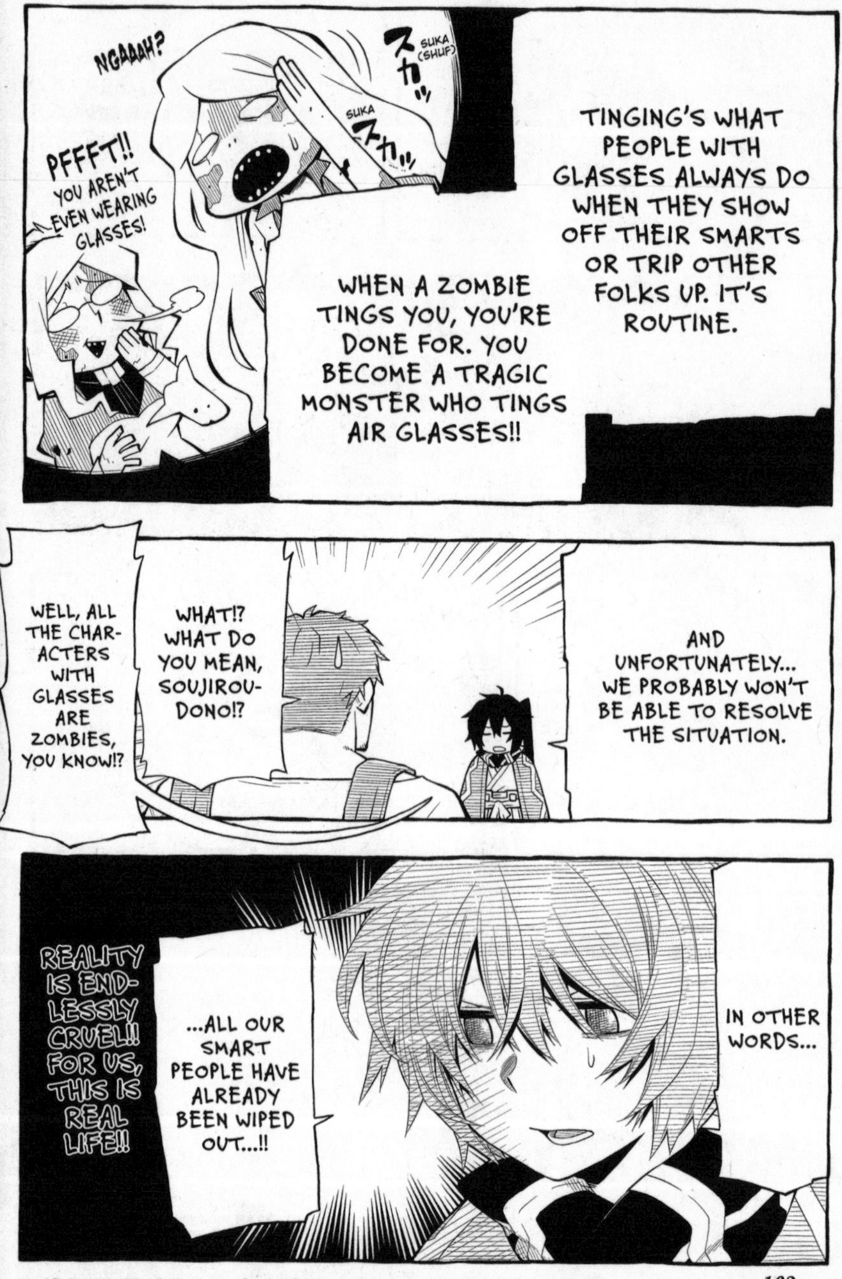
スカッ SUKA (SHUF)
TINGING'S WHAT PEOPLE WITH GLASSES ALWAYS DO WHEN THEY SHOW OFF THEIR SMARTS OR TRIP OTHER FOLKS UP. IT'S ROUTINE.
NGAAAH?
スカッ SUKA
WHEN A ZOMBIE TINGS YOU, YOU'RE DONE FOR. YOU BECOME A TRAGIC MONSTER WHO TINGS AIR GLASSES!!
PFFFT!! YOU AREN'T EVEN WEARING GLASSES!
AND UNFORTUNATELY... WE PROBABLY WON'T BE ABLE TO RESOLVE THE SITUATION.
WHAT!? WHAT DO YOU MEAN, SOUJIROU-DONO!?
WELL, ALL THE CHAR-ACTERS WITH GLASSES ARE ZOMBIES, YOU KNOW!?
IN OTHER WORDS...
...ALL OUR SMART PEOPLE HAVE ALREADY BEEN WIPED OUT...!!
REALITY IS END-LESSLY CRUEL!! FOR US, THIS IS REAL LIFE!!

TO BE CONTINUED NEXT TIME IN "THE BESPECTACLED ONES TAKE FLIGHT" (MAYBE).

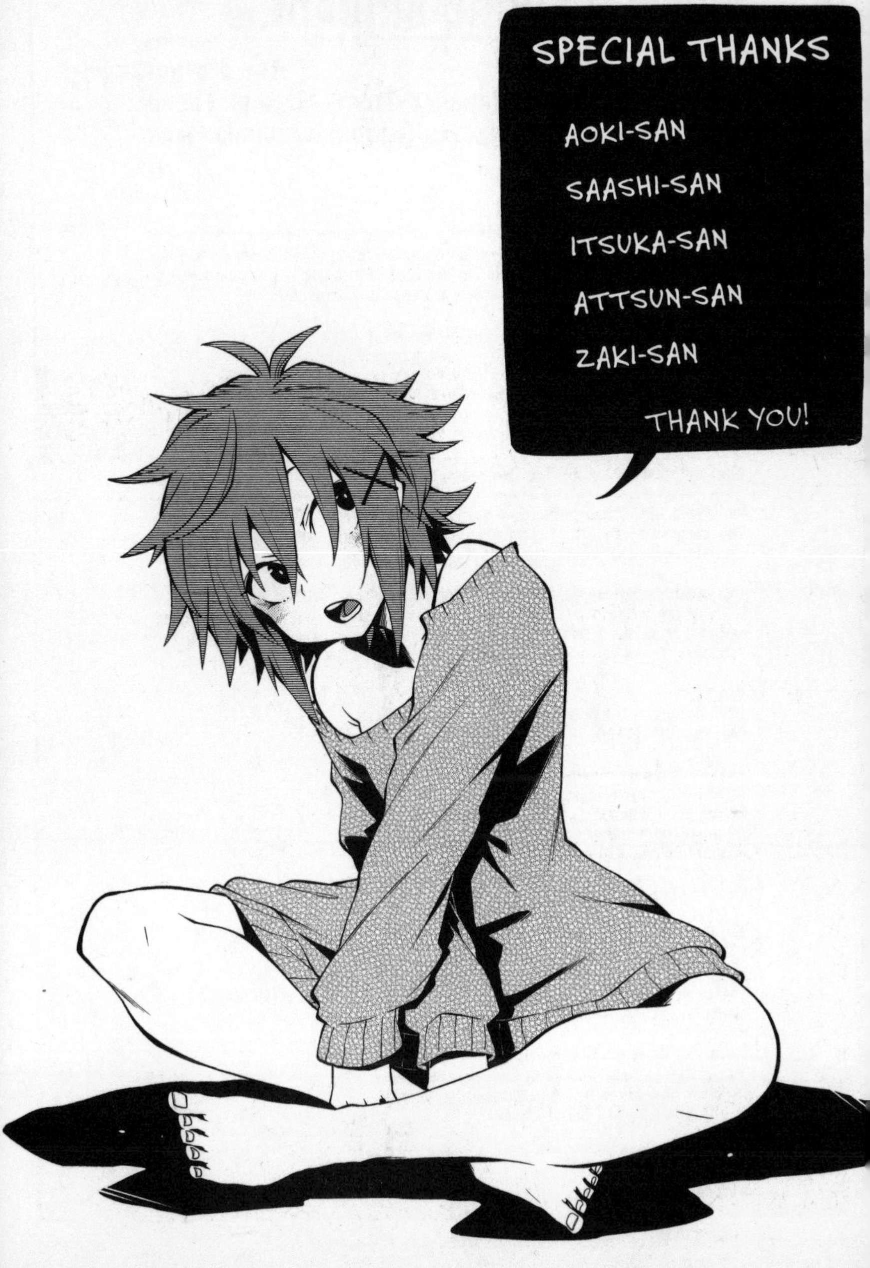
SPECIAL THANKS
AOKI-SAN
SAASHI-SAN
ITSUKA-SAN
ATTSUN-SAN
ZAKI-SAN
THANK YOU!

LOG HORIZON
THE WEST WIND BRIGADE ❼

ART: KOYUKI
ORIGINAL STORY: MAMARE TOUNO
CHARACTER DESIGN: KAZUHIRO HARA

Translation: Taylor Engel
Lettering: Brndn Blakeslee

LOG HORIZON NISHIKAZE NO RYODAN volume 7
© KOYUKI 2016
© TOUNO MAMARE, KAZUHIRO HARA 2016
First published in Japan in 2016 by KADOKAWA CORPORATION, Tokyo.
English translation rights arranged with KADOKAWA CORPORATION,
Tokyo, through Tuttle-Mori Agency, Inc., Tokyo.

English translation © 2017 by Yen Press, LLC

Yen Press
1290 Avenue of the Americas
New York, NY 10104

Visit us at yenpress.com
facebook.com/yenpress
twitter.com/yenpress
yenpress.tumblr.com
instagram.com/yenpress

First Yen Press Edition: November 2017

Yen Press is an imprint of Yen Press, LLC.
The Yen Press name and logo are trademarks of Yen Press, LLC.

The publisher is not responsible for websites (or their content) that are not owned by the publisher.

Library of Congress Control Number: 2015952586

ISBNs: 978-0-316-47450-4 (paperback)
978-0-316-47451-1 (ebook)

10 9 8 7 6 5 4 3 2 1

BVG

Printed in the United States of America